Images of Modern America

THREE RIVERS FESTIVAL

Front Cover: The raft race sponsored by radio station WLYV took place on Sunday, July 10, 1977. The banks of the St. Joseph River were teeming with people who came out to watch the colorful and intriguing handmade rafts race down the river from the City Utilities Park to the Columbia Street Bridge. Here, teams wait in the early morning sun to launch their carefully constructed rafts into the river at Johnny Appleseed Park. (Courtesy of the Three Rivers Festival Archive.)

Upper Back Cover: The annual bed race took place on Thursday, July 11, 1974, during the sixth Three Rivers Festival. (Courtesy of the Three Rivers Festival Archive.)

Lower Back Cover (from left to right): Tug-of-war contest in Swinney Park during the 17th festival (courtesy of the Three Rivers Festival Archive); the WPTA 21 Alive float in the 22nd annual parade (courtesy of the Three Rivers Festival Archive); guests enjoy the sun and flying in the air on the giant swing during the 47th festival (photograph by Erin Graf, courtesy of the Three Rivers Festival Archive).

Images of Modern America

THREE RIVERS FESTIVAL

Lori Angela Graf

ARCADIA PUBLISHING

ISBN 978-1-4671-2843-8

Published by Arcadia Publishing
Charleston, South Carolina

Printed in the United States of America

Library of Congress Control Number: 2018930617

For all general information, please contact Arcadia Publishing:
Telephone 843-853-2070
Fax 843-853-0044
E-mail sales@arcadiapublishing.com
For customer service and orders:
Toll-Free 1-888-313-2665

Visit us on the Internet at www.arcadiapublishing.com

This book is dedicated to the generous volunteers who have helped to plan, organize, and host the Three Rivers Festival for the past 49 years.

Contents

ACKNOWLEDGMENTS

This book would not have been possible without the help of many individuals—I hope I leave none of them out. First, I would like to thank Jack Hammer, executive director of the Three Rivers Festival, who encouraged me to write this book and allowed me to search the festival archives for information and photographs. Thanks to the Three Rivers Festival board of directors, who have supported me throughout the writing process and answered any questions that I had. And thanks to Tommie Manny, one of the original festival board members, for her insight into the planning of the first festival.

While the festival archive has hundreds of photographs, others contributed to the project. I would like to thank Emily Maggart, my partner in crime and fellow cat lady, who helped me sort through and organize hundreds of photographs. Thanks to George Hays and Tom Pellegrene for providing me with photographs from the Fort Wayne newspapers archives. My big sister, Erin Graf, provided me with beautiful photographs of the past three festivals.

An author always needs a second or third set of eyes, and I was lucky enough to have several sets. A shout-out goes to Michelle Lane, a good friend, coworker, and confidant, who lent me her eyes and brain to proofread, make suggestions, and give much needed encouragement. Thanks to Rachel Klein, my millennial snowflake and top banana, who was always willing to read over my writing and let me bounce words and thoughts at her. Tim Schieferstein read over my author proposal, which started this whole project in motion, and lent me his vast festival knowledge.

Finally, thanks to Melanie Martz, my best friend and soul sister, for listening to me complain when I was tired of writing and for telling me to just get it done. To my mother, Gayle Buchs, for always encouraging me and offering to take care of my kids when I needed quiet time to write. And last, but definitely not least, to my children, Tori, Kaiden, and Zerek, my monsters who make me laugh each and every day. Life would not be the same, nor as fun, without you!

Unless otherwise noted, all images appear courtesy of the Three Rivers Festival Archive.

Introduction

Every summer in July, half a million people descend on downtown Fort Wayne, Indiana, for the annual Three Rivers Festival. Patrons of the festival enjoy nine days of fun events, entertainment, and food, all of which have brought together friends and family for nearly five decades. The mission of the Three Rivers Festival is to celebrate Fort Wayne's and the region's diversity, culture, and spirit through exciting, entertaining events and activities for all ages. People from all over Indiana and the tristate region come to the Three Rivers Festival to take part in the many events the festival offers each year. Some of the most popular festival events include the opening day parade, Junk Food Alley, the bed race, and the chalk walk.

In 1968, Dean Phillips, of the Convention and Visitors Bureau, came up with the idea of holding a community festival. With the support of Mayor Harold Zeis, Phillips, along with Paul Shaffer, Joan White, Bob Walda, Elston Ehrler, Tommie Manny, and Ruth Whearly, sought to hold a festival for the community that promoted business and industry, all while celebrating Fort Wayne's culture and diversity and helping to revitalize the downtown area. These have been the goals that have served the festival for the past 49 years. All of this was made possible due to the support and collaboration between the city, festival organizers, and volunteers. In fact, the City of Fort Wayne continues to contribute $20,000 to the festival, as well as helping to stage events by allowing the festival to use Fort Wayne's city parks and parking lots and providing services such as barricades, permits, and signs free of charge.

In the early years of the festival, activities and events were difficult to book; because of this, early organizers would book just about any activity that could draw a crowd. This was the start of what was to become a long history of obstacles that the festival has had to overcome each year. Frequently the festival conquers at least one major obstacle. It may be strife surrounding the parade route, the City of Fort Wayne declining to renew its cash contribution due to budgetary restraints, or unforeseen weather, but it is a continuous battle. From the very beginning of the festival, the board, staff, and volunteers would rise above the protests and complaints of too much traffic, too much noise, and the disruption associated with the event.

The Three Rivers Festival was held on the Landing for the first 10 years. The Landing Historic District is a stretch of merchant buildings constructed between 1865 and 1917 along the south bank of the Wabash and Erie Canal. The canal was eventually shut down and sold to the railroad in 1881. However, the businesses along the Landing continued to thrive. Due to its location in downtown Fort Wayne and its proximity to parking, the festival made the Landing its home in 1969. In 1975, a fire set by arsonists burned down two of the buildings on the Landing. Thankfully, this did not deter the festival board from moving forward, nor did it deter festival patrons from enjoying the festivities, particularly the children. Each year, on Wednesday, the festival offered free kiddie rides on the Landing. In fact, what began as kiddie rides on the Landing has now turned into a full-fledged Children's Fest, which has become one of the communities' favorite festival events each year. In 1997, due to changing landscapes and prospering businesses, the festival moved to its permanent home in the newly built Headwaters Park, on the northeast side of downtown Fort Wayne.

In 1975, the Three Rivers Festival board of directors hired its first executive director, Bill Hausman, making the festival a year-round organization. Even though there were many obstacles, such as the Landing fires, the festival managed to attract more than 1.5 million people to Fort Wayne that year, topped the following year with over two million patrons. The festival started out hosting 60 events in 1968 and grew to 190 events in 1985. The board worked very hard to keep events affordable, so that the festival could continue to grow; about 90 percent of the events were free to the public. Volunteers have been a colossal part of the continued success of this event. Continued contribution from local businesses has helped to maintain the emphasis on affordability for festivalgoers, just as it was in those very early days. By the 1980s, the festival had grown and needed more space. Food concessions were moved into the city-county parking lot, Freimann Square became the home of Art in the Park, and the parade route was changed to accommodate the growing number of entries. Staging for the parade took place in the West Central Historic District and the Nebraska Neighborhood on the west side of downtown, where residents graciously welcomed the event.

Forty-nine years later, the festival is still Fort Wayne's largest summer celebration and the second-largest festival in the state of Indiana! The persistence that has been the hallmark of the festival continues today with the staff and board of directors always striving to provide affordable, exciting, family-oriented fun to people throughout the region. In 2006, the festival updated its mission to continue to celebrate, in a way like no other, the region's diversity, culture, and spirit through exciting, entertaining events and activities for all ages. The Three Rivers Festival remains the place to see old friends and make new ones, spend time with family, experience new things, and celebrate Fort Wayne. The cooperation between local businesses, city and county governments, local media, and the community has been and will be maintained as the festival continues to provide fun events, exciting entertainment, and the opportunity for people to create great memories into the future.

One

1969–1978

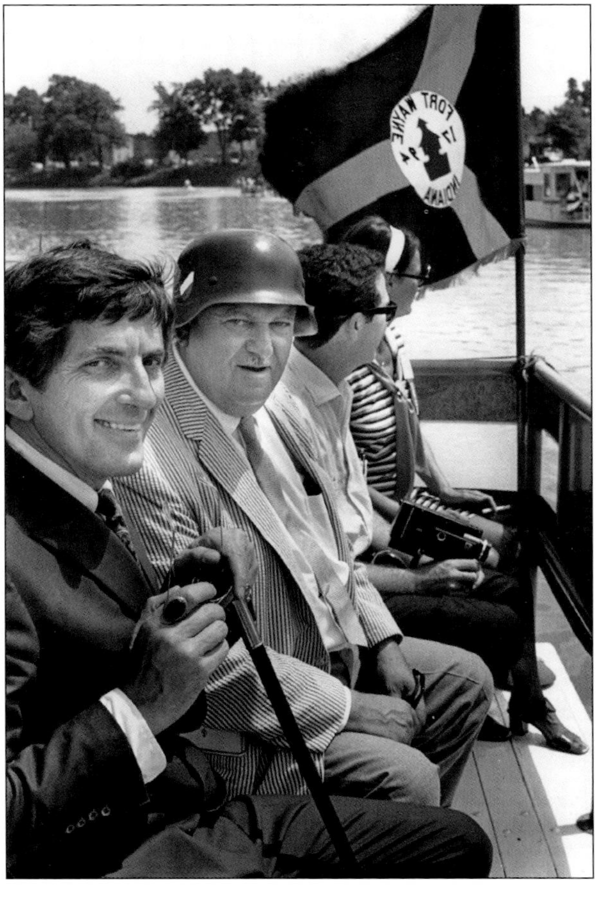

The first Three Rivers Festival Parade was held along the St. Joseph River on July 12, 1969. Decorated boats, music, and people in colorful costumes floated up the river to the amusement of the crowds. Pictured are the grand marshals Jonathan Frid (left), who played the vampire Barnabas Collins on the television show *Dark Shadows*, and John Banner, who portrayed Sergeant Schultz on *Hogan's Heroes*.

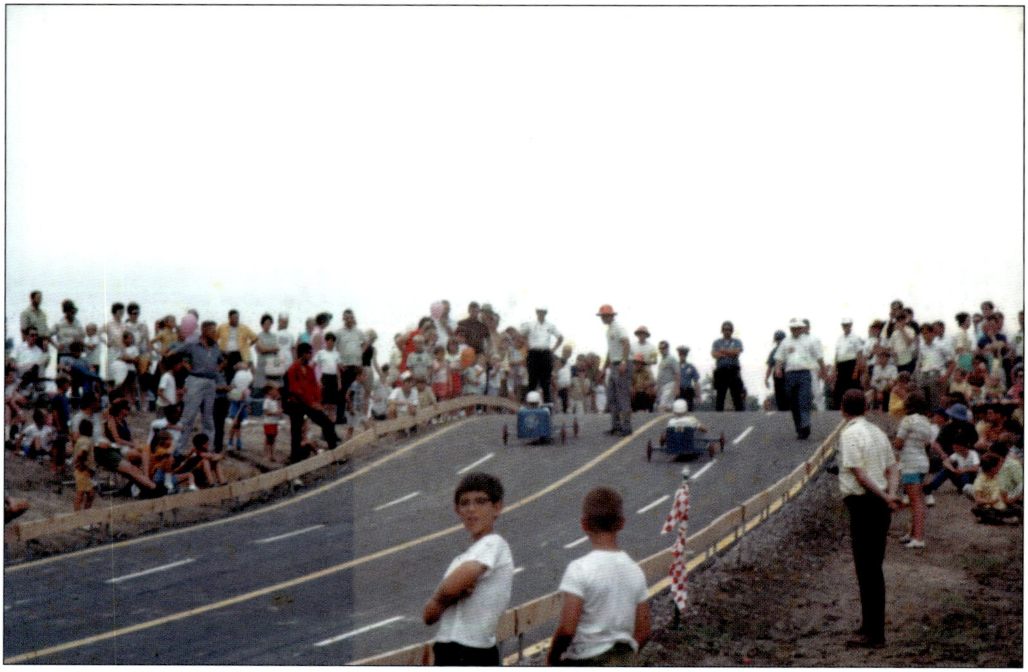

A sunny and beautiful Franke Park was the setting for the kids' soap box derby on Sunday, July 20, 1969. Moms, dads, brothers, sisters, and grandparents lined the raceway to cheer their racers to the finish line. The derby was such a success it quickly became an annual tradition for many families in Fort Wayne. Here, the crowd watches as two drivers race to the finish line. (Courtesy of Visit Fort Wayne.)

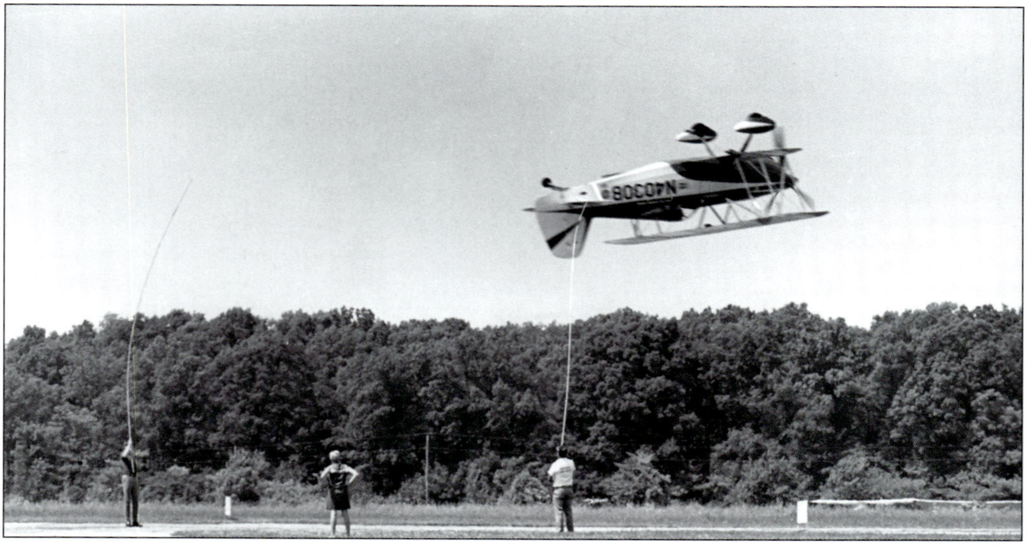

The first Three Rivers Festival featured an air show at Smith Field. Included were the Golden Knights paratroopers, US Air Force Thunderbirds, and Bill Sweet's National Air Show. The Thunderbird pilots dazzled the crowd with aerobatic and precision flying, while the Golden Knights demonstrated their sensational skydiving stunts and skills in the air. Here, a plane from Bill Sweet's National Air Show flies across Smith Field upside down.

Saturday, July 18, 1970, brought a sunny, fun-filled day for children in Franke Park during the second annual festival. Children could participate in several different contests, including watermelon eating, bike decorating, apple eating, a clown contest, and a freckle contest. A magic show and demonstration by the Fort Wayne Fire Department was also provided for the children's enjoyment. Pictured is freckle contest winner Randy Meyers.

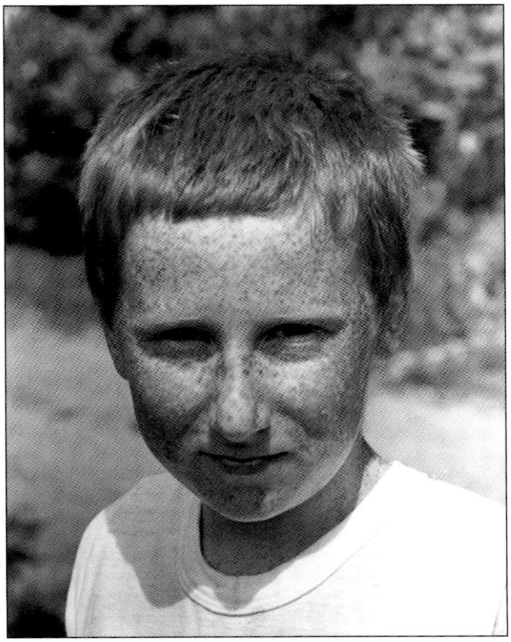

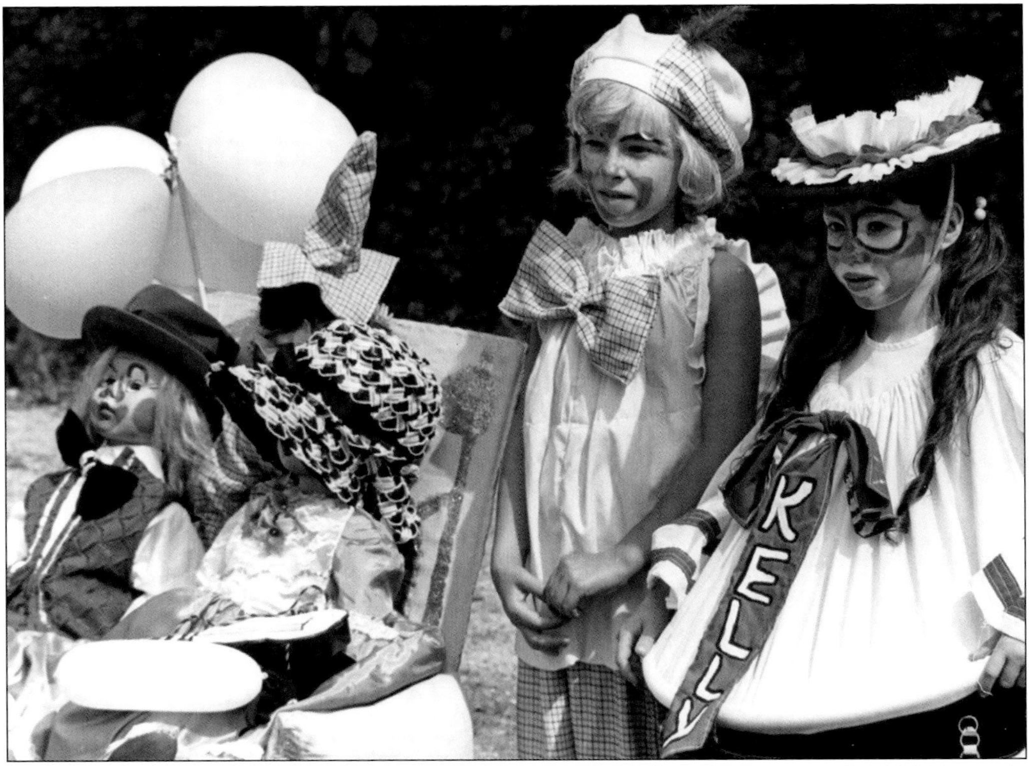

Attendance at the second annual Three Rivers Festival grew by 25 percent, with 125,000 people attending 66 events over nine days. One of the more popular events was the children's day at Franke Park. Hundreds of families enjoyed the day in Franke Park, participating in contests and activities. Pictured are the 1970 clown contest winners, Roxanne Gillingham (left) and Kelly Snyder (right).

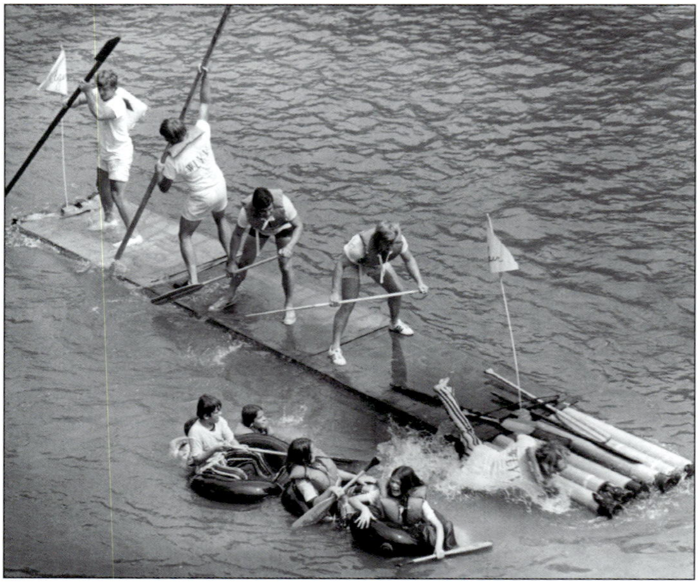

The raft race took place for the first time on the morning of Saturday, July 11, 1970. Following the annual boat parade, hundreds of participants enjoyed a fun and competitive day on the St. Joseph River as they raced their handmade and human-propelled rafts to the finish line. Here, some participants get a little wet on their way to the finish. (Courtesy of the *Journal Gazette*.)

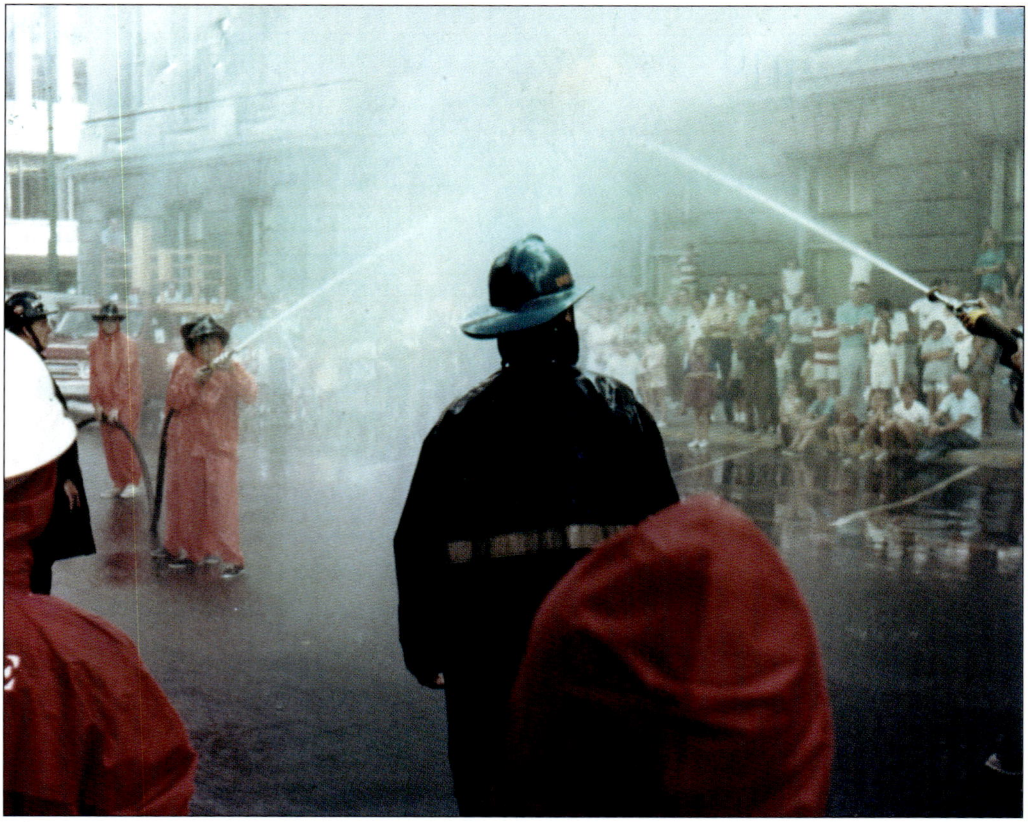

The Four County Water Battle was fought between the fire departments of Allen, Adams, Huntington, and Wells Counties. The battle took place on Court Street in downtown Fort Wayne on Wednesday, July 15, 1970. Using fire hoses and fire hydrants, the firemen competed in several contests to see which county was the best. Here, fire departments battle with hoses to push an overhead ball to the opponent's side.

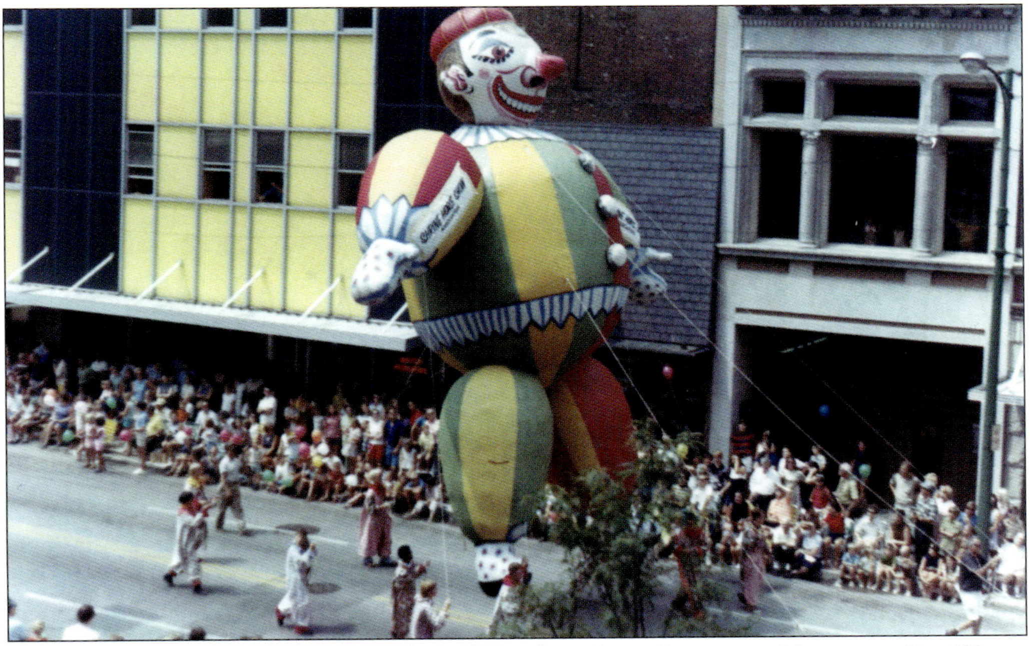

The third annual Three Rivers Festival Parade was brought to the streets of downtown Fort Wayne for the first time in 1971. The parade featured 42 balloons, many of which were the same ones that thrilled crowds at the Macy's Thanksgiving Day Parade. Here, a giant clown balloon is led down South Calhoun Street by a group of colorful clowns from the Shriners.

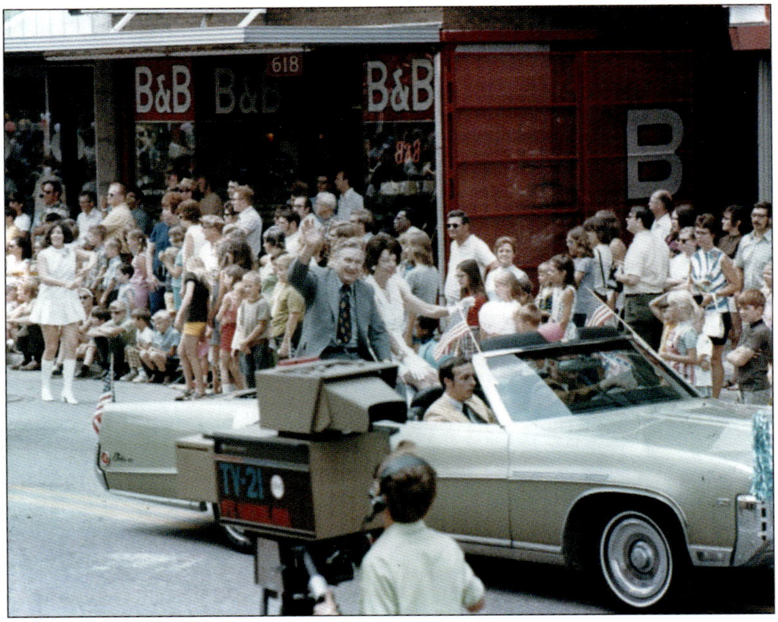

The annual Three Rivers Festival Parade is the official opening event of the festival. The parade has featured marching bands, clowns, balloons, antique cars, and floats with fun themes. Here, Mayor Harold Zeis and his wife, Elda, wave from a car during the 1971 parade.

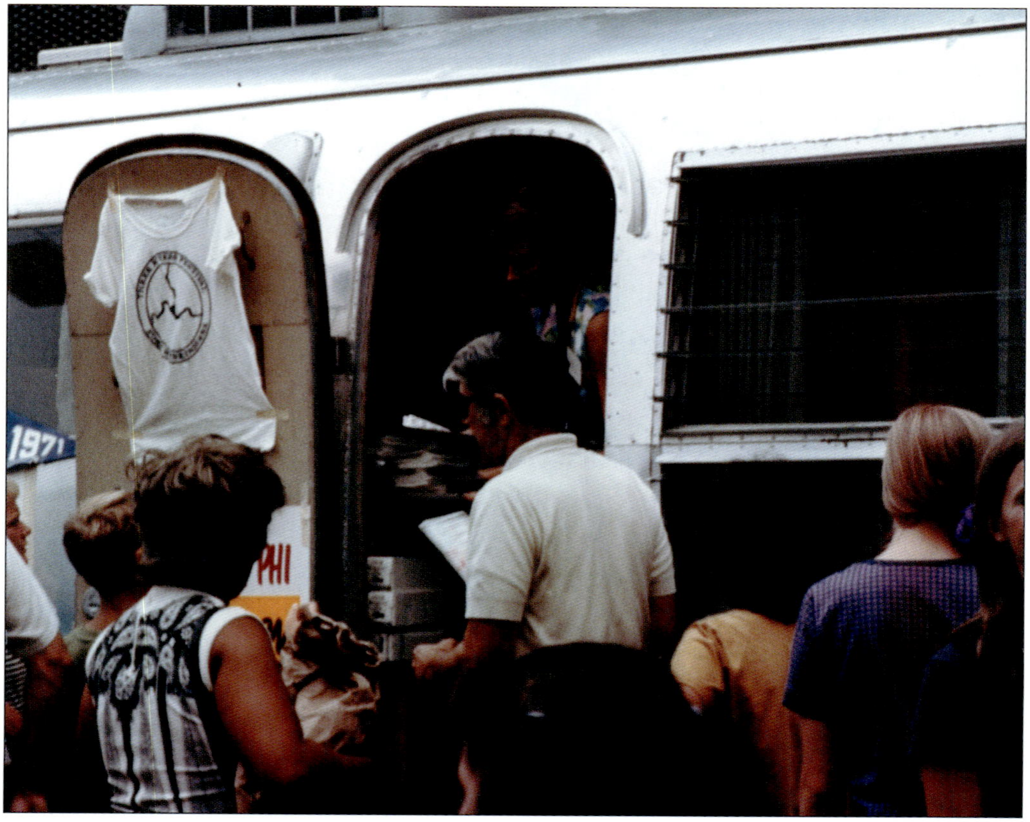

The Beta Sigma Phi sorority hosted the official Three Rivers Festival information and souvenir booth from 1969 through 1972. The ladies of Beta Sigma Phi volunteered their time to answer questions, hand out festival guides, and sell festival souvenirs. The booth was open each day from 10:00 a.m. to 7:00 p.m. Festival visitors are pictured stopping by the information booth during the 1971 festival.

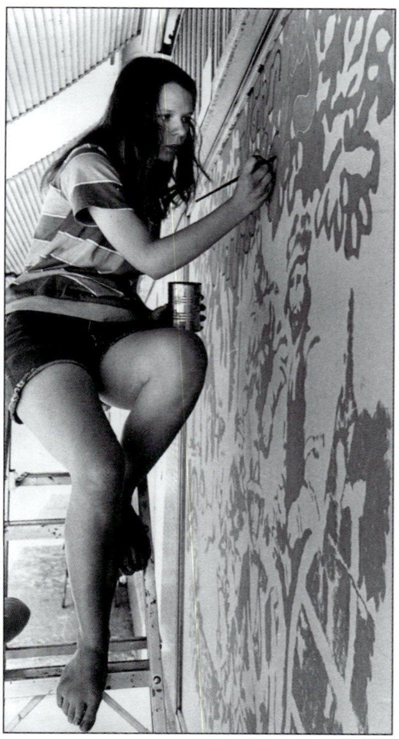

Community participation has always been a goal of the Three Rivers Festival, which includes engaging the youth of Fort Wayne. The annual Student Paint On gathered high school students to paint windows in downtown Fort Wayne. This annual event ran from 1971 to 1987, allowing student artists to showcase their work to the city. A student is pictured working on her window mural during the Student Paint On in 1971.

The 1972 Three Rivers Festival Bicycle Tour took place on Sunday, July 16, at 8:00 a.m. The sunny, 66-degree day was perfect for participants as they rode their bicycles 62 miles from the Landing on Columbia Street to Hicksville, Ohio, and back to Fort Wayne. Here, cyclists ride down Harrison Street on their way to Hicksville.

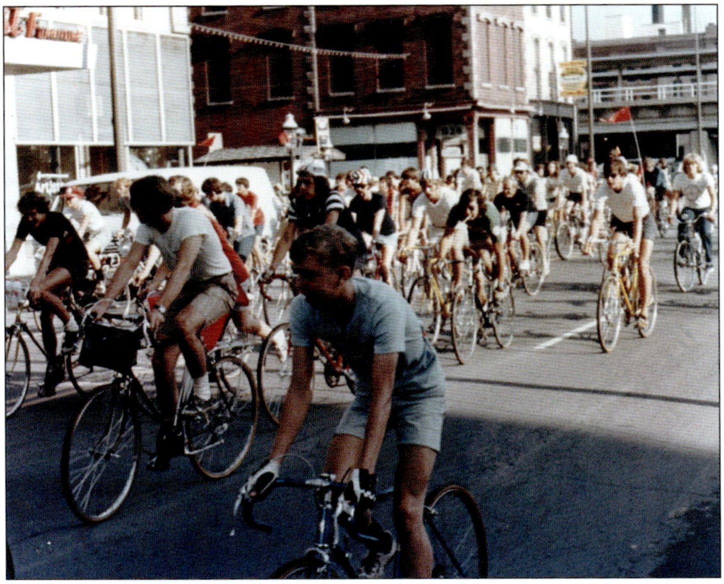

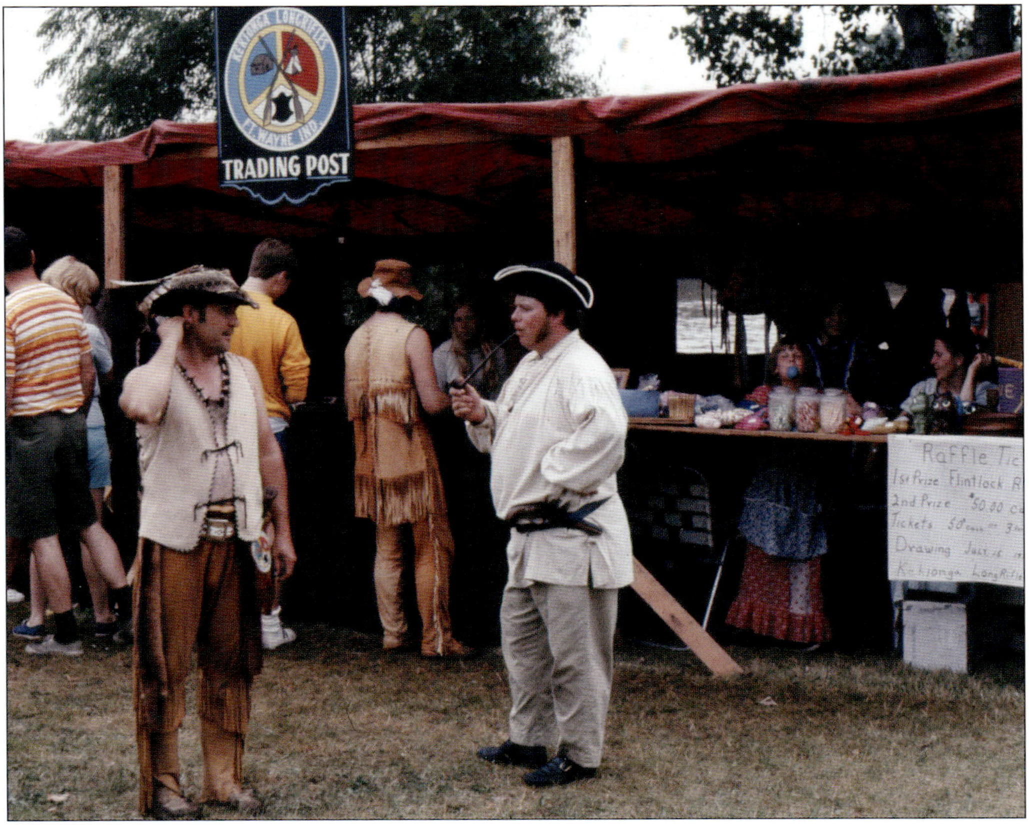

Fort Wayne was established in 1794 near the Miami village of Kekionga. A trading post was established near the fort where both settlers and Native Americans could go for goods. In honor of this history, the Kekionga Long Rifles and Troop 40 of the Boy Scouts of America hosted a two-day reenactment of the trading post, trapper's camp, and Kekionga village. Pictured are trading post reenactors at the 1972 festival.

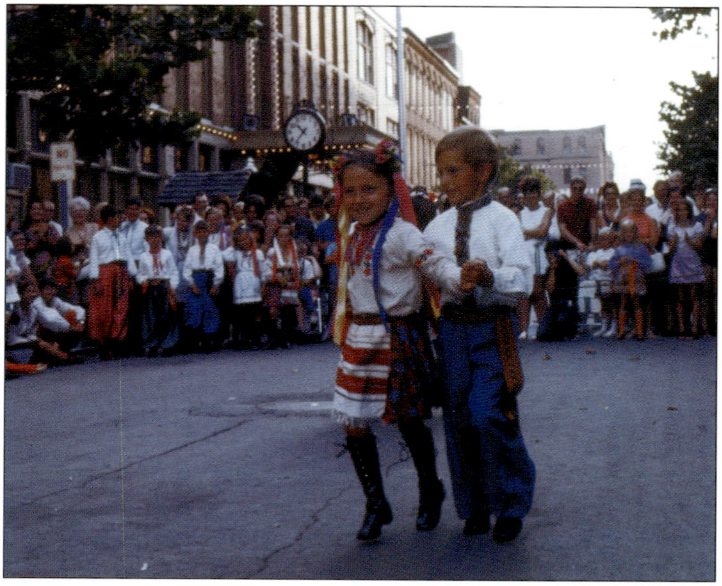

International Village was held for the first time during the 1972 Three Rivers Festival. People from all over the world call Fort Wayne home, making the city a rich blend of cultures and traditions. International Village brings the people of Fort Wayne together to celebrate their diversity. Each day of the festival was devoted to a cultural group. Here, Macedonian children are pictured dancing on the Landing.

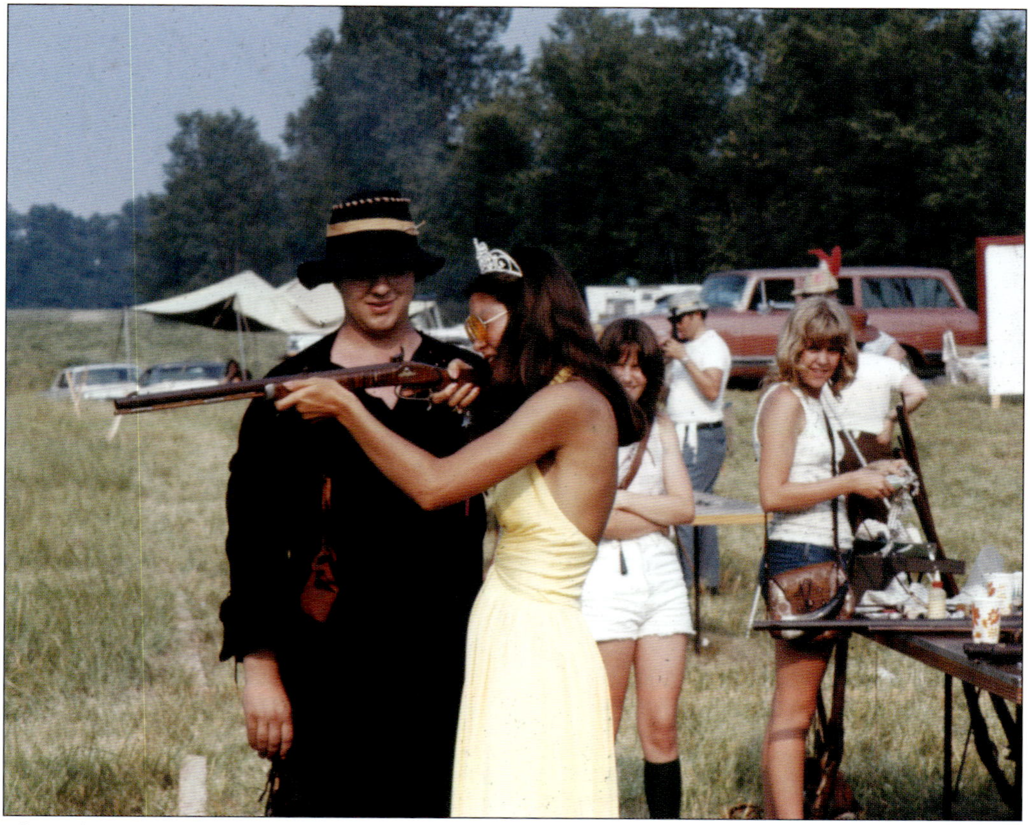

The Kekionga Long Rifle Club hosted a muzzle-loading rifle match during the fifth annual Three Rivers Festival, held on the Harvester Union recreation grounds. The weather was beautiful on the day of the match, with wind speeds around seven miles per hour and temperatures in the mid-80s. Pictured is Cindy Holmes, 1973 Three Rivers Festival queen, as she tries her hand at shooting a long rifle.

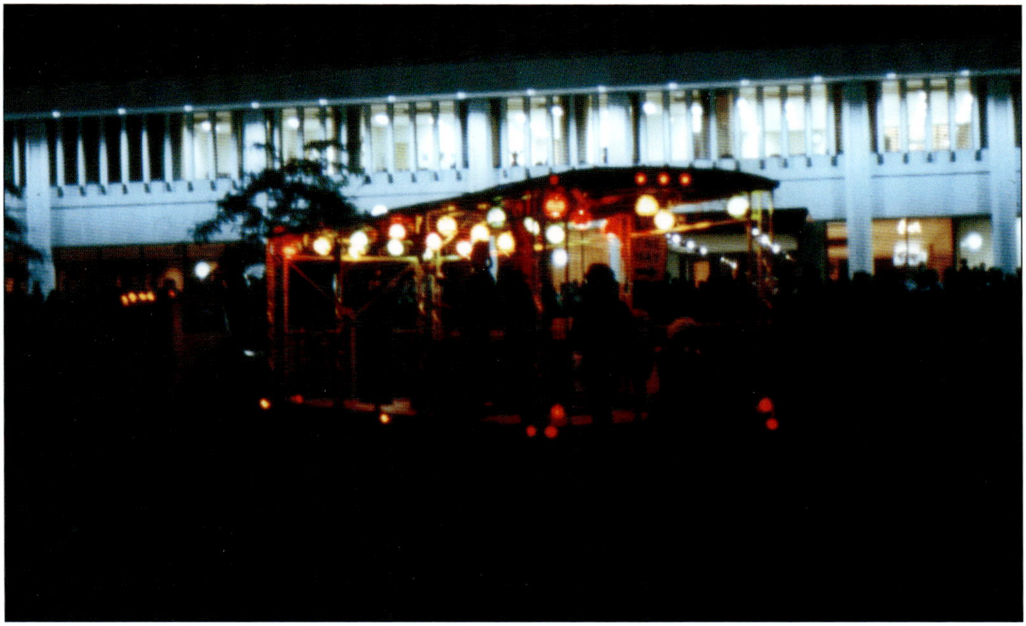

Shrine-A-Rama, later the Parade of Lights, started in 1971 to the delight of the community. Colorful floats, horses, bands, clowns, dune buggies, and pedal pushers decorated in thousands of lights amazed and entertained fans for decades. In 1974, the parade moved to downtown, where it remained until the last parade in 2010. Here, a lighted horse-drawn trolley passes by the city/county building on Main Street in 1973.

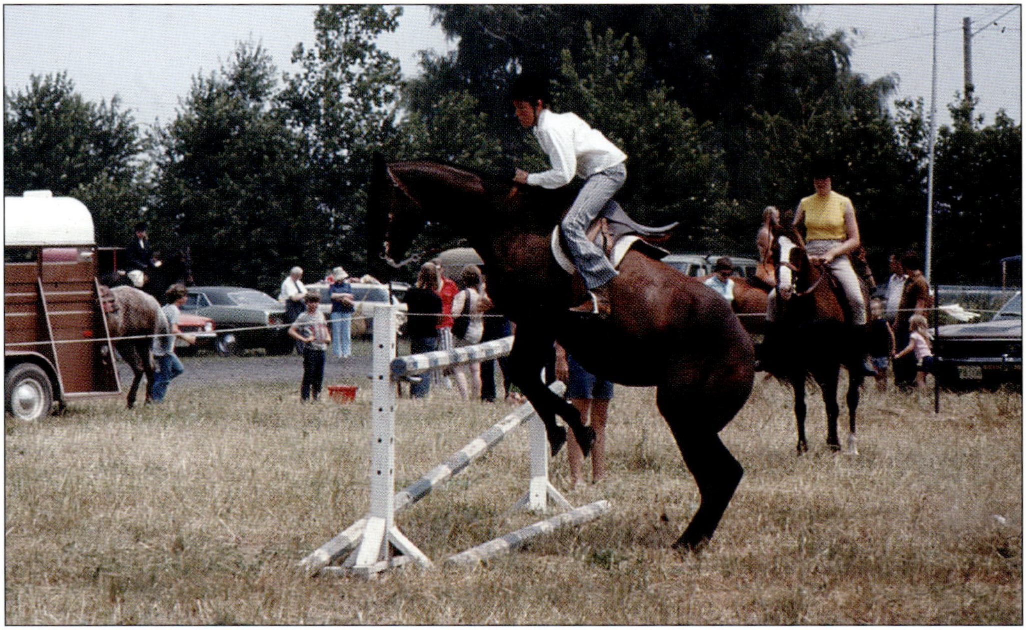

Planning a nine-day festival is no easy feat. Most events held during the festival are planned by the festival board, committees, and staff. In addition, a number of events are planned each year by local organizations, which allow them to participate in the festival while raising awareness for their group. Pictured are participants in the Allen County 4-H Club horse show, held on Sunday, July 8, 1973.

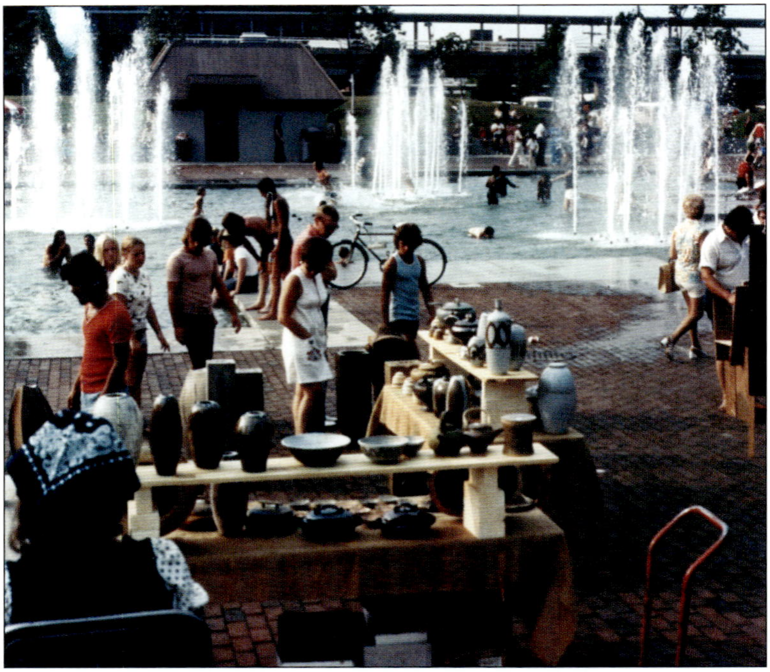

The first annual Art in the Park was held on Saturday, July 6, 1974, in Freimann Square. Art in the Park is a juried fine arts show featuring hundreds of artists from across the United States. Here, festival attendees admire pieces at a pottery booth, while others enjoy the cool water of the Freimann Square fountain.

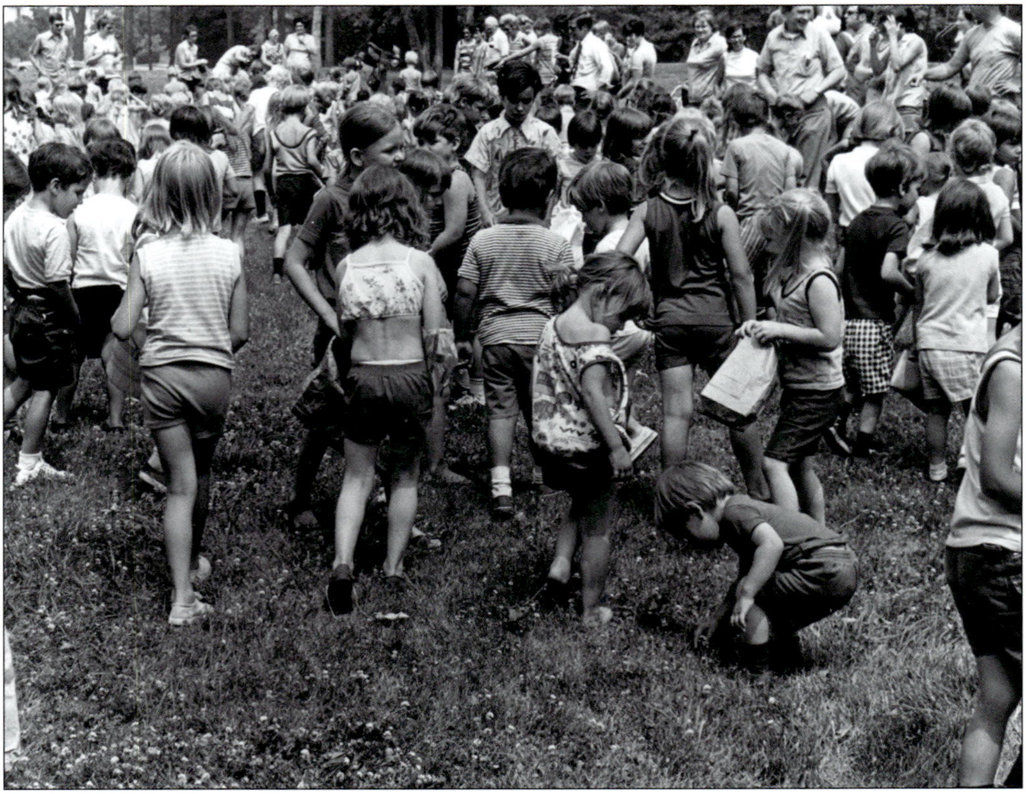

The fourth annual kids' peanut hunt was held on Tuesday, July 9, 1974, in Swinney Park. Thousands of peanuts were hidden in the grass by festival volunteers for the children to find. On the day of the event, hundreds of children came out to hunt for peanuts and win prizes.

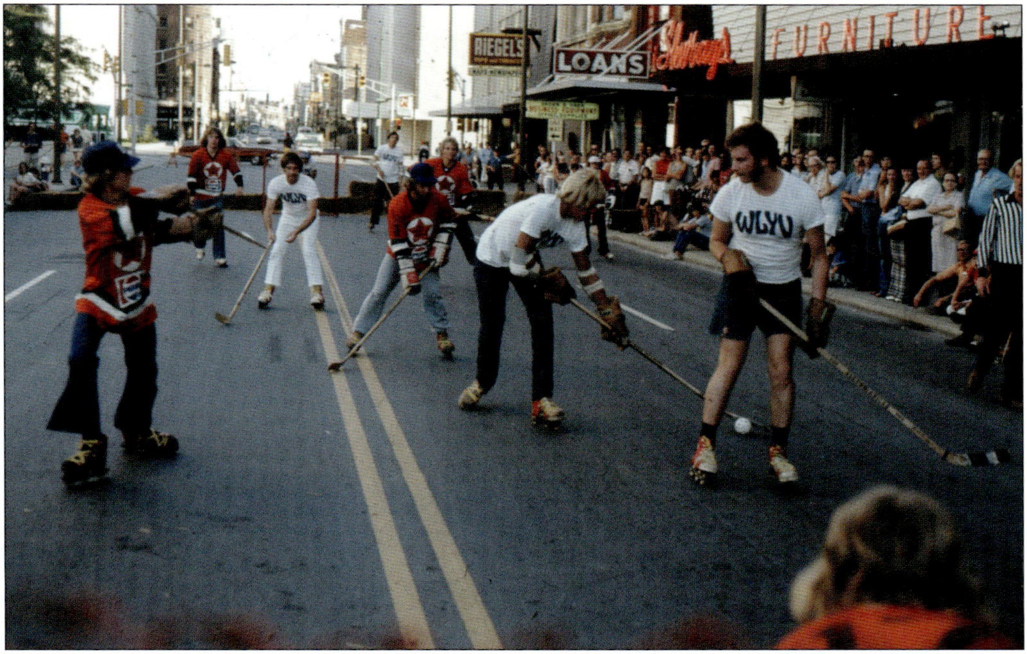

The Fort Wayne Komets played a game of skeeling against WLYV on Friday, July 12, 1974. Hundreds of people came out to watch their favorite professional hockey team battle it out with their favorite disk jockeys in an exciting game of hockey played on three-wheeled roller skates. Here, the crowd watches as the Komets and WLYV fight for the puck on South Calhoun Street.

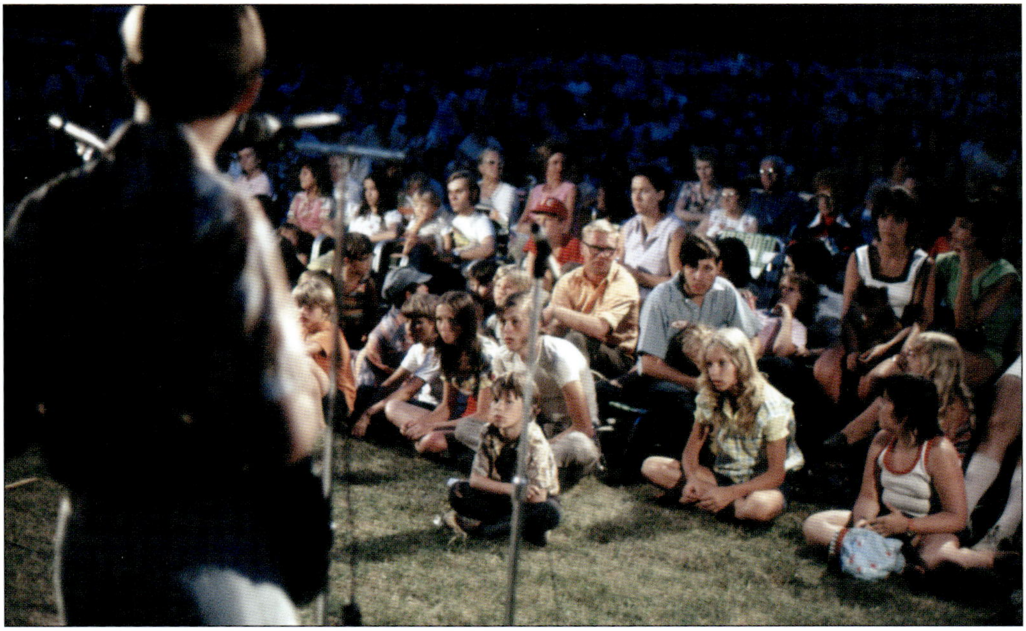

What is a festival without music? Music has been an integral part of the Three Rivers Festival since its beginning. Hundreds of bands have taken to the stage to entertain festival attendees. Here, music lovers enjoy the 1975 country & western music festival at Franke Park featuring Joe Taylor & the Redbirds, Bill Nix & the Ideals, Paula Jo Taylor & the Last Resort, and Vic Rigsby the Ridiculous.

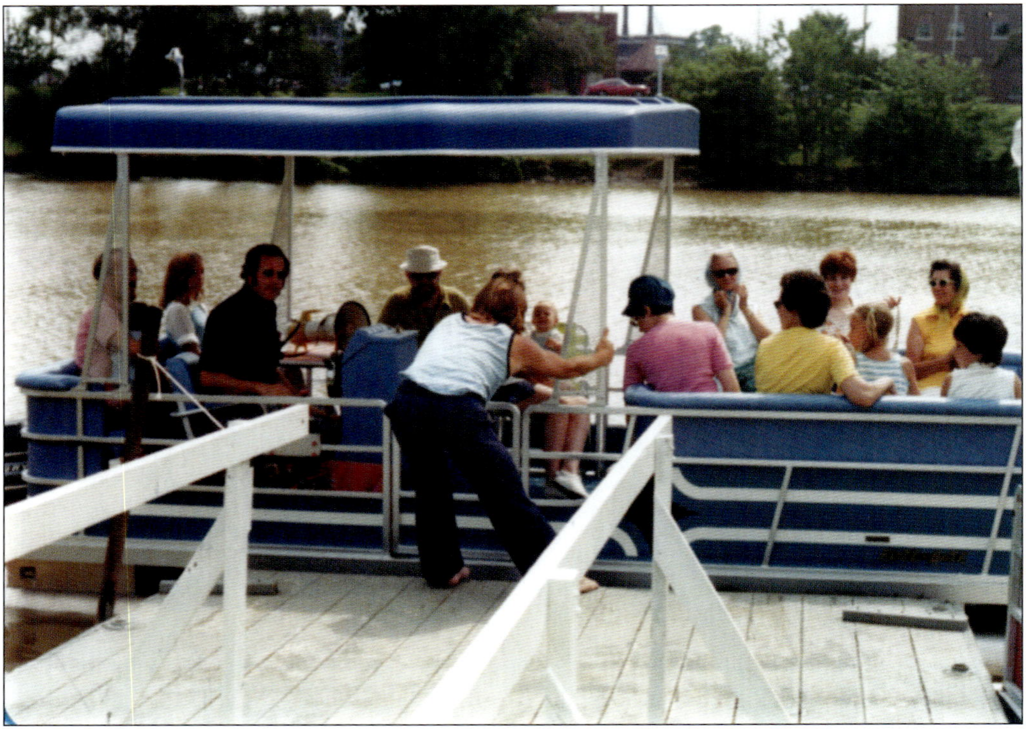

The theme of the 1975 Three Rivers Festival was "Good Time '75." Thousands of festival attendees had a good time on the St. Joseph River during the excursion boat rides. Boats took guests down the river to enjoy views of the city while learning the history and importance of the river system to Fort Wayne and the surrounding area. Here, festival attendees are arriving back at the dock.

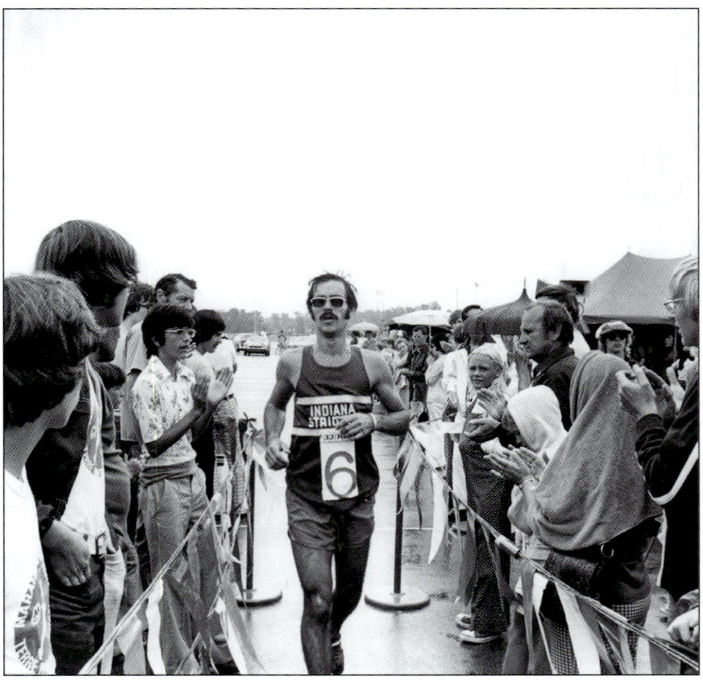

In keeping with the theme, new events were planned in 1975. One of these events was a marathon, which ran a winding course from the Allen County War Memorial Coliseum to Foster Park and back, covering 26.2 miles. The marathon was an AAU–sanctioned qualifying race for the Boston Marathon. Here, a runner crosses the finish line.

Main Street, from Barr to Clinton Streets, was the location of the 1975 Down-on-the-Tarm tractor pull hosted by the Indiana Tractor Pulling Association. Tractors and drivers from all over Indiana competed for honors in three different classifications. The crowd watches in anticipation as the driver lines up his tractor to begin his pull.

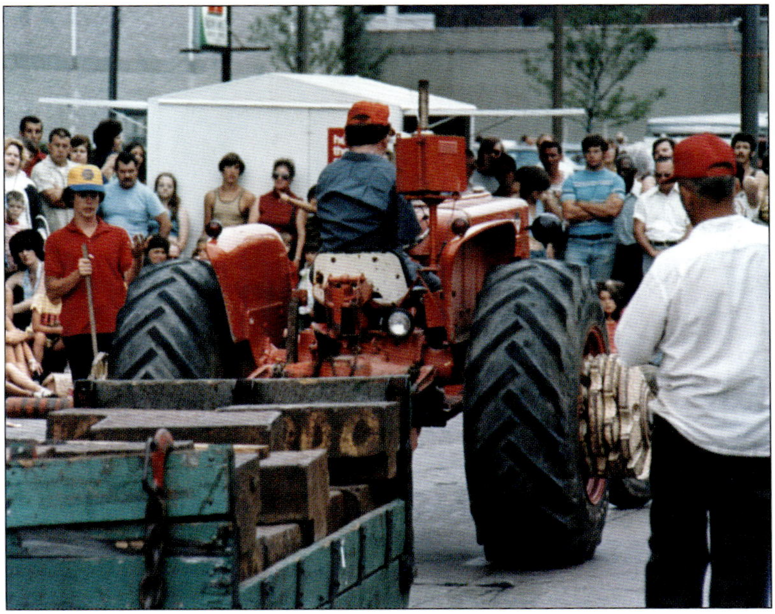

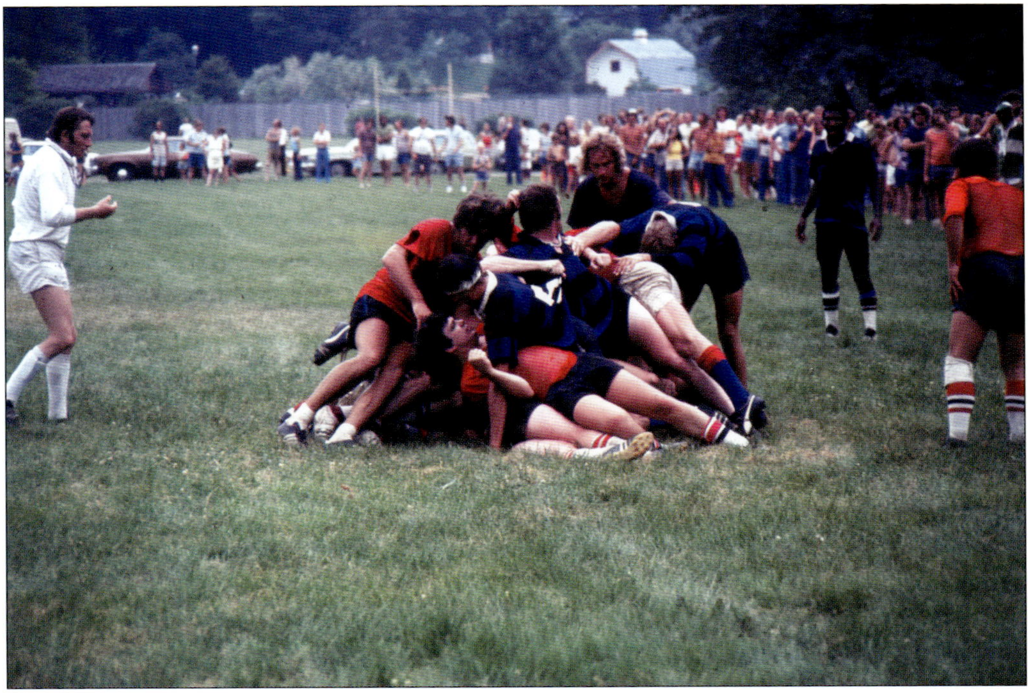

Eight teams from St. Louis, Cincinnati, Chicago, Gary, South Bend, Indianapolis, Kalamazoo, and Fort Wayne competed in the 1975 Three Rivers Festival rugby tournament. The tournament was held over two days starting on Saturday, July 5. The tournament championship and consolation games between the winners of Saturday's games took place on Sunday, July 6. Here, the crowd watches as the players fight over the ball in a pileup.

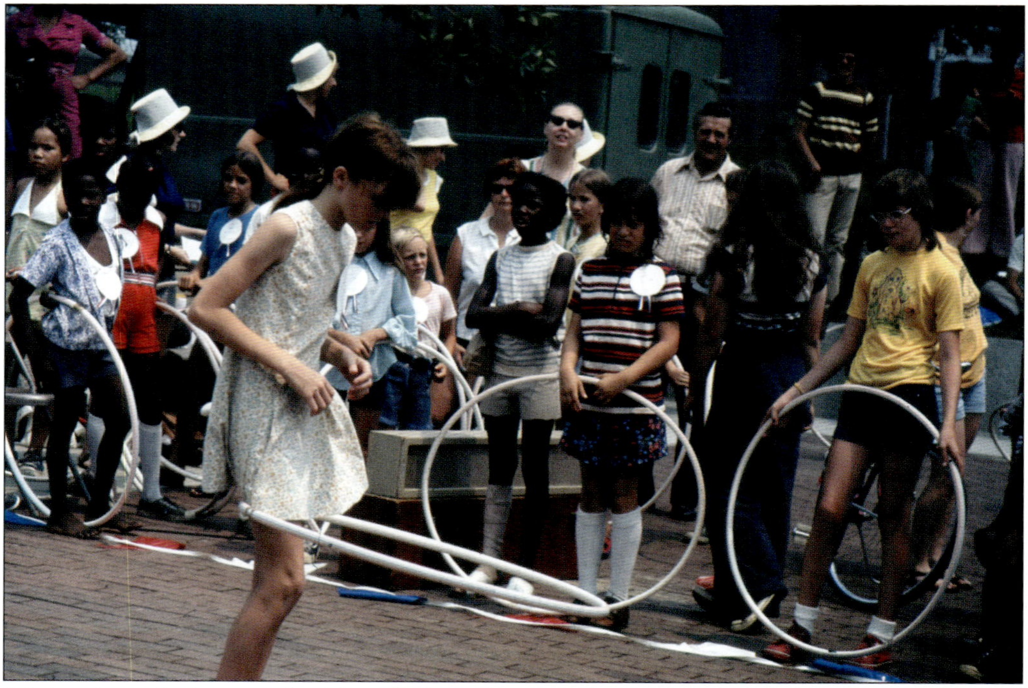

Wednesday, July 9, was full of fun-filled children and family activities during the 1975 festival. Fun-A-Rama took place in Freimann Square and provided games, contests, a pet show, and musical entertainment for children. Down on the Landing, children could experience thrills on the free kiddie rides. Rides included a merry-go-round, Ferris wheel, dragon ride, animal swing, and tractor and pony rides. Pictured are children participating in the hula-hoop contest.

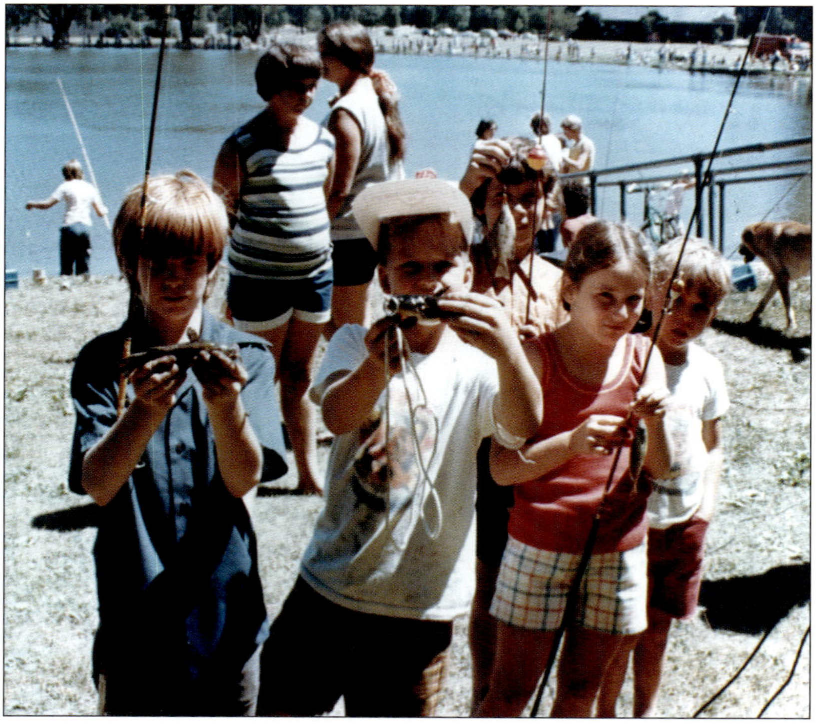

Local radio station WXKE hosted a fishing derby for children 15 and under at the Franke Park pond on Monday, July 12, 1976. Prizes were awarded for the biggest fish caught in each age group. Pictured is a group of children proudly showing off the fish they caught during the derby.

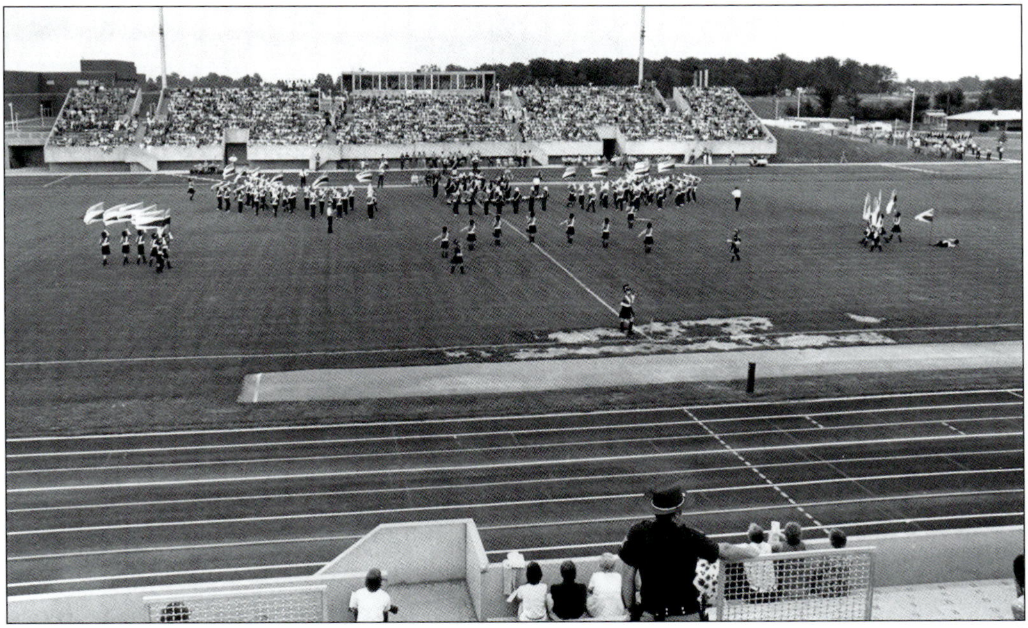

On the eve of the 1976 Three Rivers Festival, a drum and bugle corps from Drum Corps International gave an outstanding performance to a packed stadium at Northrop High School. The corps was made up of talented high school and college musicians and performers from across America. The Northrop High School football stadium stands were filled with people enjoying the music and performance of Drums Across America.

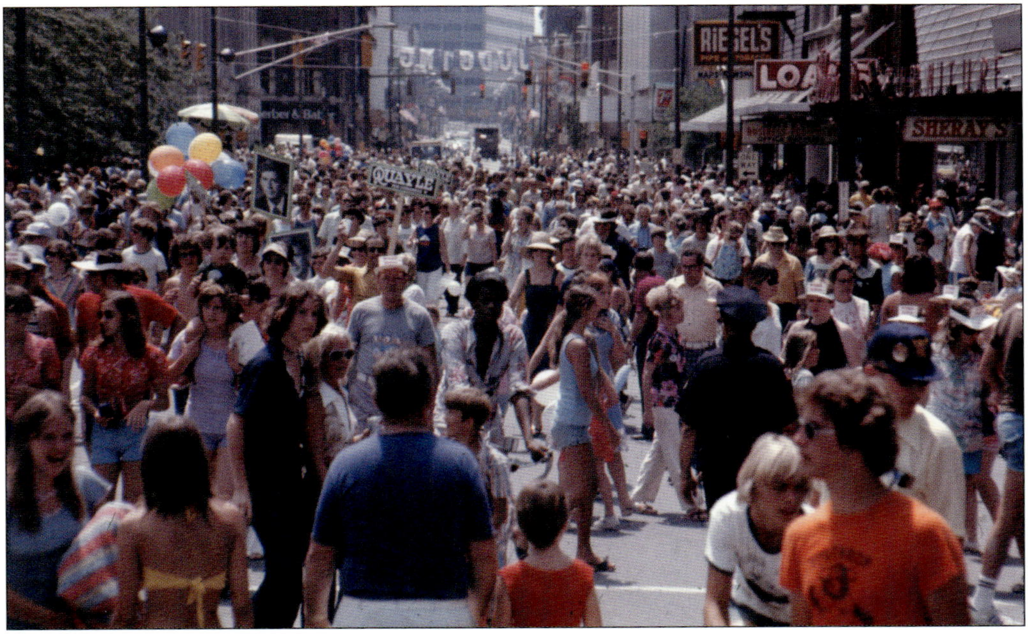

A yearly tradition for the Three Rivers Festival, the parade kicked off the 1976 festival on the morning of Saturday, July 10, with Earl Finckle as grand marshal. The streets were lined with thousands of happy and enthusiastic parade watchers, who came out to see colorful floats, balloons, and bands. The route then fills with people as they head to other festival events after the end of the parade.

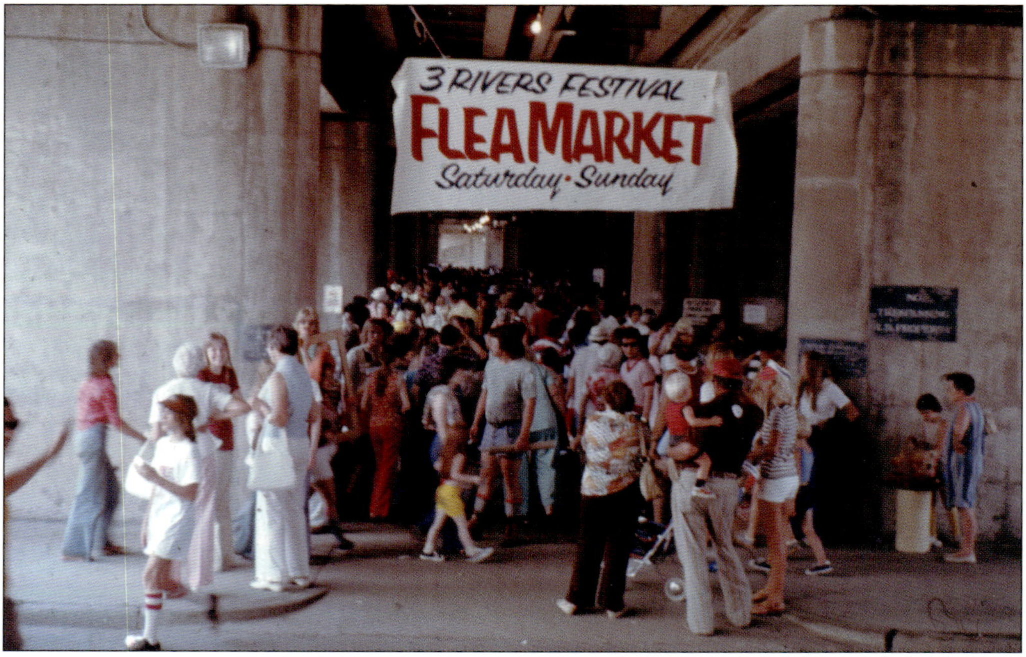

North of the Landing, underneath the historic Nickle Plate Railroad elevation, once the route of the Wabash and Erie Canal, festival attendees could shop for antiques, collectables, and other items at the Three Rivers Festival flea market. The market was open each day of the festival. Here, shoppers enjoy their time at the flea market in 1976.

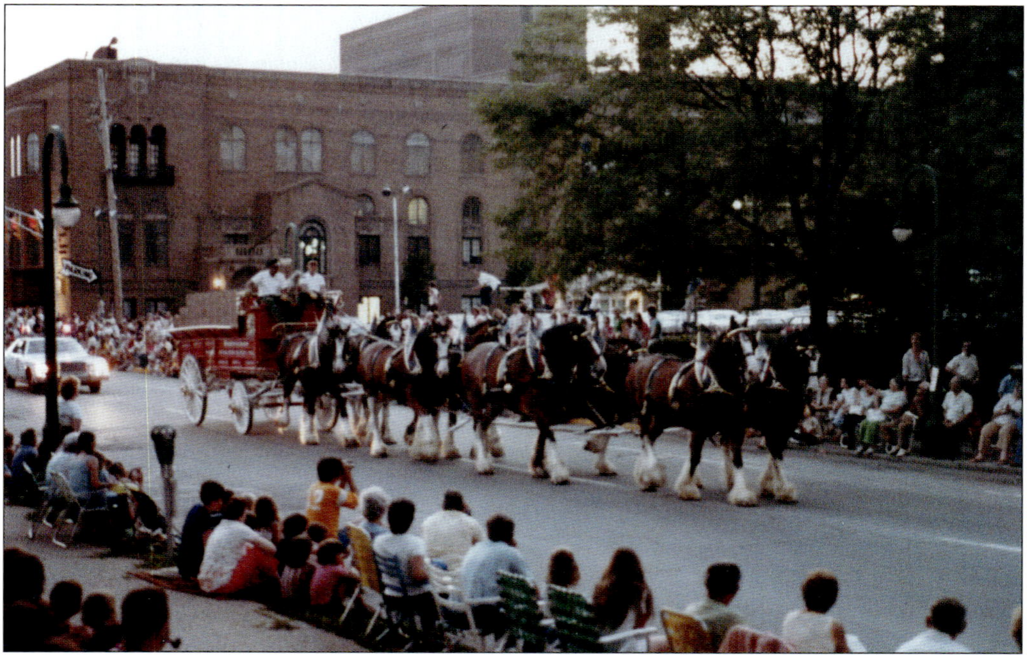

The 10th annual Three Rivers Festival opening day parade was held on Saturday, July 9, 1977. The warm, 80-degree day brought thousands of people downtown to see the colorfully decorated floats, clowns, horses, marching bands, and the Drums across America drum and bugle corps. Here, the famous Budweiser Clydesdale team pulls a historic wagon down South Calhoun Street.

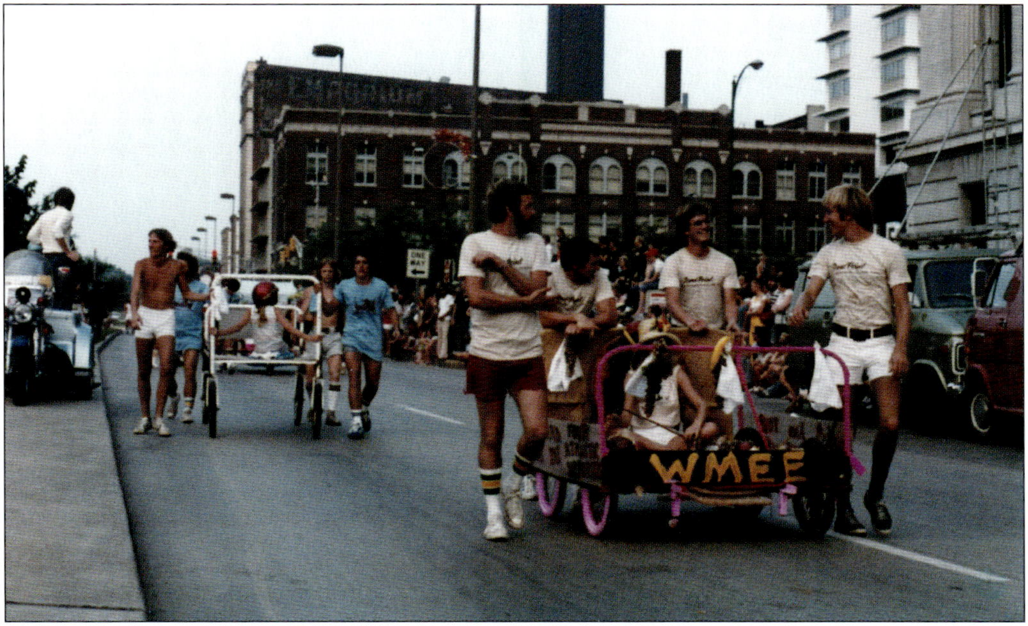

The 1977 Three Rivers Festival had 143 events. These included annual favorites such as the bed race and parade, along with several new attractions. New events for the year included a cutting horse exhibition, a mini concert caravan, reenactments at Historic Fort Wayne, a skateboard grand prix, and more. Here, bed race teams walk their beds past the crowd as they line up for the start.

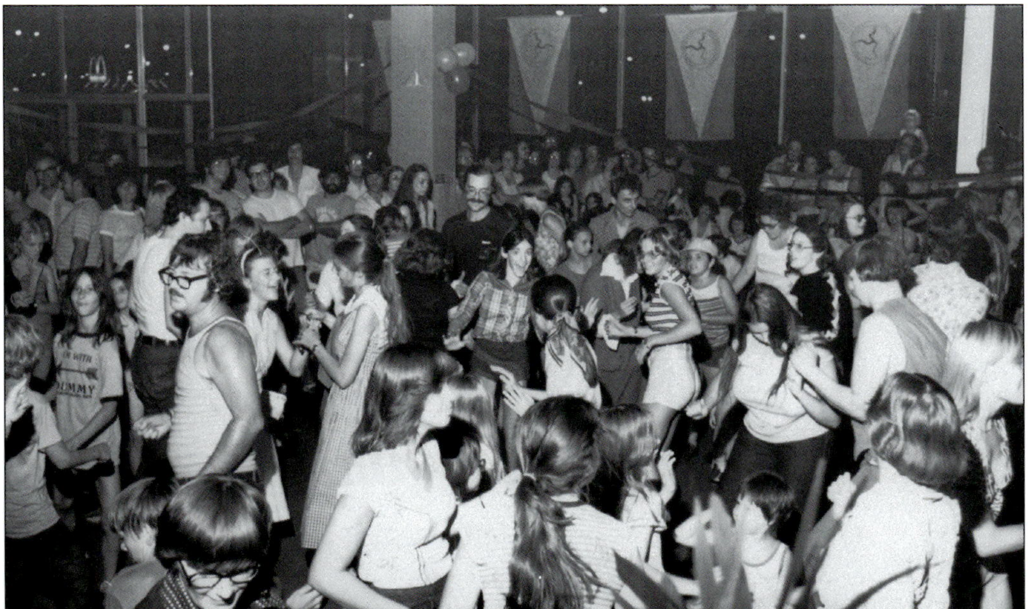

Guys and gals of all ages danced the night away to the hits of the 1950s and 1960s at the Fabulous 50s Sock Hop, held in Southgate Plaza. Participants enjoyed a night of dance contests and trivia games. A store turned dance hall was filled with people of all ages enjoying a night of dancing, fun, and community spirit.

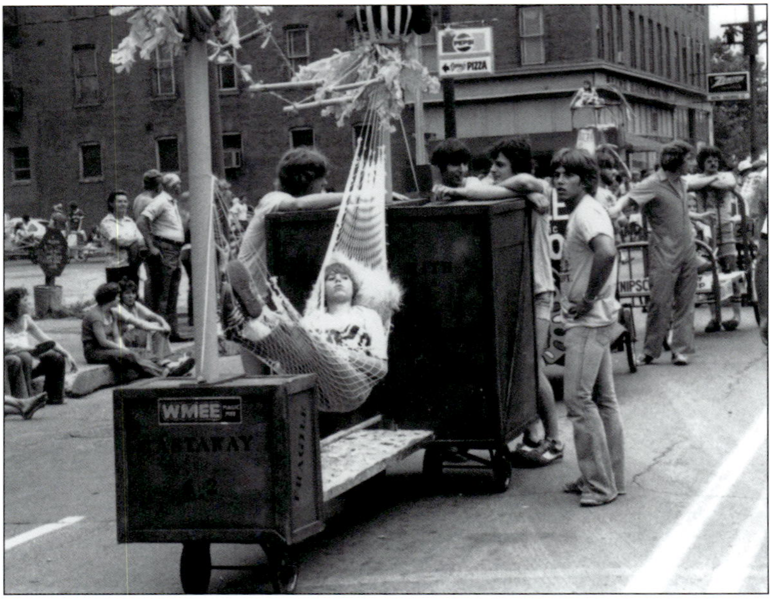

The year 1978 was the 10th anniversary of the Three Rivers Festival. The year started off on a bad note, with the Great Blizzard of 1978 blowing into the city in January, which slowed festival staff in their planning. Once the blizzard was over and the snow melted, 200 events were planned for the enjoyment of the city. Here, teams line up for the start of the bed race on Main Street.

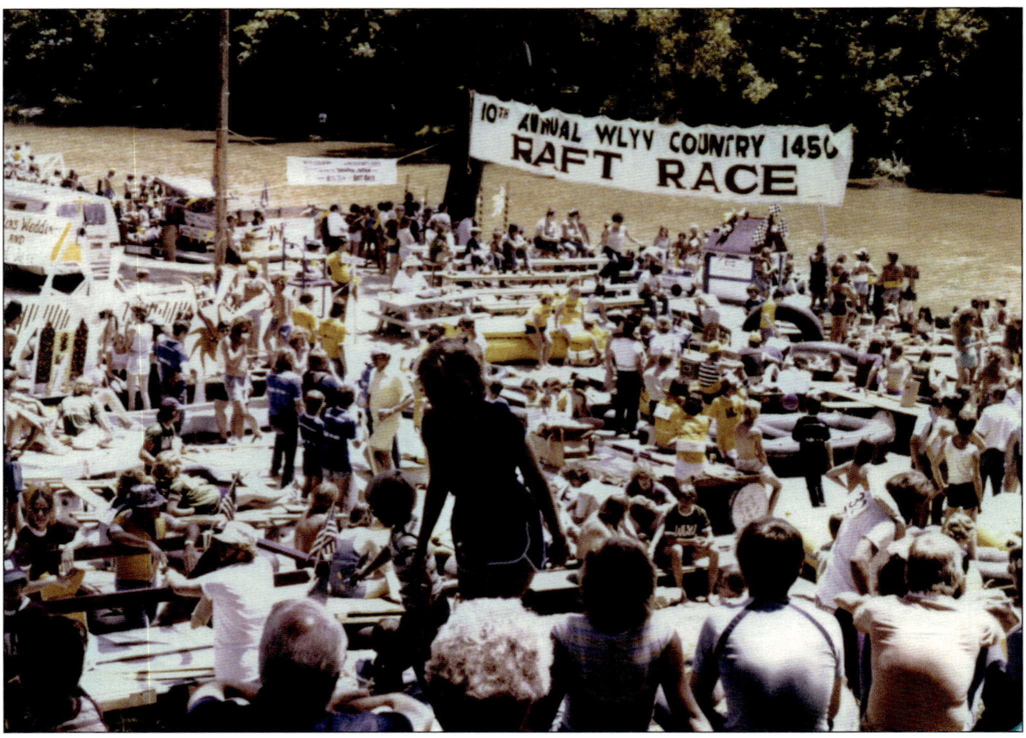

The blizzard and melting snow did not stop people from preparing for the annual raft race. While the St. Joseph River was rising to an alarming level, participants worked diligently on building their rafts for the upcoming race. The raft race went off without a hitch on the first Sunday of the festival. Here, participants wait to launch their rafts into the river for the 1978 race.

Two

1979–1988

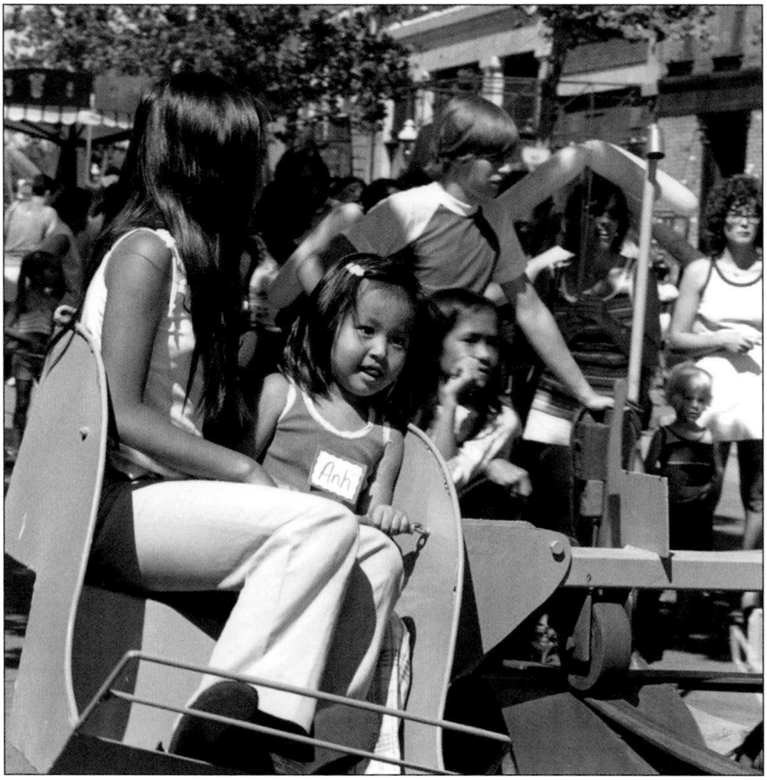

Since the first festival in 1969, one of the main goals of the Three Rivers Festival board of directors and staff has been to keep festival events free or low cost, so that all members of the community can participate. Pictured are children enjoying free amusement ride thrills in Franke Park on Wednesday, July 11, 1979, during the 11th annual Three Rivers Festival.

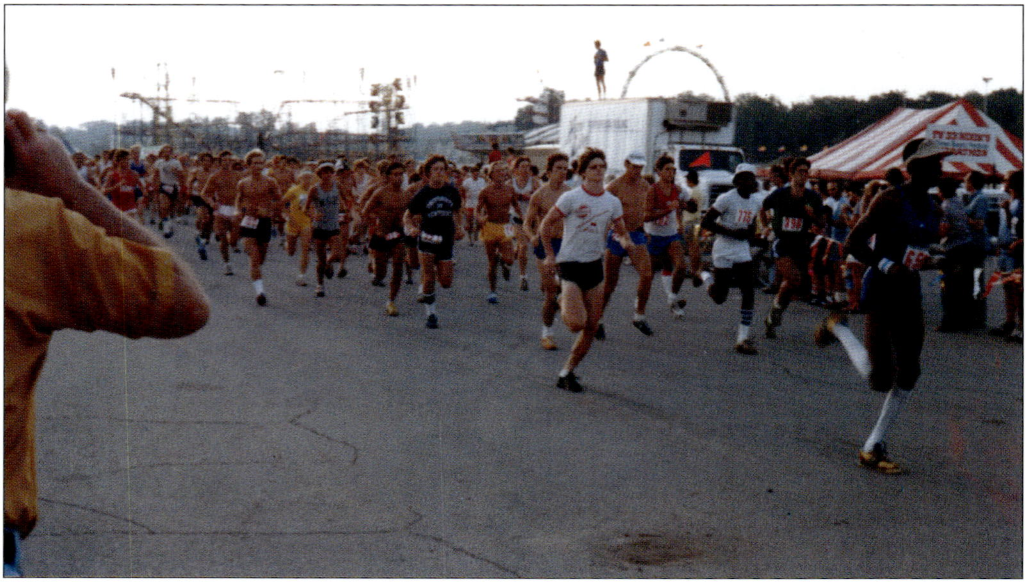

The year 1980 brought a new decade and the 11th annual Three Rivers Festival. The festival celebrated the dawning of the decade with the theme of "Vision '80." The festival looked toward the future with the idea of providing celebration and wholesome entertainment, and inspiring community pride in the city and state. Pictured is the start of the Three Rivers Festival Marathon.

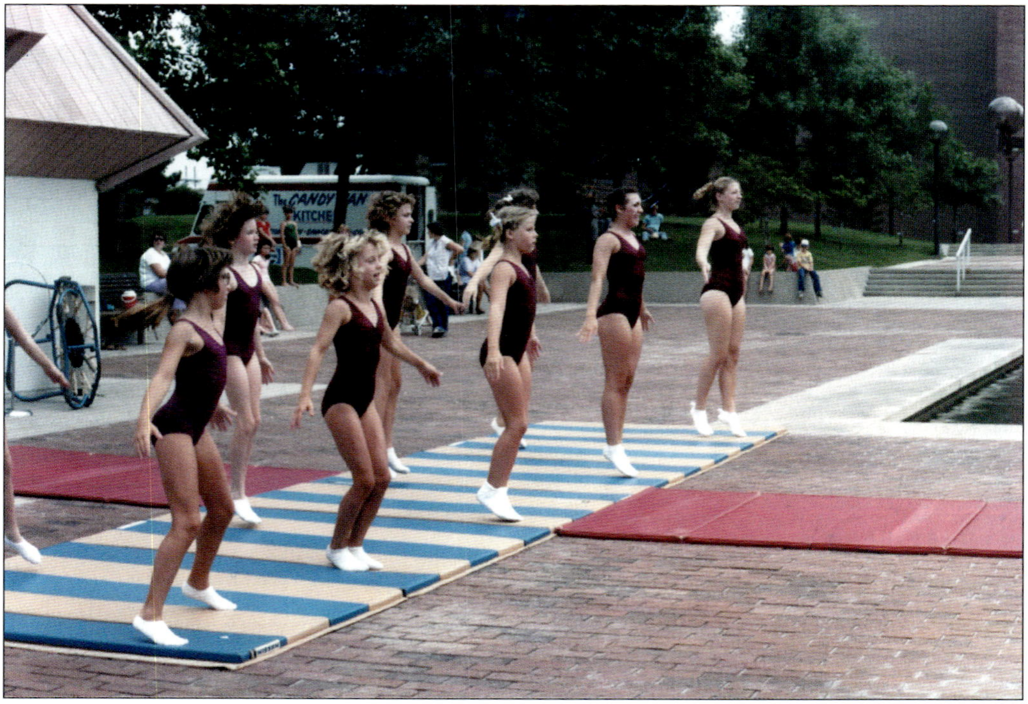

Visitors of the Three Rivers Festival enjoy a variety of events over the course of nine days. Along with fan favorites such as Junk Food Alley, the raft race, and the parade, the public can also attend events hosted by local organizations. Here, young gymnasts from the Southeast Family Branch YMCA show off their tumbling skills during an educational gymnastics demonstration on Wednesday, July 15, 1981.

From 1969 through 1980, each festival had a theme. The board of directors and the executive director, Bill Hausman, decided in 1981 that the festival had grown to such a size and importance to the city that a few words could not describe the festival; therefore, the 1981 festival was simply named 3 Rivers Festival 13. Here, shoppers look for unique items at the festival's antique show in 1981.

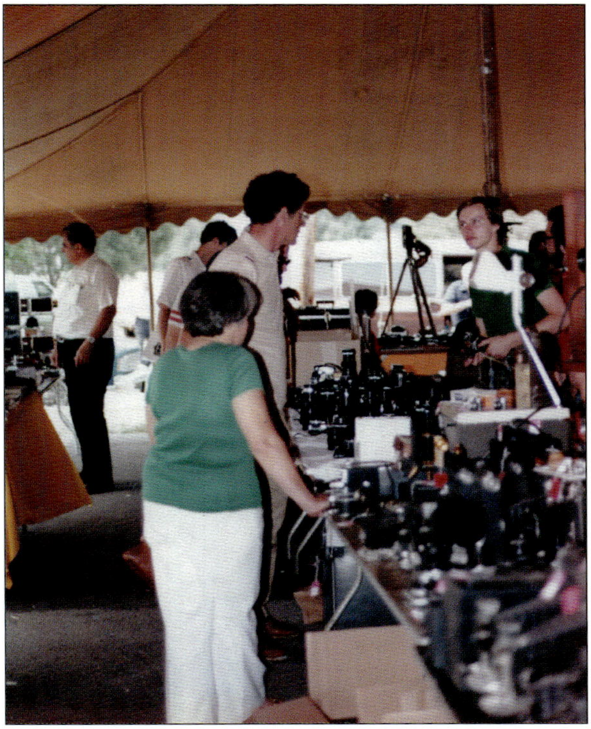

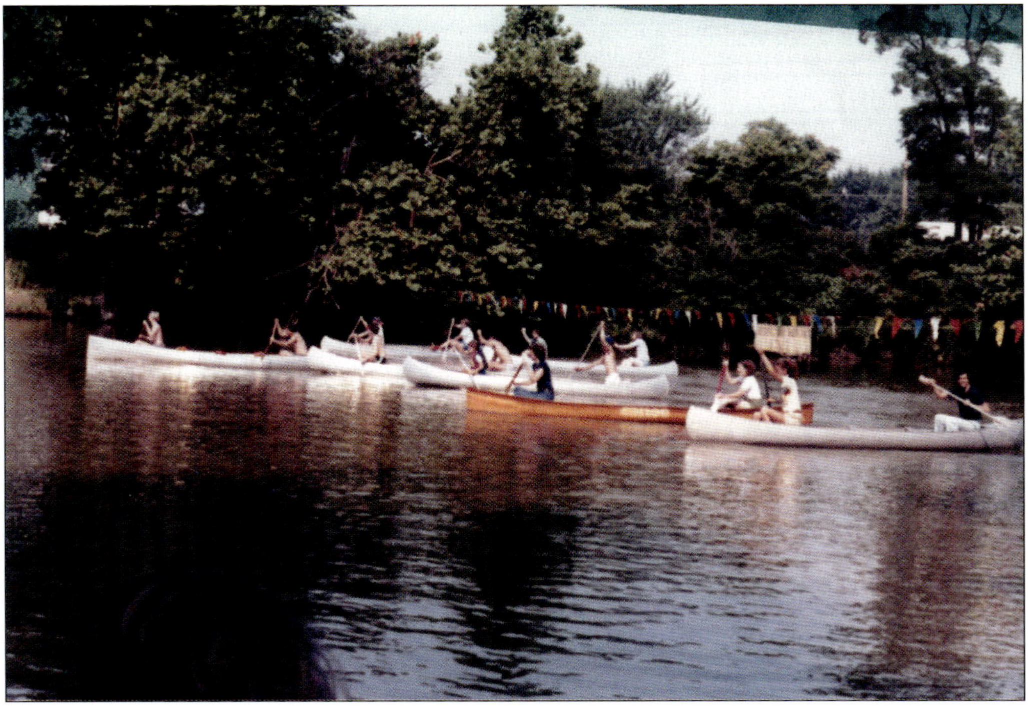

Fort Wayne is situated at the confluence of the St. Mary's, St. Joseph, and Maumee Rivers, the three rivers the festival was named after. The city's rivers host several annual festival events. On Saturday, July 18, 1981, a canoe race took place on the St. Joseph River with a course that ran from Shoaff Park to the Old Fort. Canoes lined up on the river at 9:00 a.m. to start the race.

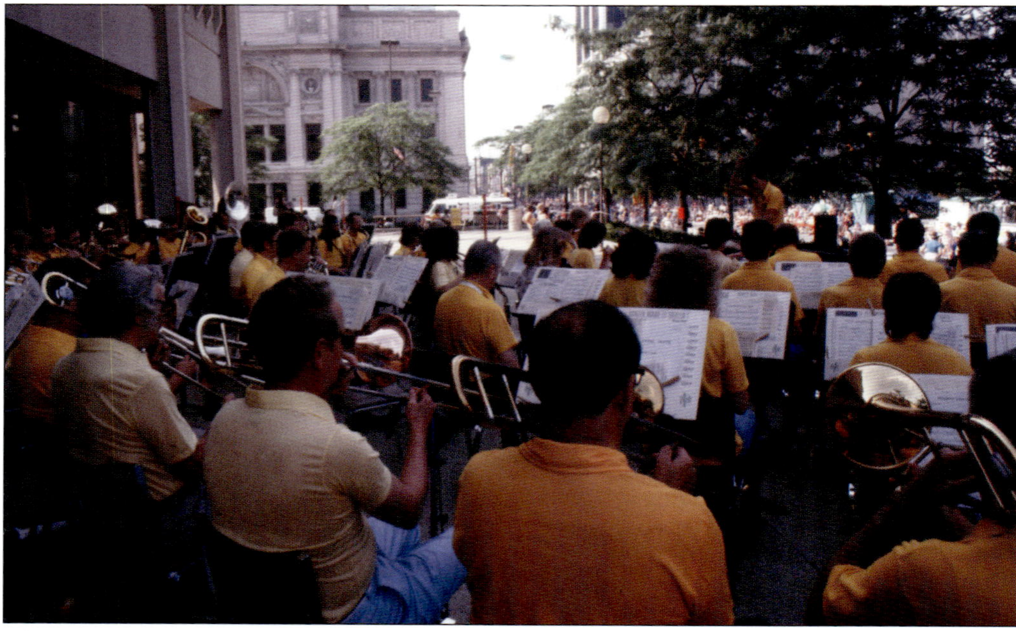

The year 1982 started off with record amounts of ice, snow, cold, rain, floods, and tornados in Fort Wayne. After the Great Flood of 1982, the people of Fort Wayne needed something to celebrate and looked forward to the festival in July. The 14th annual Three Rivers Festival kicked off at 10:00 a.m. on Saturday, July 10, with opening ceremonies and a parade. The Community Band, shown here, performs during the opening ceremonies.

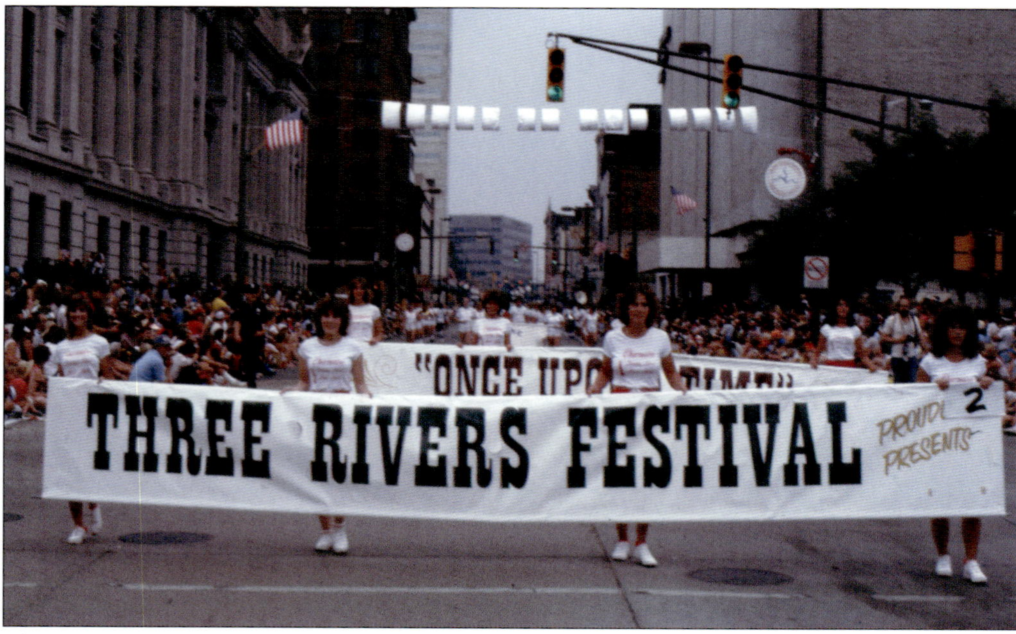

The Great Flood of 1982 left hundreds of homes and businesses damaged. The people of Fort Wayne rallied to save their homes as the rivers rose. Pres. Ronald Reagan visited during the flood and helped lay sandbags. While the city was still recovering from the flood, thousands of community members came out to watch the 14th annual parade. Here, young women carry the official Three Rivers Festival parade banner.

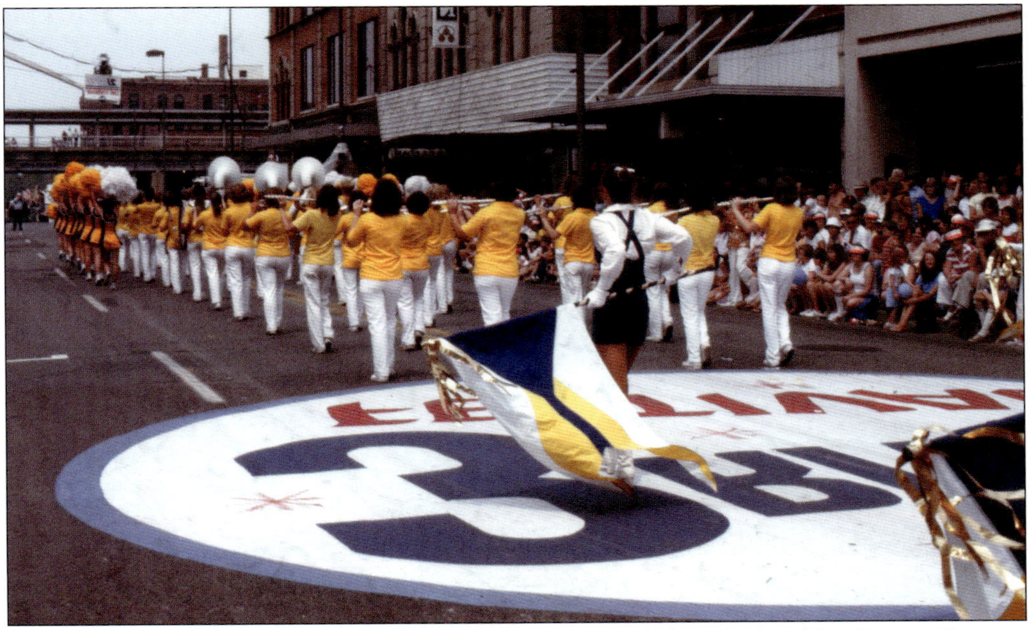

Twenty new events were introduced to the festival in 1982, including the Sand Bag Passing Contest, the World's Biggest Pretzel, and the Jell-O Jump, where participants dove into a pool full of Jell-O for prizes. The parade kicked off the festival with a "Once Upon a Time" theme. The Bishop Dwenger High School Marching Saints pass by television crews at Main and Calhoun Streets.

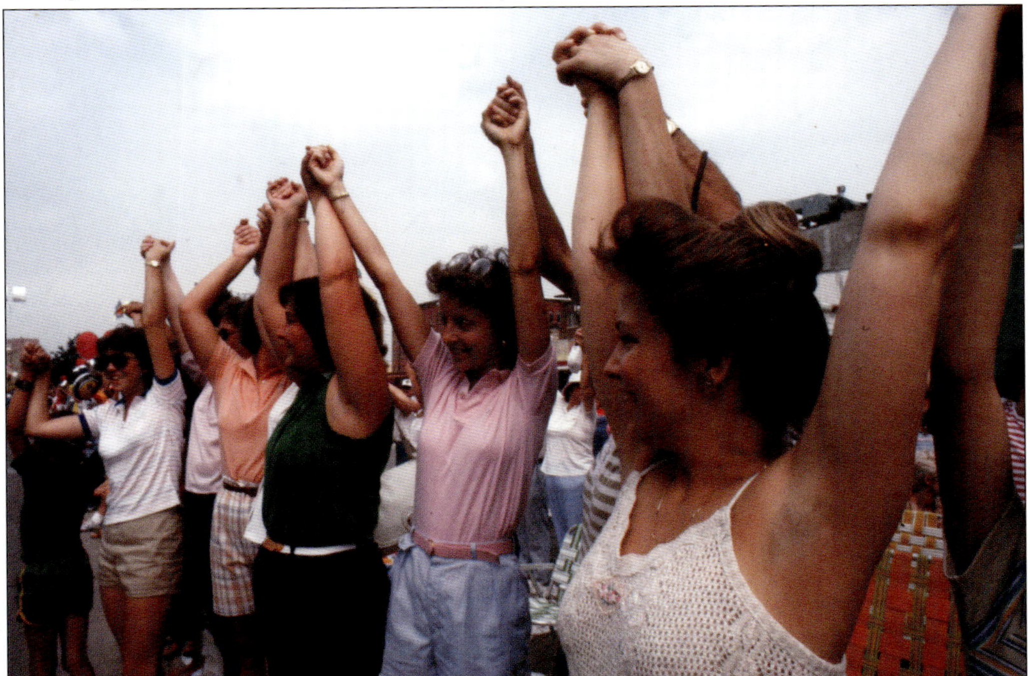

What better way to put the Three Rivers Festival on the map than by attempting to break a world record. "Put Your Hands Together Fort Wayne" took place on July 9, 1983, at 9:15 a.m. in an attempt to break the Guinness world record for the largest number of people holding hands. Twenty thousand people were needed to break the record.

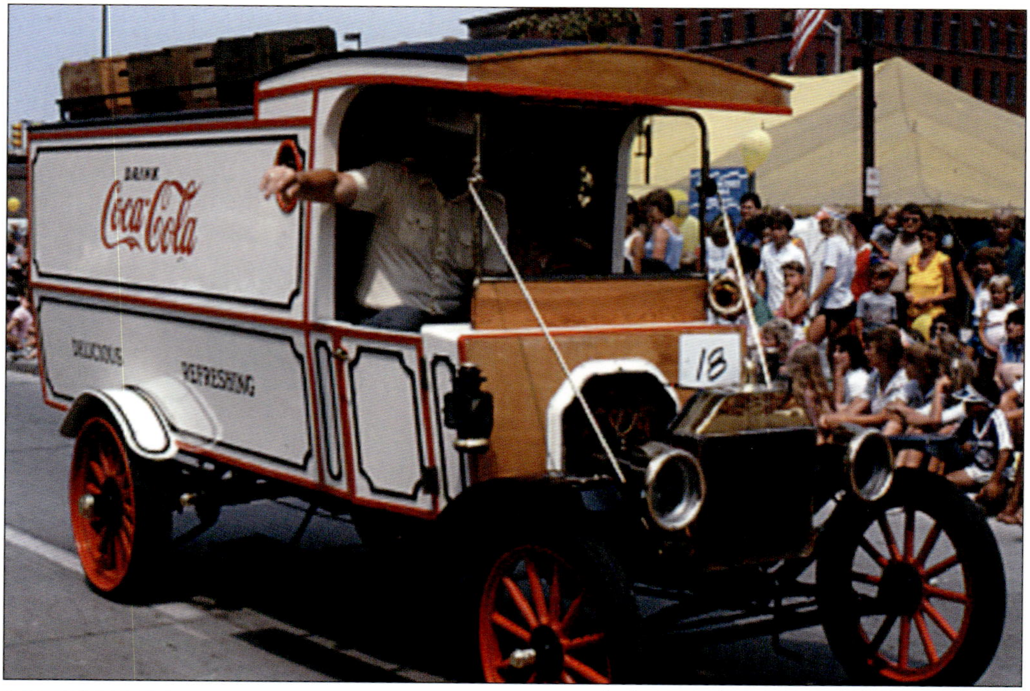

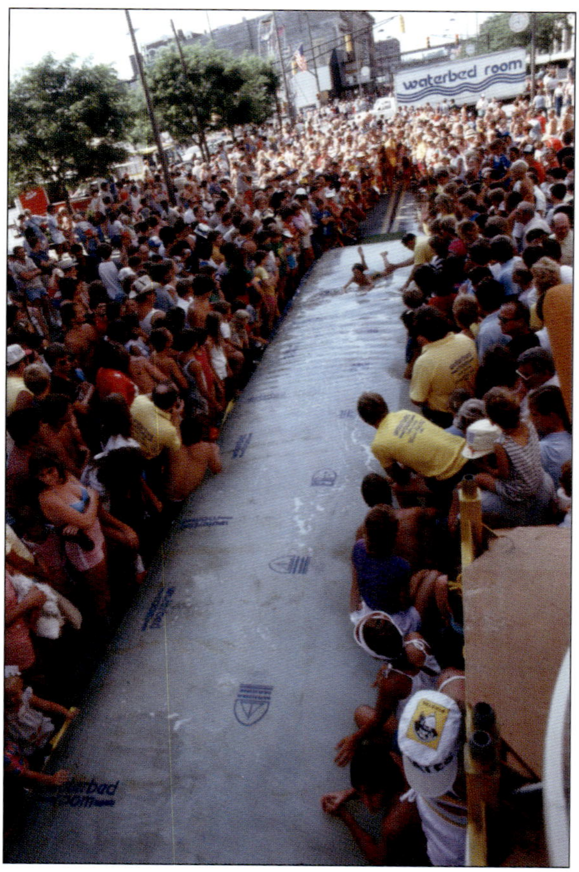

In honor of Fort Wayne having just been named an All-America City and "America's Most Livable City," the festival kicked off with the Future's Looking Good Parade. The 1983 parade welcomed special guests Tony Butala of The Lettermen and Mike Augustniak of the New York Jets. Here, an antique Coca-Cola delivery truck passes by excited parade watchers.

During the 15th annual Three Rivers Festival in 1983, the Waterbed Room hosted the Waterbed Slide On. Contestants took a running start and dove onto a 100-foot-long waterbed to see how far they could slide. Prizes were awarded for winners in men's, women's, and children's categories. The crowed is cheering on a young girl as she starts her slide.

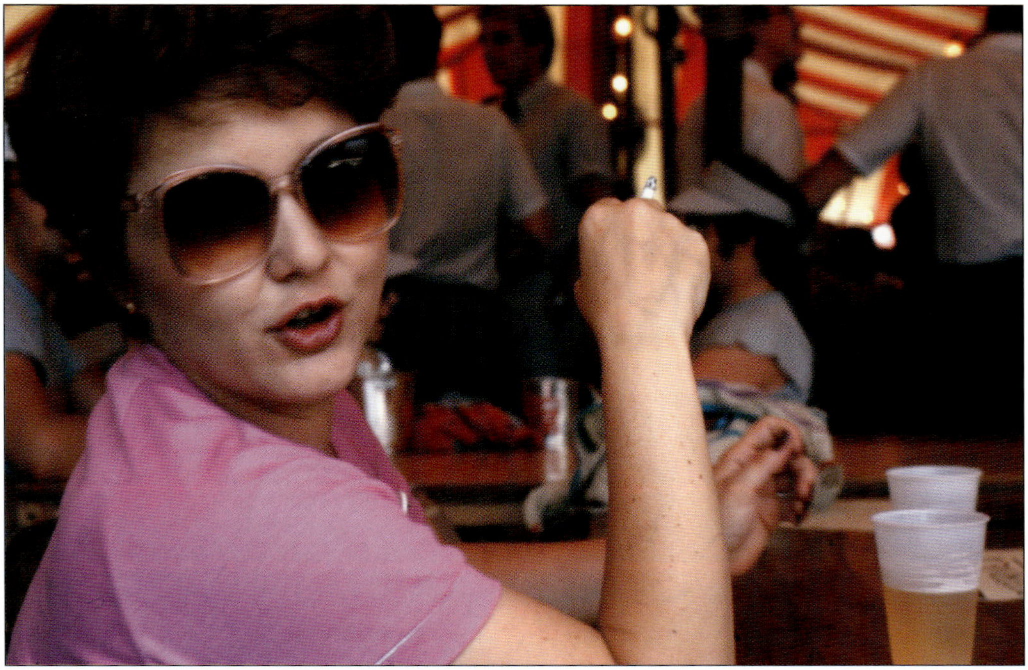

The Three Rivers Festival turned sweet 16 in 1984 with the introduction of new events such as the annual Waiter & Waitress Contest, Zoo Olympics, and a Great American Pie Bake-Off. For the first time, a shuttle bus was offered on Children's Day to take people from Franke Park to downtown activities. Here, parade chairwoman Rosemarie Bostleman enjoys a concert at the festival beer tent in 1984.

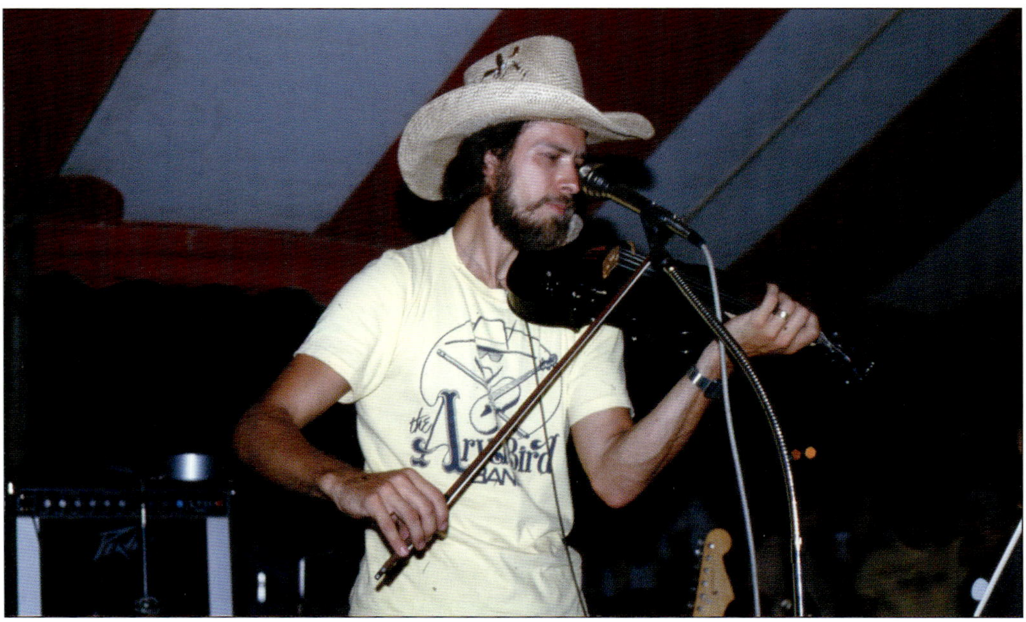

Music plays a big part of the Three Rivers Festival. Each year, the festival staff and board work hard to bring both national and local talent from different genres to multiple stages for the enjoyment of the community. In 1984, the Arvel Bird Band played its bluegrass music for the crowd inside the beer tent.

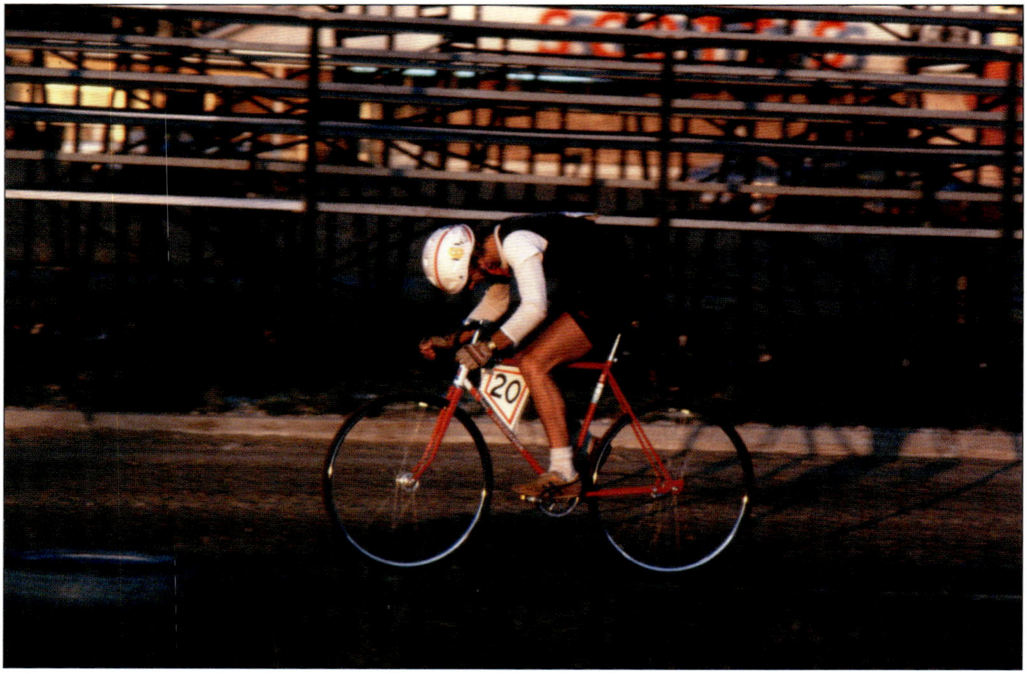

The Little 500 Challenge was held on Saturday, July 7, 1984, on the Bishop Luers High School track. The sunny, 73-degree day welcomed teams of cyclists to compete for prizes in adult and youth male, female, and coed divisions. The winning team from Indiana University competed in the finals, held at 7:00 p.m.

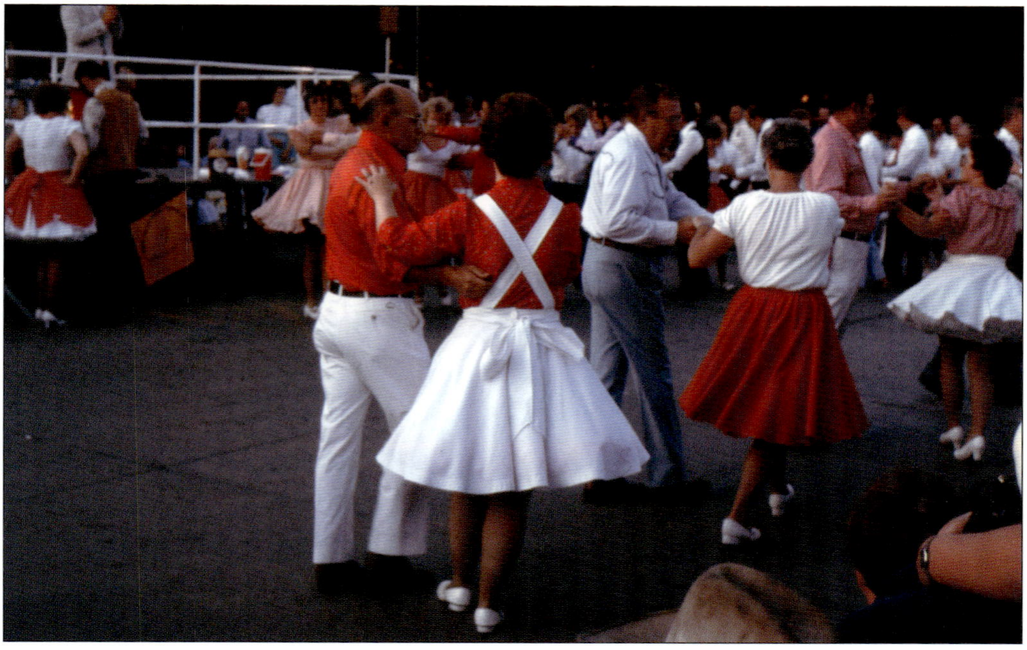

Dancers in a beautiful array of attire came out to the city/county building parking lot on Wednesday, July 11 to do-si-do with their partners at the Western-style square dance. The Fort Wayne Area Callers Association instructed the dancers in a whirl of steps for two fun-filled hours, to the enjoyment of the dancers and audience.

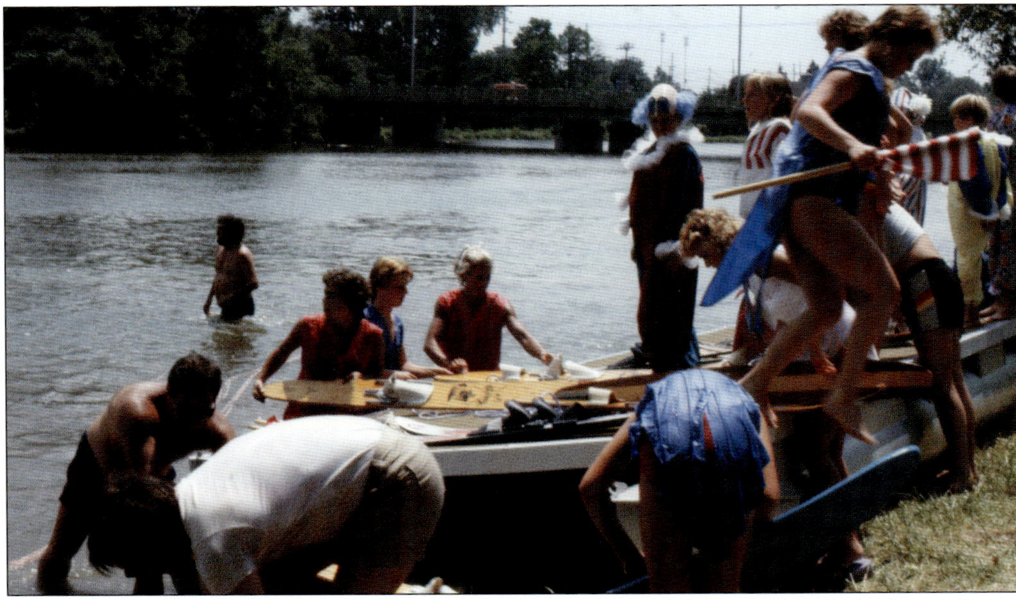

Sunday, July 15, was the final day of the festival's sweet 16 celebration. The Lake James Sports Club held a water-ski show on the St. Joseph River at Indiana University–Purdue University Fort Wayne (IPFW). The show featured barefoot skiing, a 10-man pyramid, towed hang gliding, ballet, trick skiing, and a 360 around the boat. The day and the festival concluded with the annual firework finale. Here, water-skiers are preparing for the water-ski show.

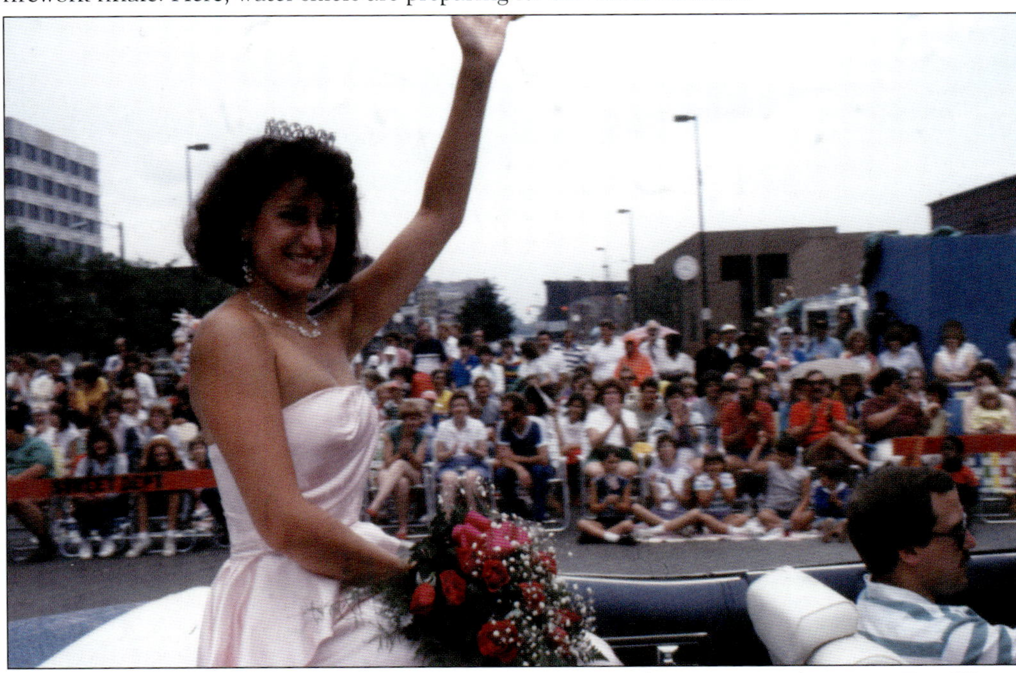

The 1985 Three Rivers Festival was held from July 13 to July 21. During this time, Fort Wayne was without a mayor. Mayor Win Moses resigned from office after pleading guilty to violating election laws. However, on Friday July 9, 1985, Moses was once again voted in as mayor of Fort Wayne through a special Democratic caucus. Pictured is Amy Moniker, Miss Fort Wayne, riding in the annual parade on Saturday, July 13, 1985.

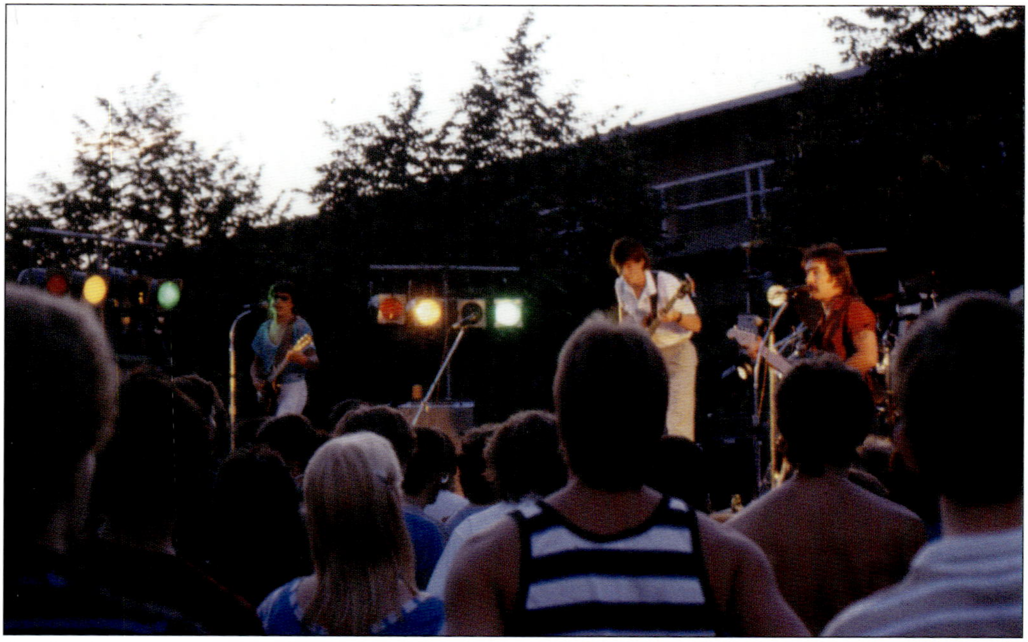

As the largest summer celebration in Fort Wayne, the Three Rivers Festival provides many opportunities for the community to gather together outdoors in the summer heat. Concerts have always been a main attraction for the festival. The 1985 festival had several stages throughout the city providing musical entertainment in a variety of genres. Above, music lovers gather at the city/county building stage to hear Mon-Taj play rock 'n' roll favorites.

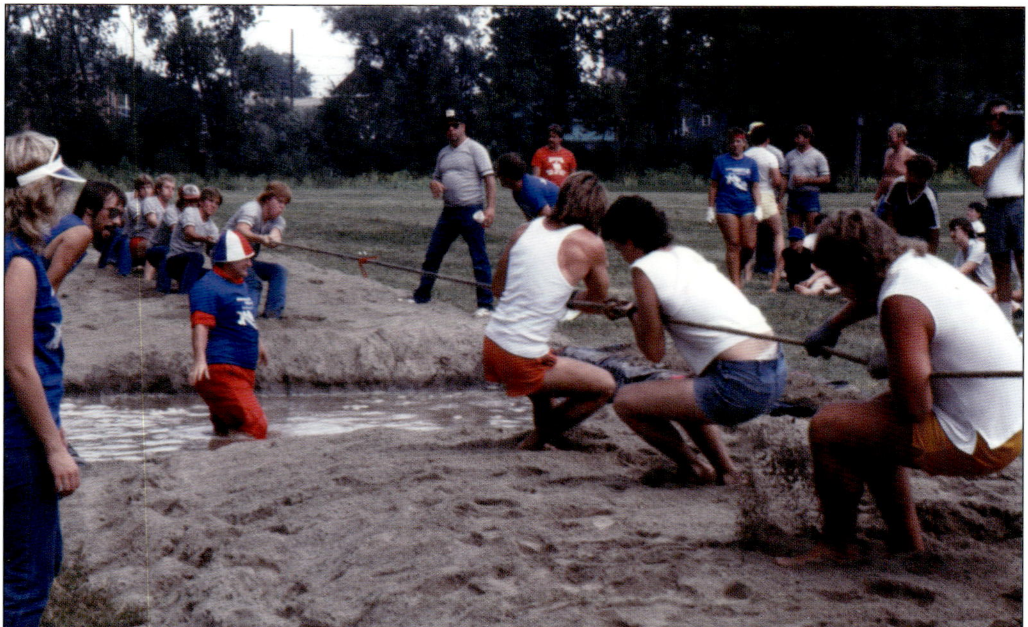

Swinney Park was the scene of the 1985 tug-of-war contest. The contest took place on the last day of the festival, which turned out to be a hot 88 degrees. Teams of men battled it out on the new tug track. The winning team received the coveted trophy and title of tug-of-war champions. Pictured are opposing teams attempting to pull their rivals into the moat.

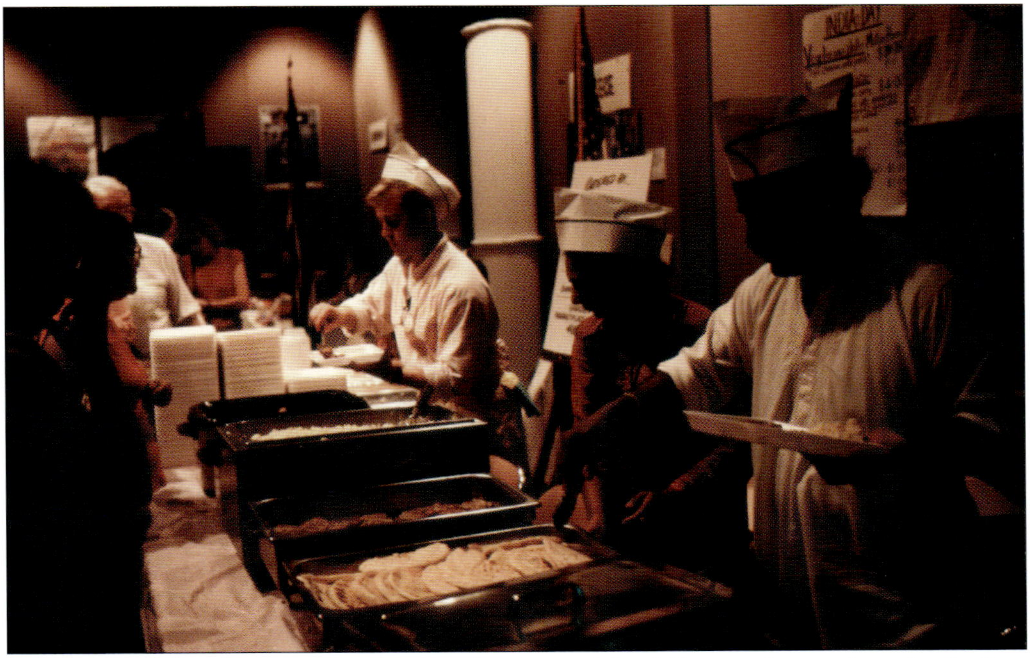

International Village was a weeklong event that featured the different cultures of people who live, work, and play in Fort Wayne. International Village allowed the people of Fort Wayne to learn about the customs, foods, traditions, and heritage of those who came from different parts of the world to make Fort Wayne their home. Pictured is India Day at the 1985 International Village.

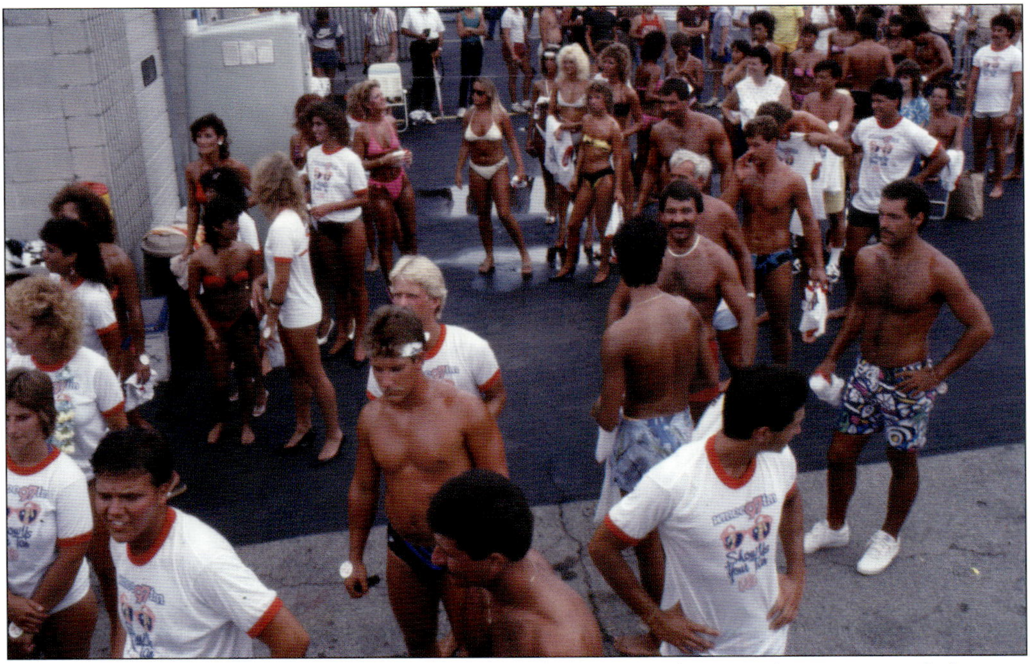

During the 1980s, dark tans were fashionable, and many people spent their summers baking in the sun. The Three Rivers Festival gave these sunbathers a place to show off their tans during the 1986 Show Us Your Tan Contest. A total of 97 contestants, both male and female, competed for prizes and the title of best tan. Here, tanned contestants wait to be called to the stage.

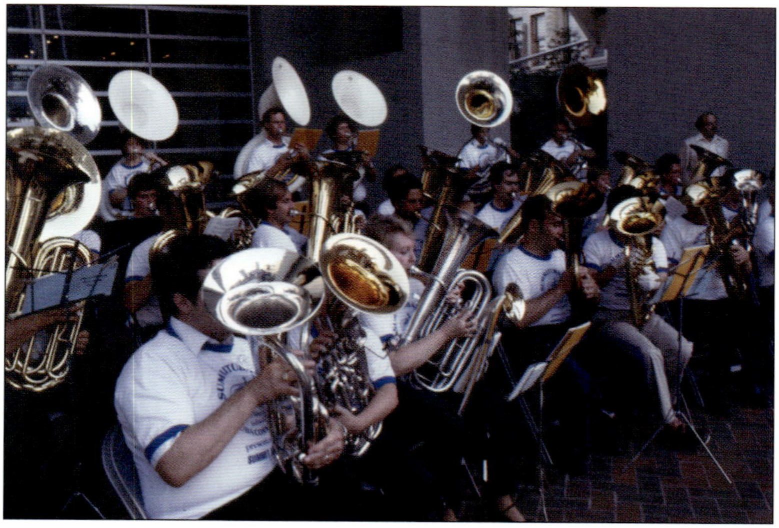

A unique concert took place at Summit Square on Wednesday, July 16, 1986—the Summit Tubafest Concert. The tuba and euphonium band played a spirited concert directed by "Mr. Tuba," Harvey Phillips. Musicians played tubas of different sizes during the concert.

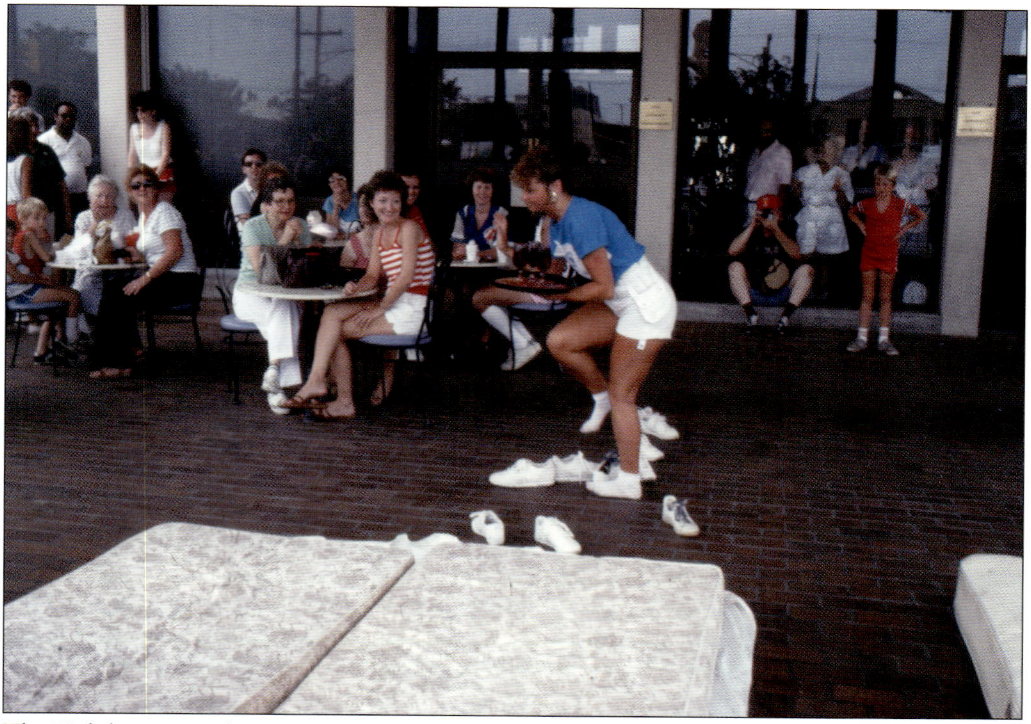

The Holiday Inn in downtown Fort Wayne hosted the festival's third annual Waiter & Waitress Contest in 1986. Waiters and waitresses from local restaurants, in full uniform, carried full bottles of wine and wineglasses through obstacles around the outside of the hotel for prizes and trophies. Here, a waitress takes off her shoes while balancing a tray of wine glasses as she completes the obstacle course.

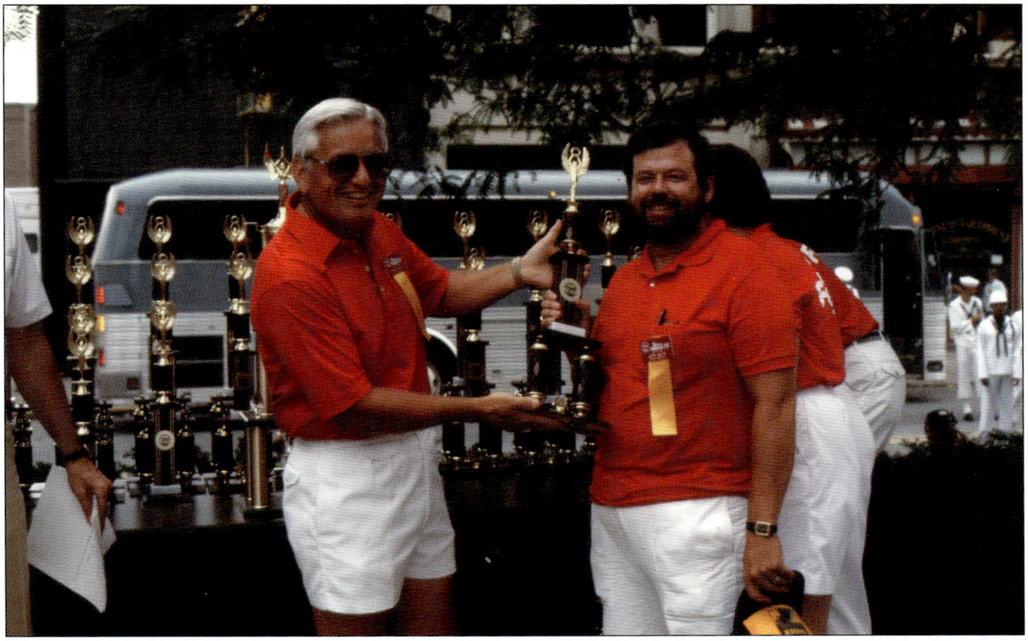

The Three Rivers Festival became a nonprofit organization in 1974. Since then, the festival has been run by a volunteer board of directors and a small staff. The festival board and staff work all year to plan and organize Fort Wayne's largest summer celebration. Board member Jerry White is pictured helping hand out awards during the 1987 parade.

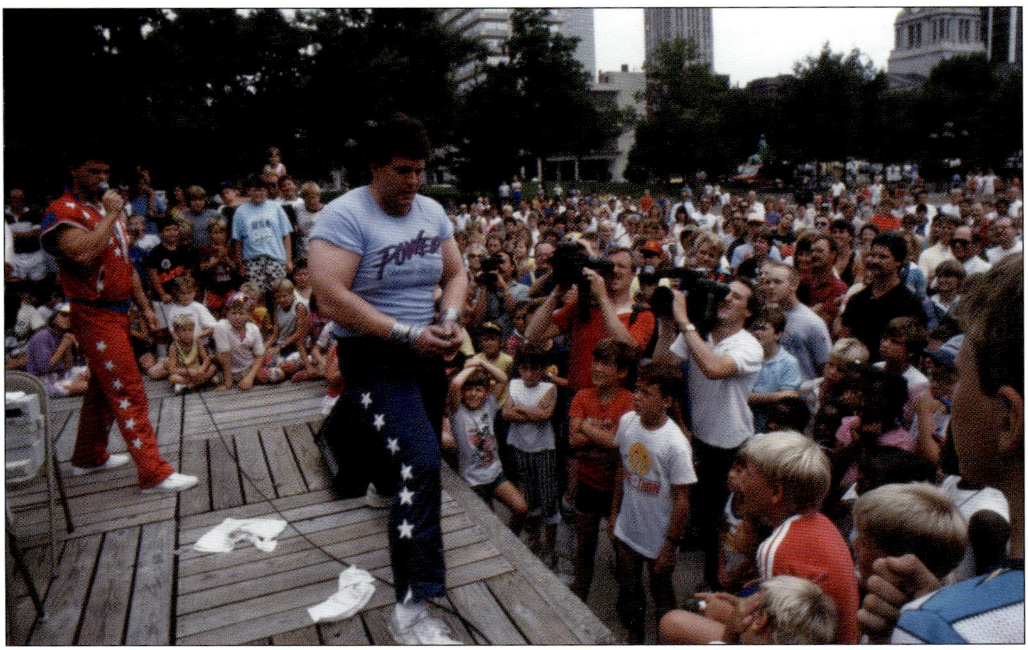

The 1987 festival hosted the Power Team, featuring world-class record-holding athletes. Over the course of three days, the Power Team demonstrated its strength in steel handcuff breaking, steel bar bending, breaking stacks of flaming bricks, and more. Here, a member of the Power Team shows off his big muscles to the delight of the crowd.

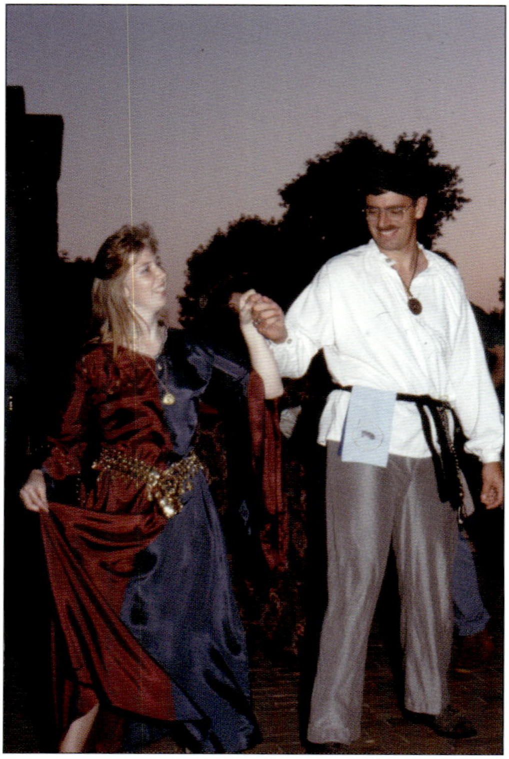

The Shire of Shadowed Stars transported festival attendees back in time to the Renaissance when it hosted a medieval fighting demonstration, followed by medieval dancing in Freimann Square. Fighters dressed in chain mail and boiled leather armor recreated the medieval field of honor. After the epic battles, knights and ladies dressed in their finest Renaissance clothes and danced the night away. Here, a couple demonstrates a medieval dance in 1987.

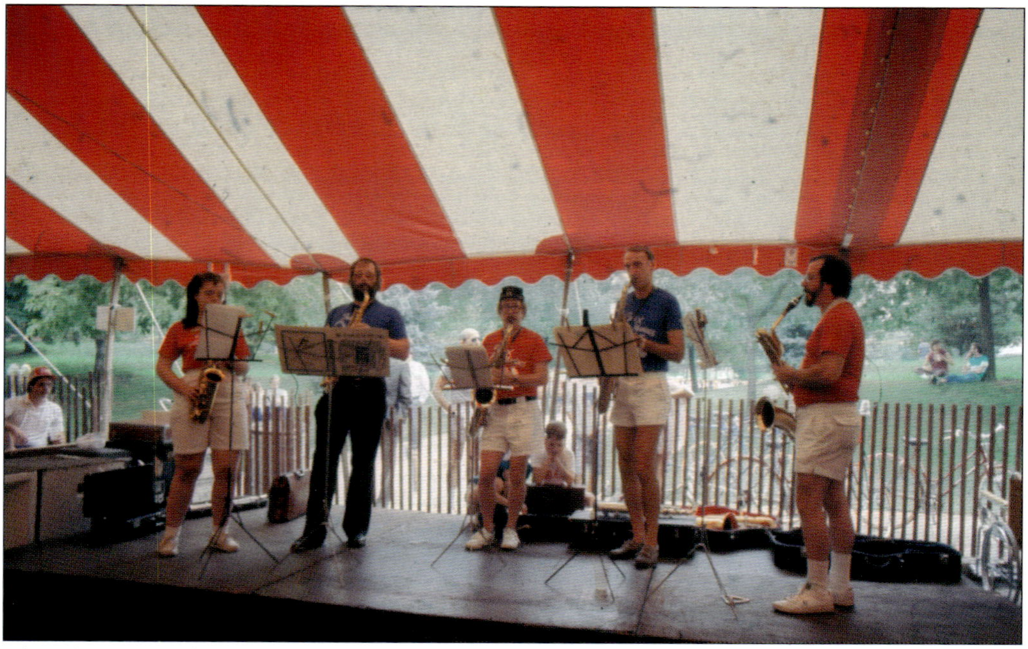

The Three Rivers Festival hosted an array of musical talent on its three stages during the 1987 festival. Nightly music could be found at the city/county building, Freimann Square, and the official Three Rivers Festival beer tent. Rock, country, folk, and jazz were just a few of the musical genres that could be enjoyed by all. Here, the Sax Maniacs entertain a lunchtime crowd from the beer tent stage.

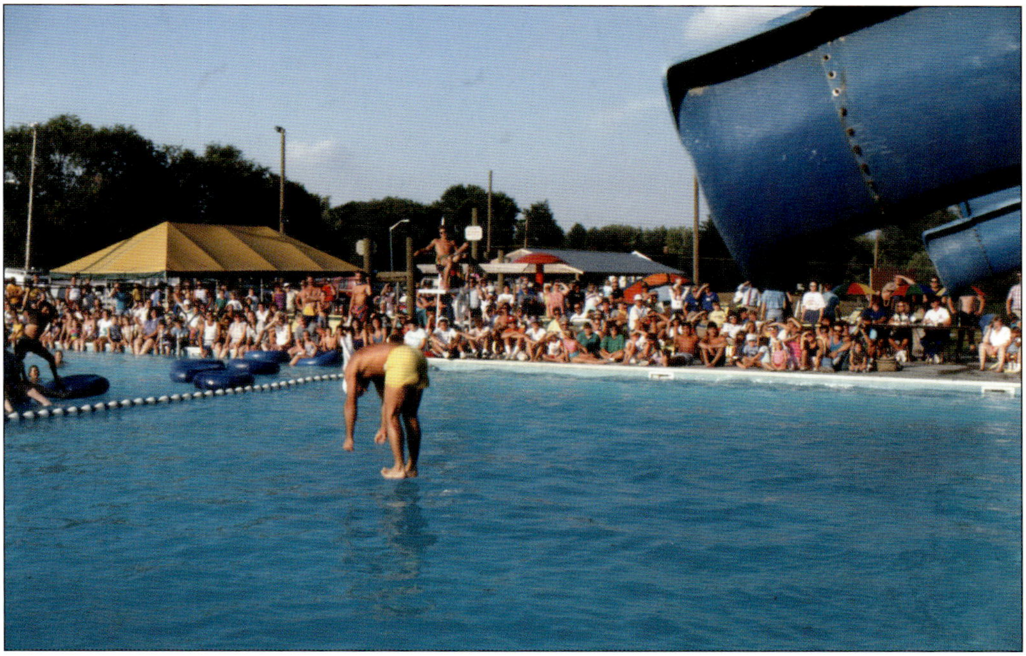

In 1988, the Three Rivers Festival celebrated its 20-year anniversary in the face of challenges. An early summer drought dried up the rivers and caused the raft race to be cancelled for the first time, and a large thunderstorm with brilliant lightning caused the beer tent and Junk Food Alley to be closed for an evening. However, Mother Nature could not stop the festival, which marched on with nine days of fun in the sun. Highlights of the 1989 festival included encore performances of the Laser Light Spectacular, an expanded beer tent entertainment schedule, and a spectacular fireworks finale. Bill Hausman, the festival's first executive director, retired in 1989. Under his guidance, the festival had grown from a small downtown festival into a sprawling extravaganza of over 275 events. Pictured here is Ebenezer Floppensloper's Belly Flop Contest on July 11, 1988.

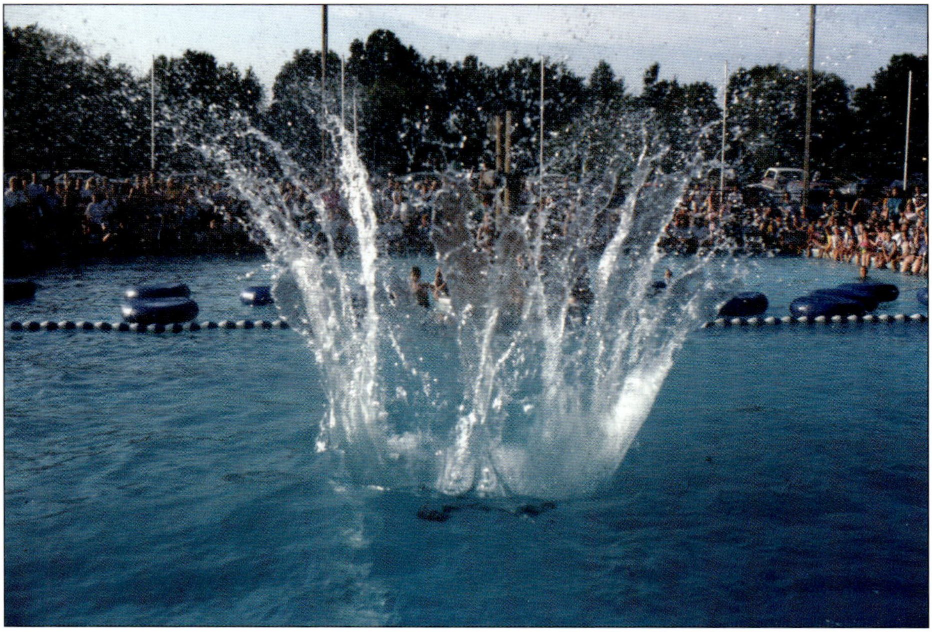

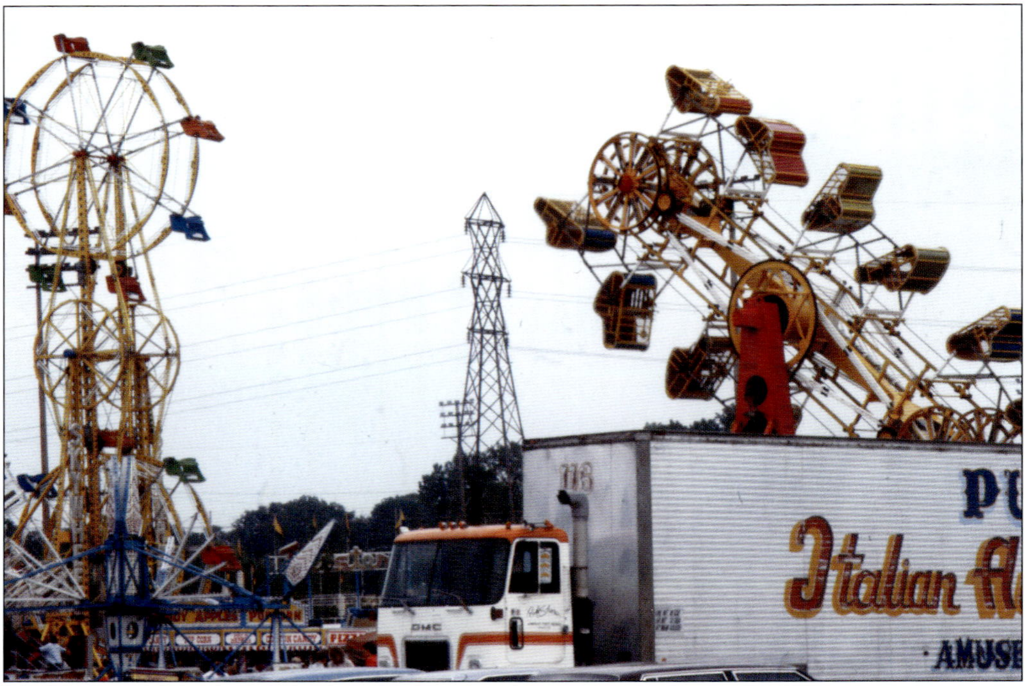

The Three Rivers Festival Giant Midway thrilled festival guests throughout the week with spectacular European and American rides, shows, concessions, and games. The midway was located in the parking lot of the Allen County War Memorial Coliseum. Festival guests could purchase an all-day wristband and ride to their heart's content. Pictured are thrill rides at the Giant Midway on Saturday, July 9, 1988.

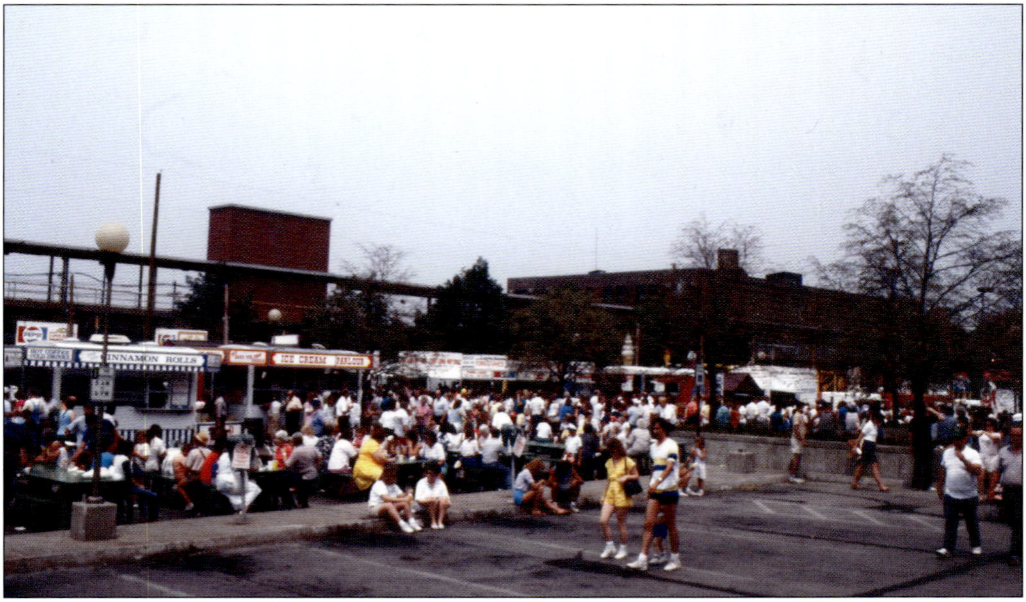

Not-All-Junk Food Alley grew over the past 20 years from a couple of concessions hosted by a local sorority to over four dozen. In 1988, it was located for a second year in the parking lot of the city/county building, after its move from Barr Street in 1987. Here, festival attendees enjoy lunch at Not-All-Junk Food Alley on Tuesday, July 12, 1988.

Three

1989–1998

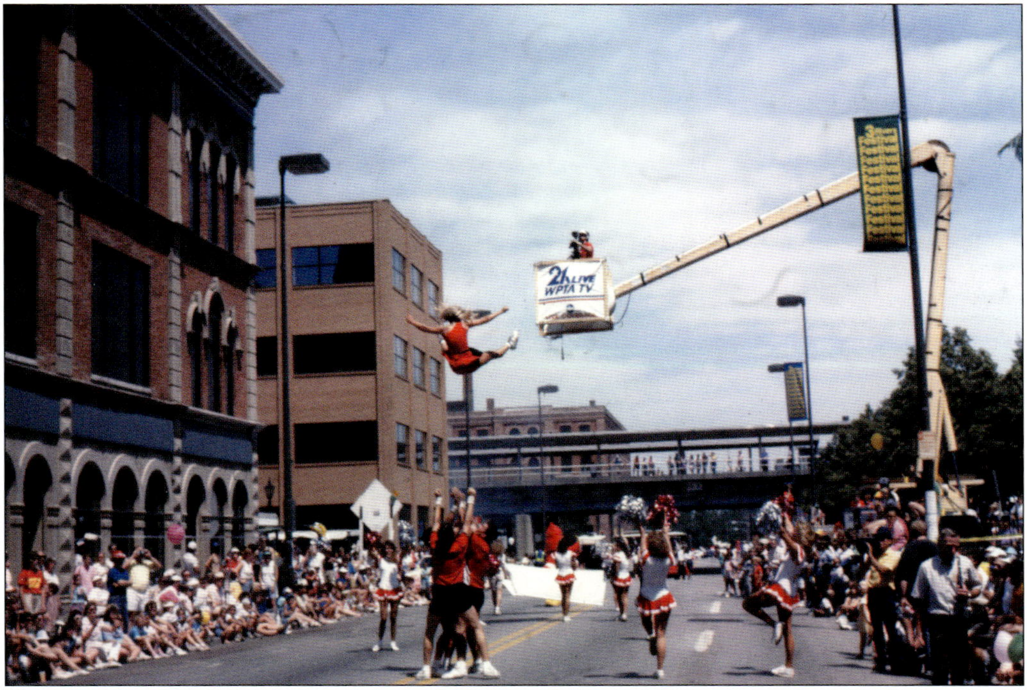

At 10:00 in the morning on Saturday, July 8, 1989, the 21st annual Three Rivers Festival parade stepped off in a moving panorama of wonderful memories and future dreams. The two-hour parade was enjoyed by thousands of people who lined the parade route and thousands more at home, who watched a live broadcast on WPTA 21 Alive. Ball State University cheerleaders are shown performing during the parade.

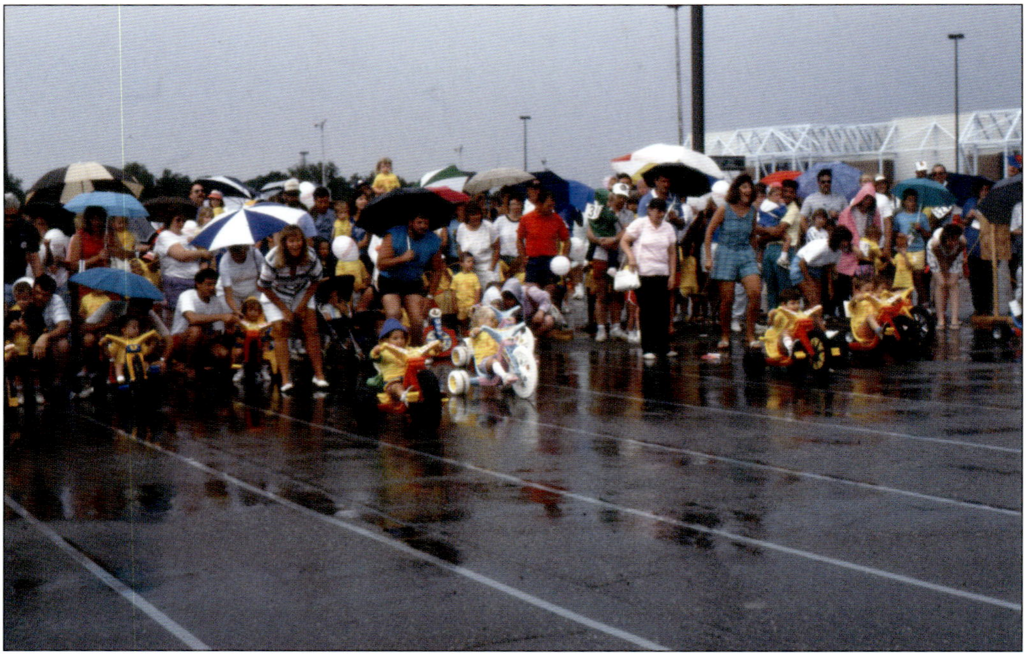

On Sunday, July 9, 1989, children aged three to six arrived at the coliseum parking lot with their Big Wheels for a race down a 100-foot racetrack during the festival's Big Wheels Race. Competitors received a T-shirt and ribbon. Here, children line up for the start of the race.

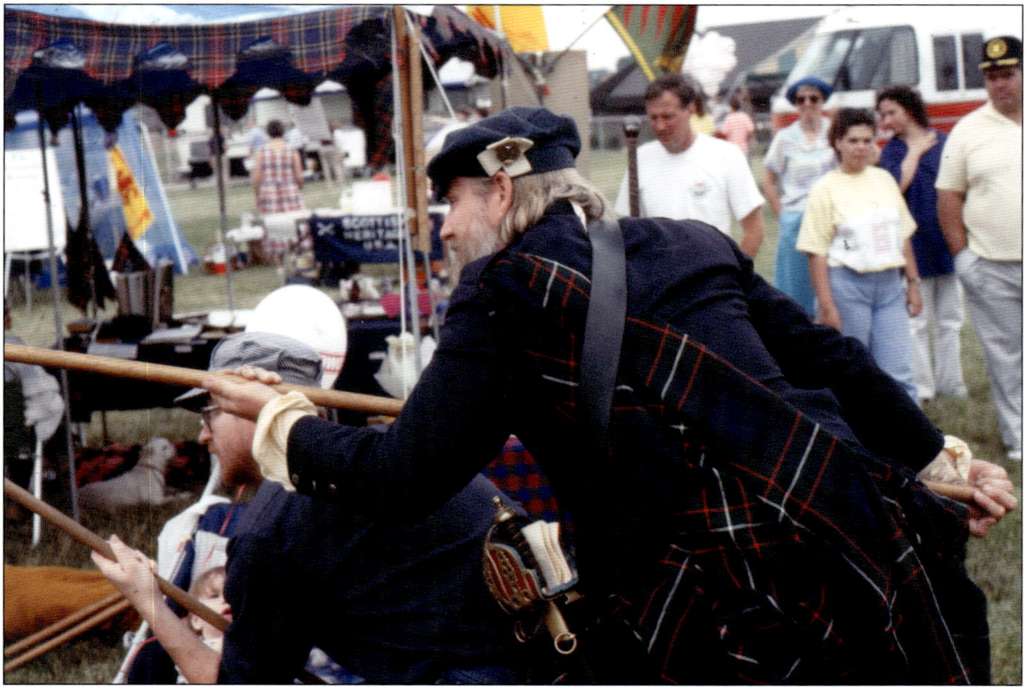

The Scottish Cultural Society sponsored the Indiana Highland Games on Saturday, July 15, 1989. The games, held at Zollner Stadium, were a salute to the Scottish heritage of the Fort Wayne community with a day full of music, sports, sheepherding, clan tents, and ethnic foods. Here, a clansman in traditional Scottish dress prepares to compete in the games.

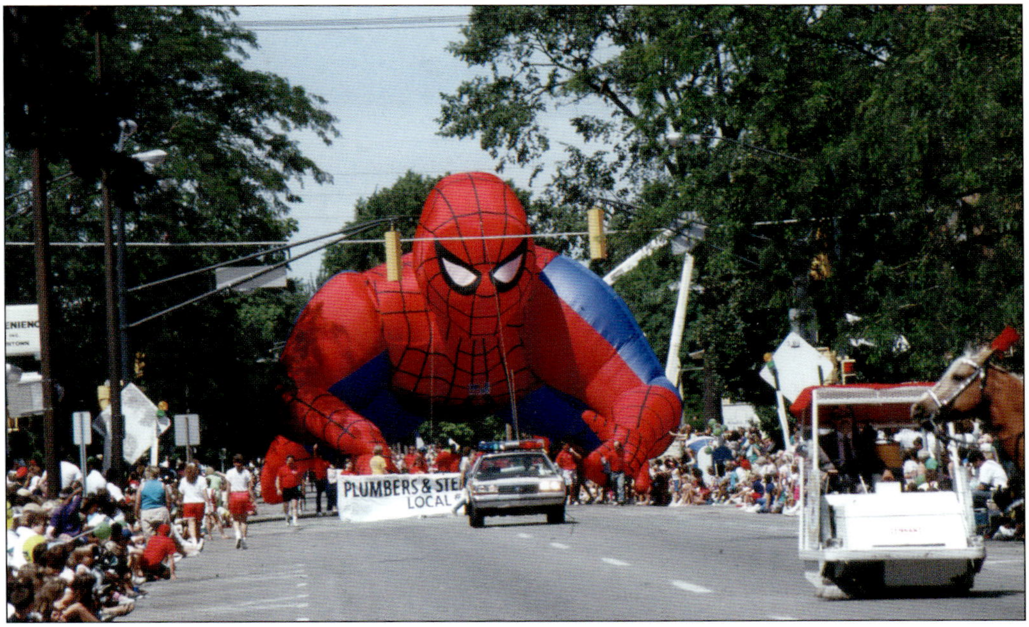

The parade theme for the 22nd Three Rivers Festival on Saturday, July 7, 1990, was "The 90's—Decade of Friendship." Each parade unit was tasked with portraying the 1990s in their floats, balloons, walking units, and marching bands. The many organizations and businesses that took part in the parade came up with creative ways to demonstrate their hopes for the decade ahead. Pictured is Spiderman making his way down Wayne Street.

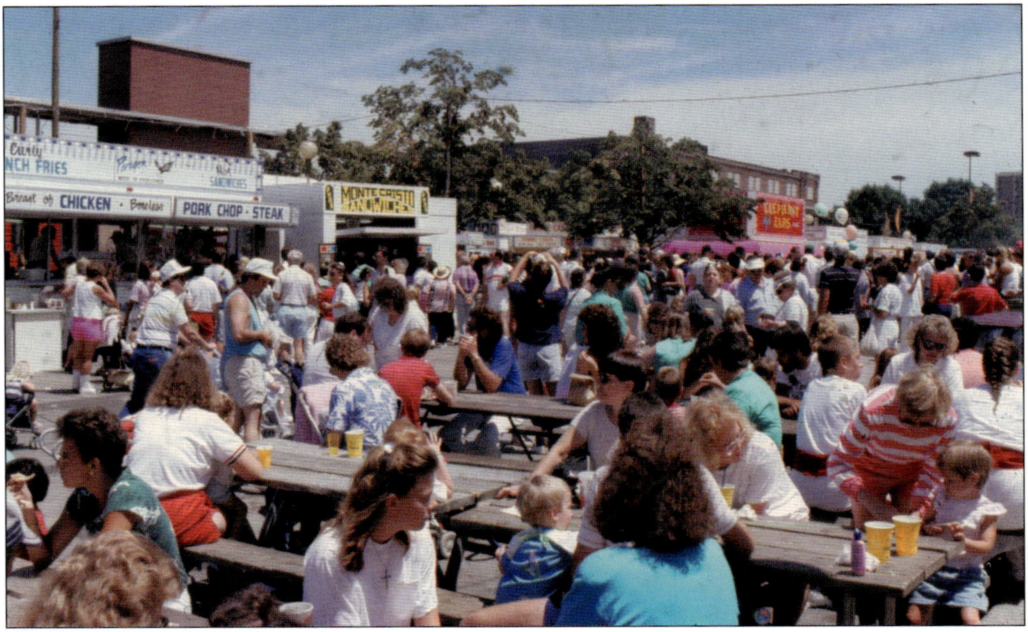

Each year, the citizens of Fort Wayne wait with anticipation for the Three Rivers Festival in July. While thousands of people line the street for the parade, even more visit Junk Food Alley to fulfill their cravings for elephant ears, Monte Cristo sandwiches, chicken on a stick, caramel apples, and much more. Pictured are festival guests enjoying the offerings of Junk Food Alley on Saturday, July 7, 1990.

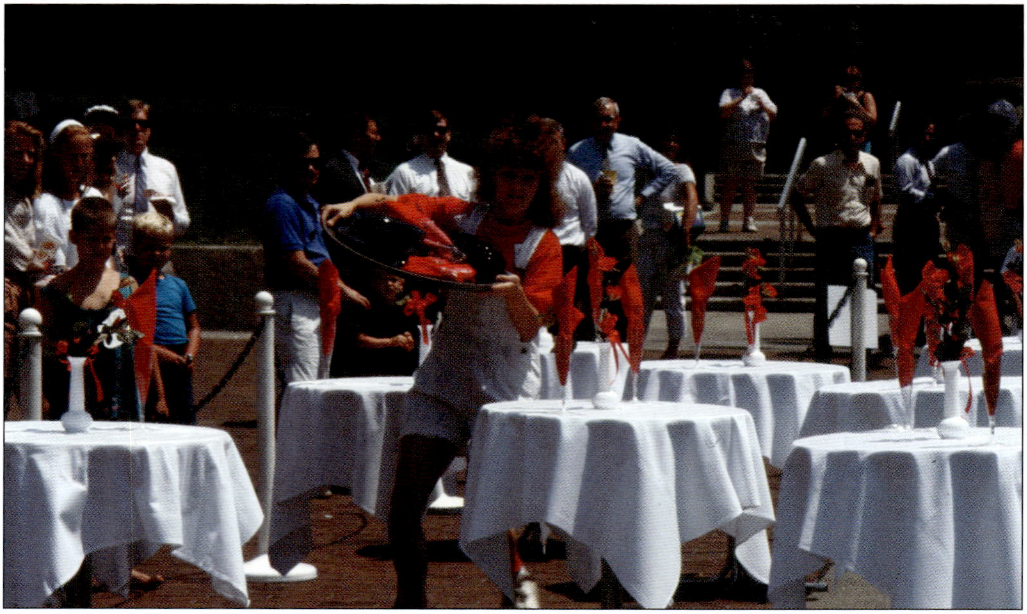

The evening of Tuesday, July 10, 1990, brought the annual Waiter & Waitress Contest to the festival. This fan favorite event challenged area waiters and waitresses to make their way through a tricky obstacle course while balancing a heavy tray. Contestants could compete as individuals or on a team. Here, a waitress races to get a table set in record time.

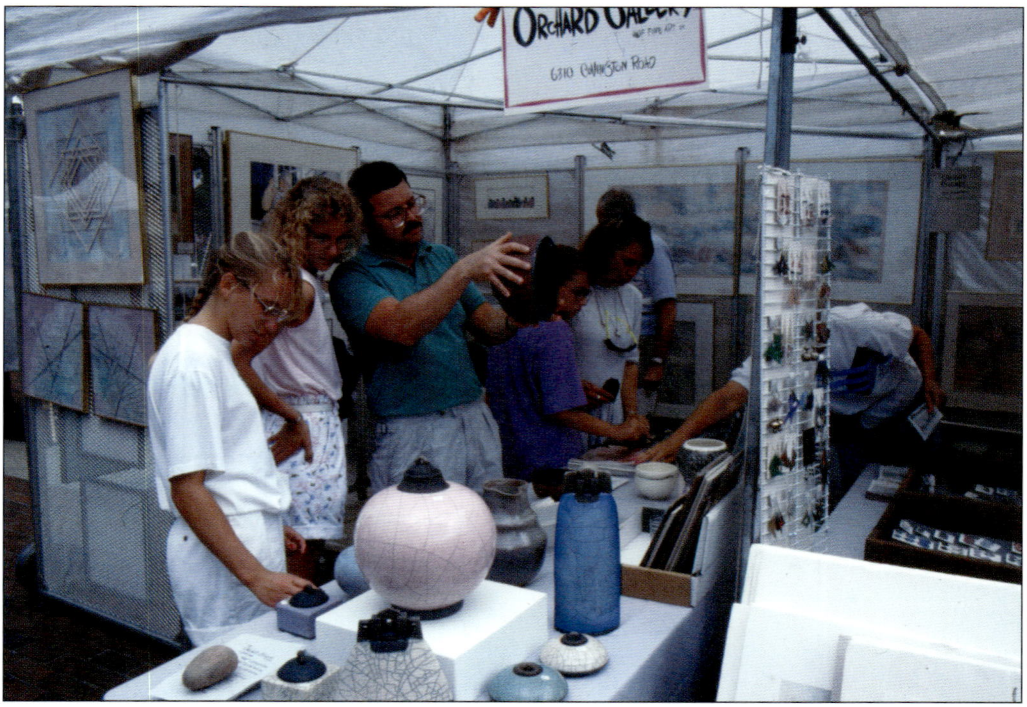

The Three Rivers Festival arts and crafts show was held in Freimann Square on Saturday, July 13 and Sunday, July 14, 1991. Dozens of talented artists displayed and sold their beautiful jewelry, painting, ceramics, fiber, and wood creations to festivalgoers. Here, a family looks at ceramic bowls on display during the arts and crafts show.

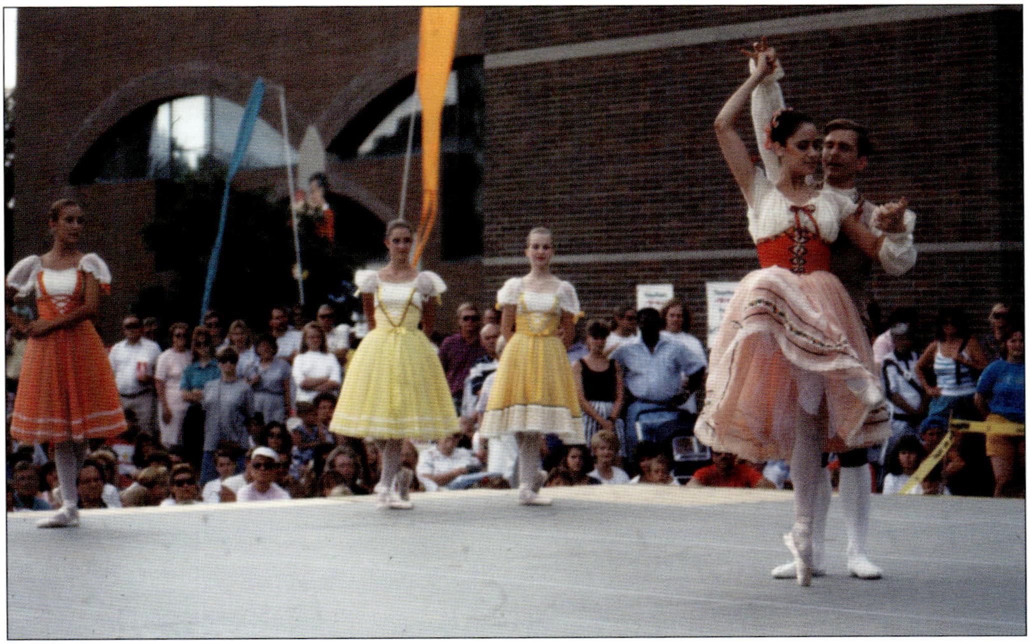

Arts United of Greater Fort Wayne hosted Sunday in the Park with Art during the arts and crafts show on Sunday, July 14, 1991. The event showcased a variety of performing and visual arts in Freimann Square and along Main Street. Festival guests were invited to bring a lawn chair and enjoy a relaxing afternoon in the park. Here, the Fort Wayne Ballet performs during Sunday in the Park with Art.

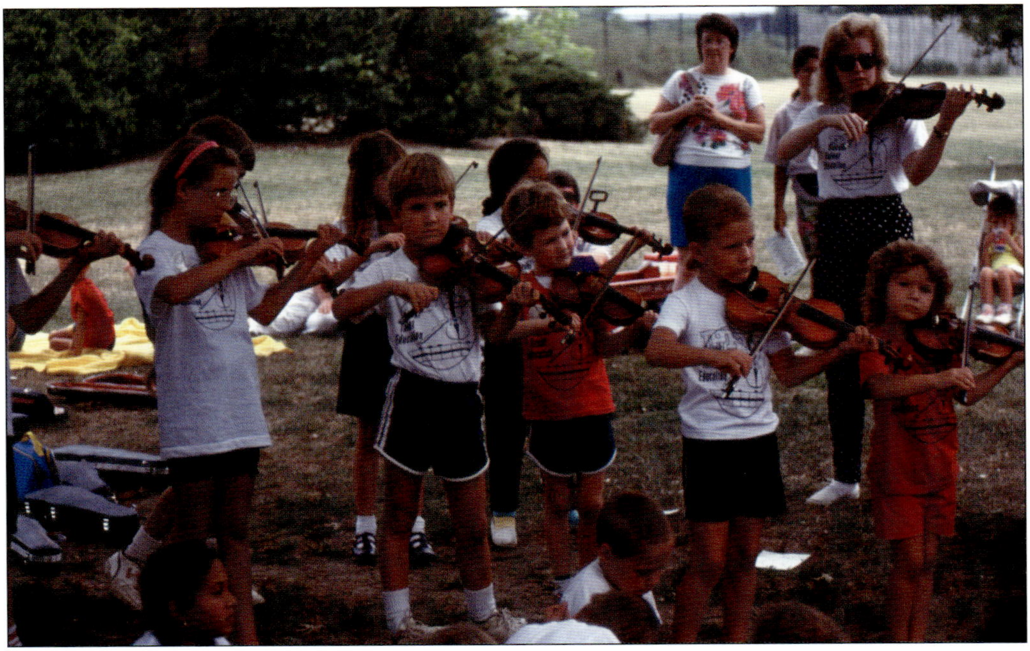

The annual Children's Festival was held at Franke Park on July 19–20, 1991. The two-day event featured a variety of activities for children of all ages. Children could have their faces painted, have fun on the amusement rides, join in a water balloon toss, and visit the Fort Wayne Children's Zoo. Children also performed during the IPFW Children's Suzuki Piano and Violin Concert.

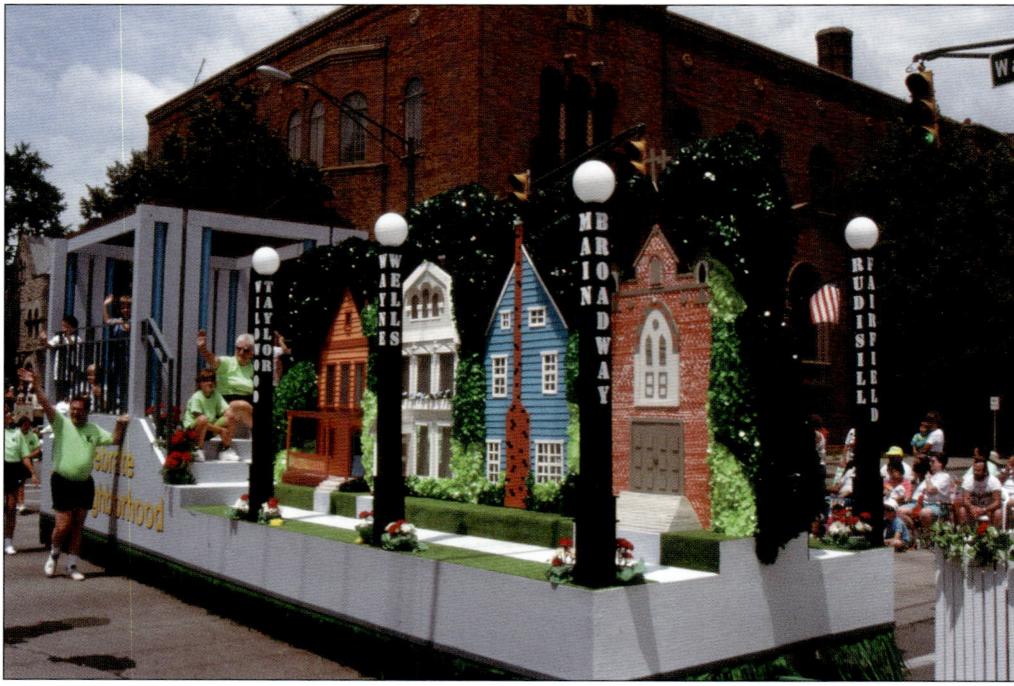

The 24th annual Three Rivers Festival parade took place on Saturday, July 11, 1992, at 10:00 a.m. The parade theme for 1992 was "Celebrate the Neighborhood," which focused on some of Fort Wayne's greatest assets. Mr. McFeely of *Mr. Rogers Neighborhood* served as grand marshal. A colorful float featuring Fort Wayne's historic neighborhoods is pictured here.

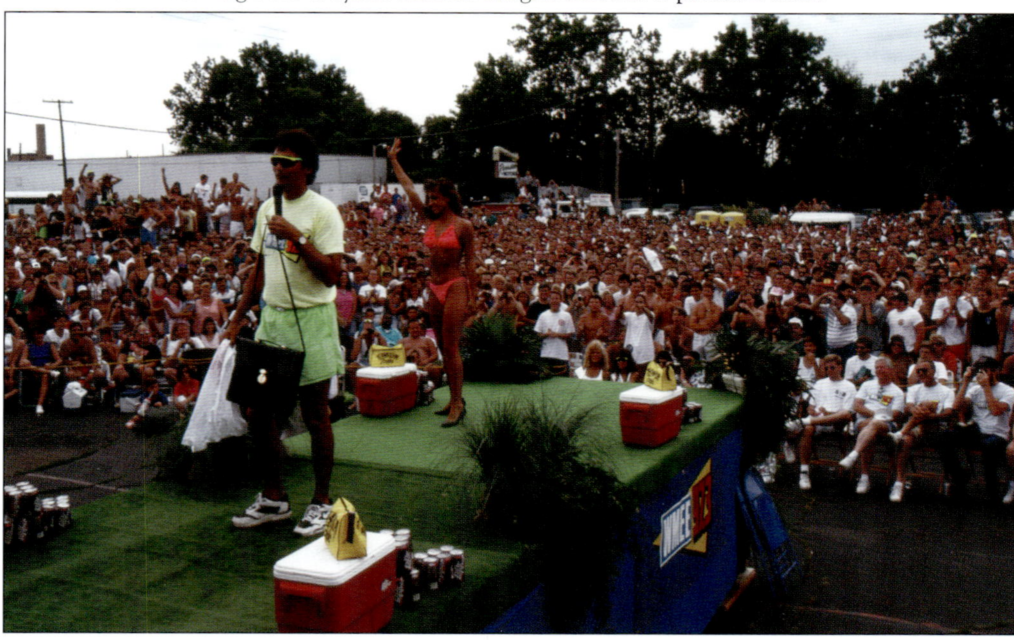

Nothing said 1990s more than a dark tan and permed hair! The WMEE/Dr. Pepper Bikini Spectacular was held on Saturday, July 11, 1992. Fifty men and 50 women took to the stage to compete for cash prizes for the best and darkest tan. It became an annual event in the 1990s due to its popularity. Pictured is WMEE DJ Charlie Butcher on stage during the 1992 contest.

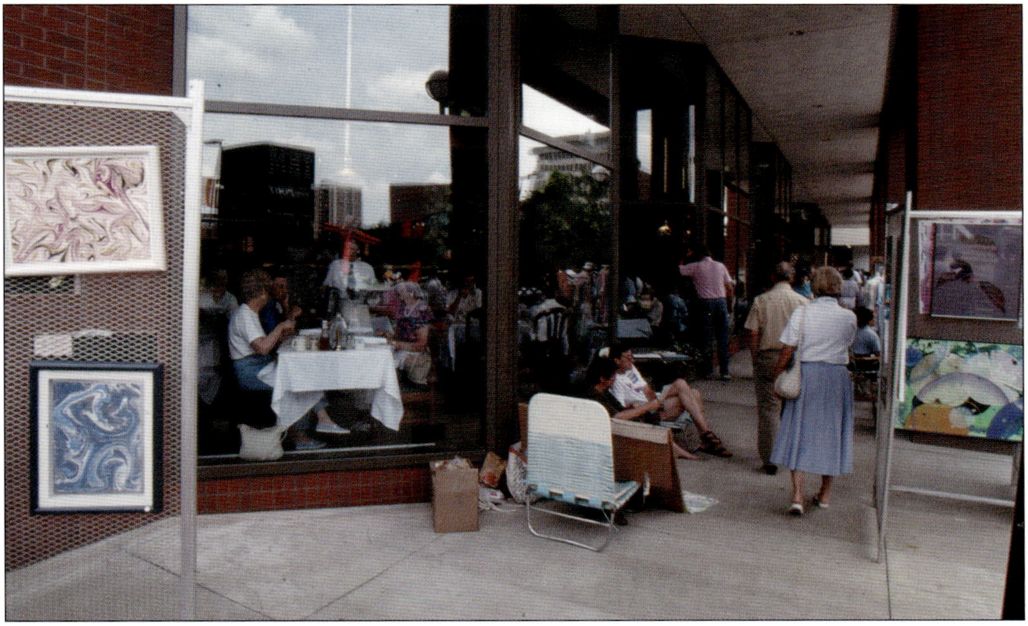

The Three Rivers Festival was not favored by Mother Nature in 1992, when rain fell on eight out of the nine days of the 24th festival. Even with all the rain, the festival marched on; attendees came out to enjoy the parade, bed race, arts and craft fair, beer tent, and all the other events. Here, festival guests enjoy art at the Artists Guild Paint Out and Sale.

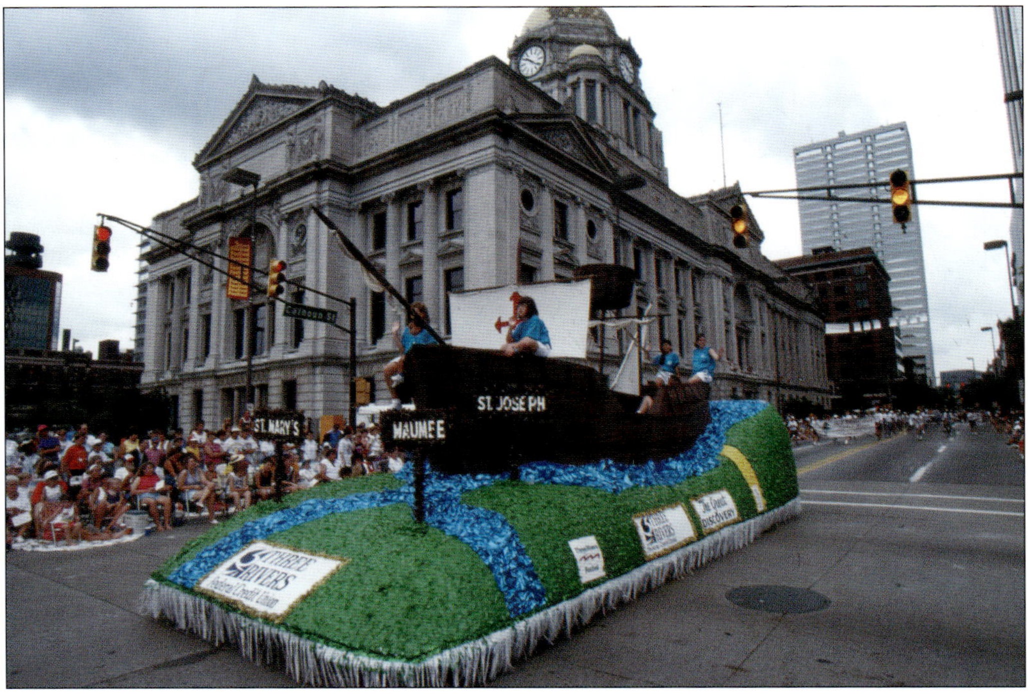

"A Sterling Celebration" marked 25 years of the Three Rivers Festival. The morning of Saturday, July 10, brought cloudy skies and rain to the 1993 opening day parade. The soaked-out parade featured 25 special floats, each displaying a theme from past festivals. The Three Rivers Federal Credit Union float, "The Great Discovery," pictured here, displayed a past parade theme.

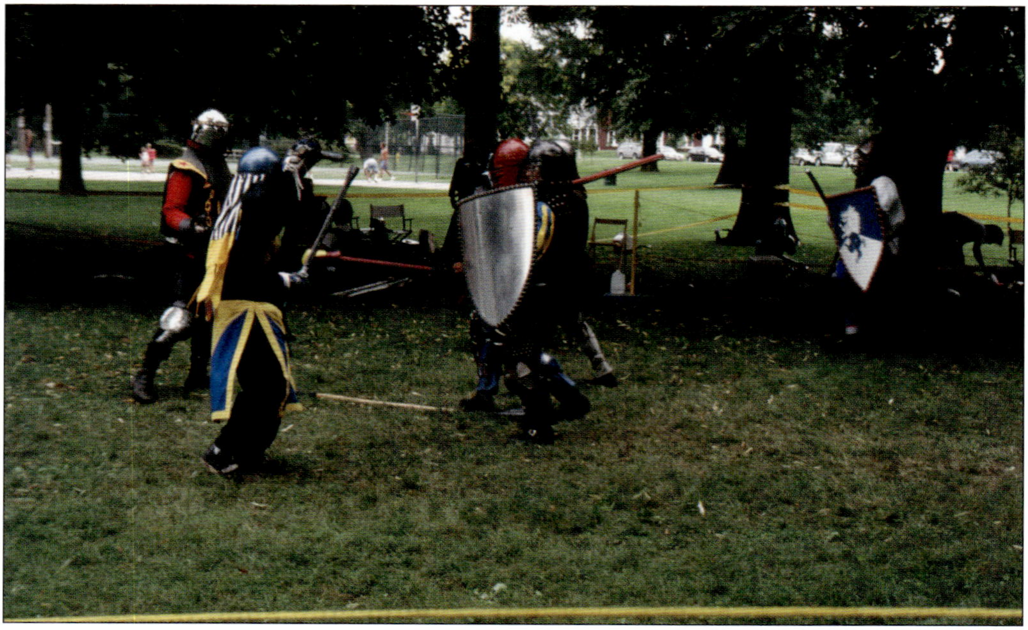

Despite the rain that opened and closed the 25th Three Rivers Festival, the community still came out to spend time with family and friends at various events. On Saturday, July 17, 1993, the Shire of Shadowed Stars hosted a medieval fair in Lakeside Park. The fair featured a festive day from the Middle Ages with tournaments, dancing, royal courts, and games. Pictured are knights competing in the sword tournament.

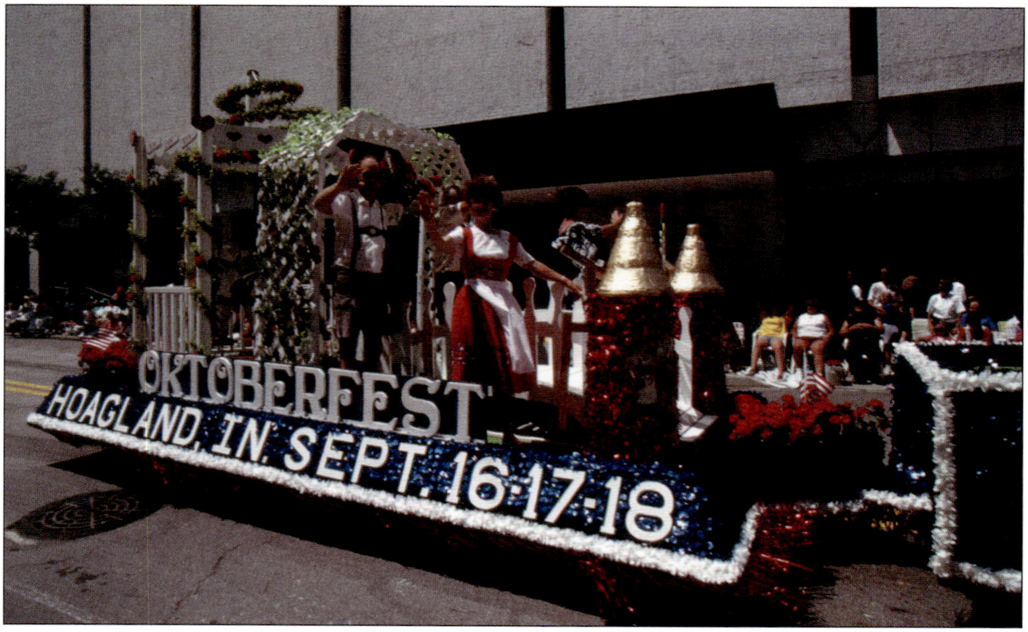

In 1994, the Three Rivers Festival turned 26, and the City of Fort Wayne turned 200. In honor of Fort Wayne's bicentennial, the annual festival parade celebrated with the theme "A Great Past, A Glorious Future." The parade portrayed significant periods in the city's history and saluted people and companies that played important roles in the city. The Hoagland Oktoberfest float depicted the German heritage of Fort Wayne.

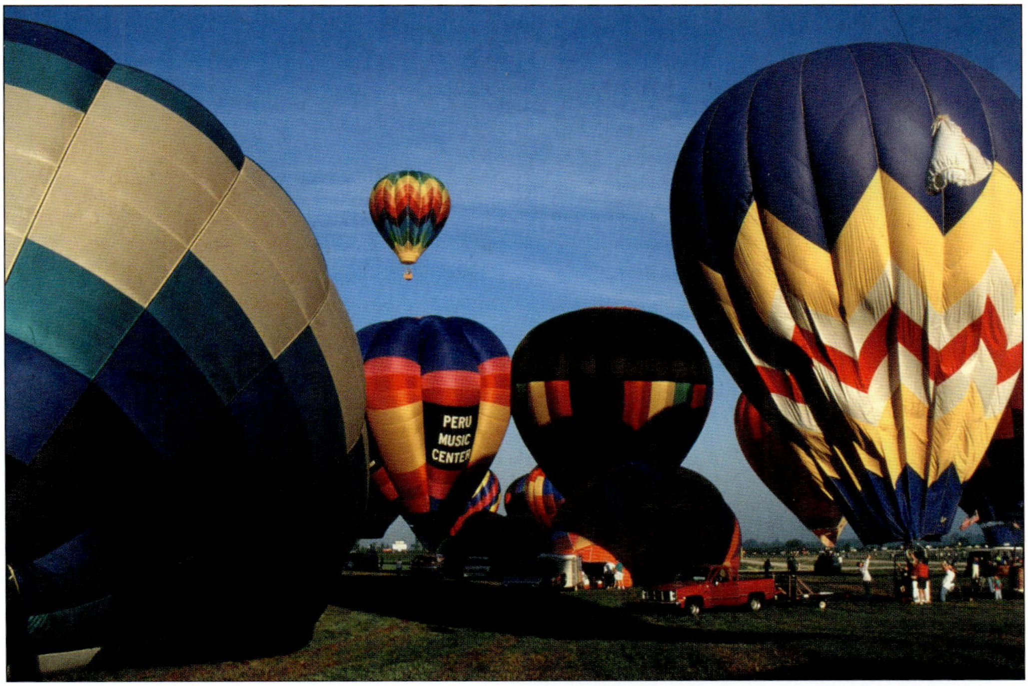

The Three Rivers Festival Standard Federal Balloon Classic took place July 15–17, 1994. It featured over 30 sport and specialty balloons. Festival guests were invited out to the Allen County Fairgrounds to watch the ascensions of the balloons each morning and evening, at 6:00 a.m. and 6:00 p.m. On Saturday, festival guests enjoyed a pancake and sausage breakfast from 6:00 to 7:00 a.m. and a chili cook-off from 2:00 to 9:00 p.m. Saturday evening, the TRF26 Balloon Glow ignited the twilight as darkness approached and tethered hot air balloons fired their propane tanks in unison. Above, colorful balloons start to fill prior to the morning ascension on Saturday, July 16. Pictured at right is a brilliantly lit balloon during the TRF26 Balloon Glow on Saturday evening.

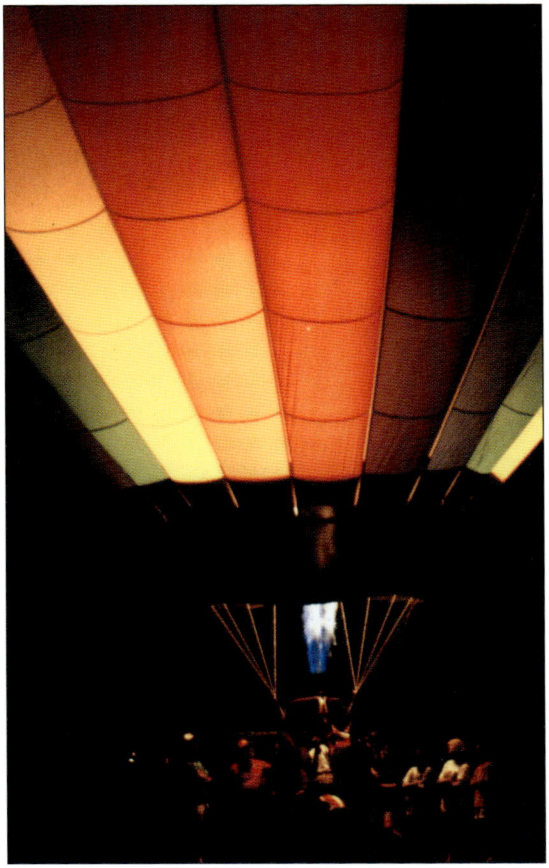

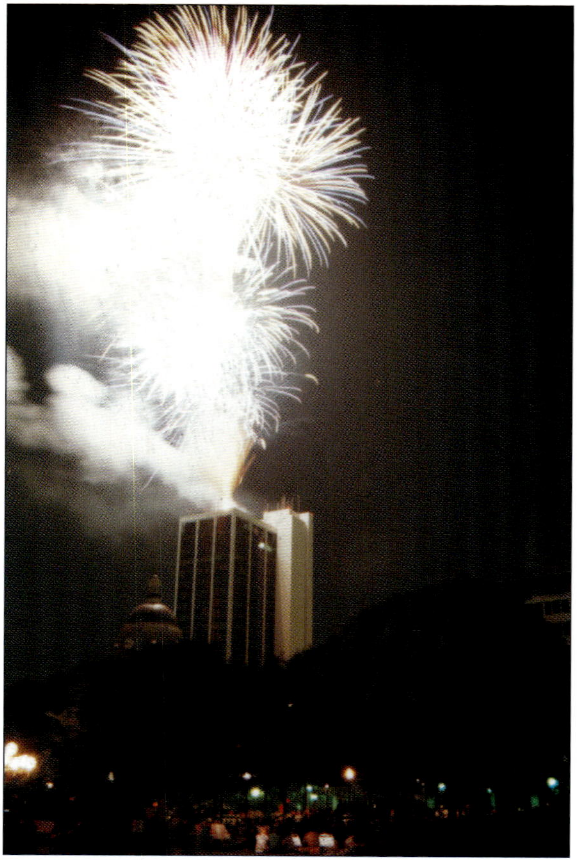

Sunday, July 17, 1994, was the last day of the 26th annual Three Rivers Festival. The Fort Wayne National Bank Fireworks Finale filled the city's sky with cascades of brilliant color to close out nine spectacular days of bicentennial and festival fun and celebration with a night as bright as the day. Prior to the fireworks, festival guests gathered in Freimann Square to hear a concert by the Community Band, while others strolled Junk Food Alley for the last time in search of the perfect treat to end a perfect week. At left is a colorful and brilliant display of fireworks from the top of the Fort Wayne National Bank Building in downtown Fort Wayne. Below, a young girl stands in front of the Freimann Square fountain while enjoying the fireworks.

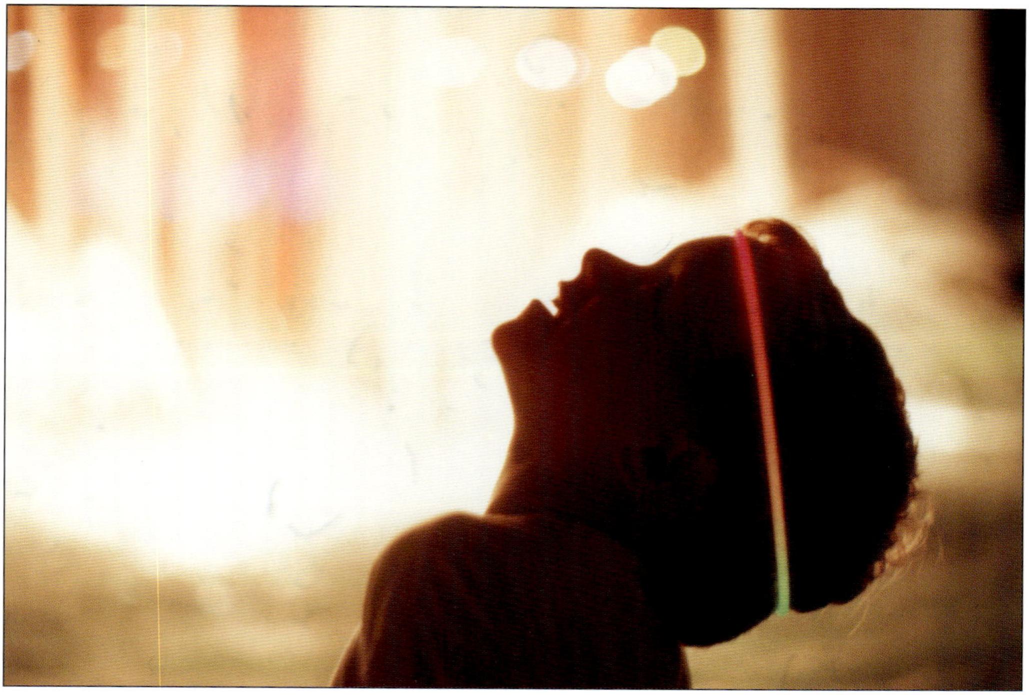

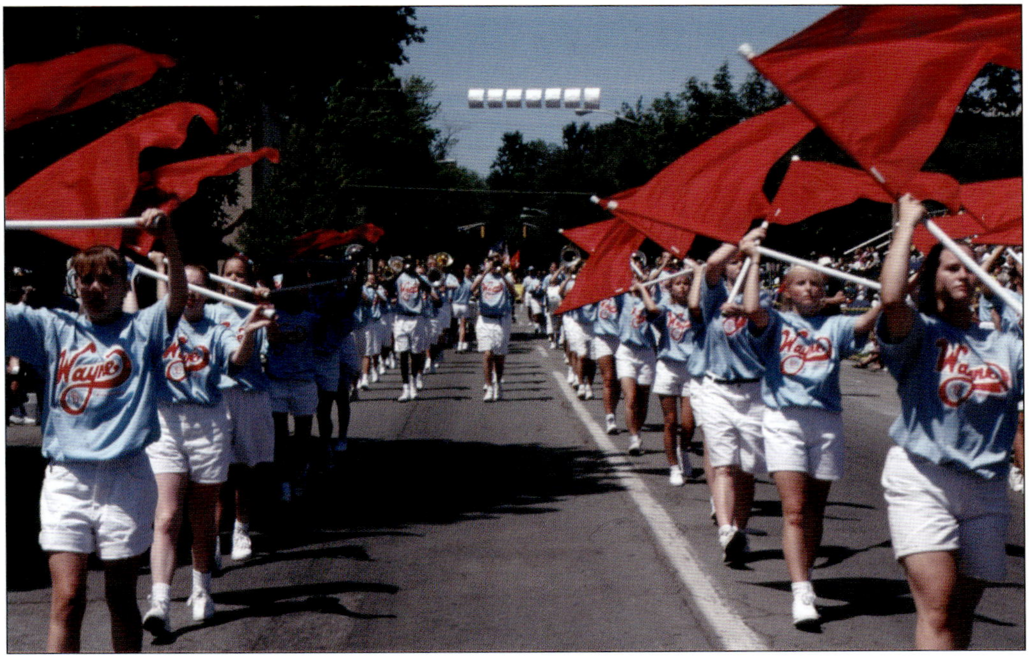

The 27th annual parade kicked off without a hitch, and the festival started off on a great note on Saturday, July 8, 1995; however, things changed mid-week. On Wednesday, July 12, 1995, record heat moved into the Fort Wayne area and hung around until Saturday. The heat caused festival staff to cancel several events, including the bed race and two flights of the Balloon Classic, and there was an early shutdown of Children's Fest. Saturday brought a downpour of rain, which flooded the streets, caused the cancellation of the Balloon Glow, and brought down a portion of the Club TRF tent. Festival volunteers and staff worked together to clean up the mess, and the tent was up and running by 7:00 p.m. Above is the 1995 Wayne High School Marching Band, and below is the Christ Child Festival's Noah's Ark parade float.

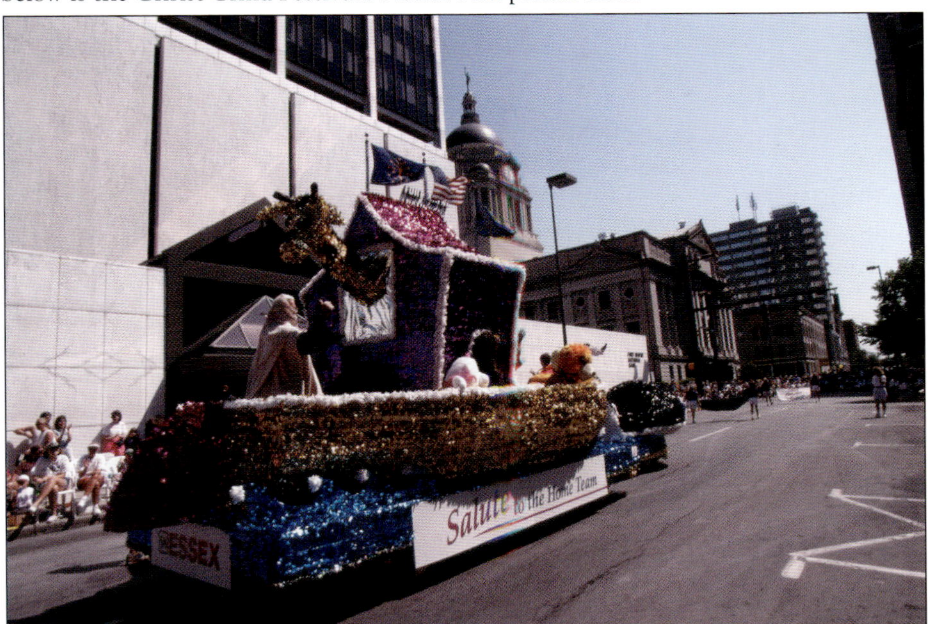

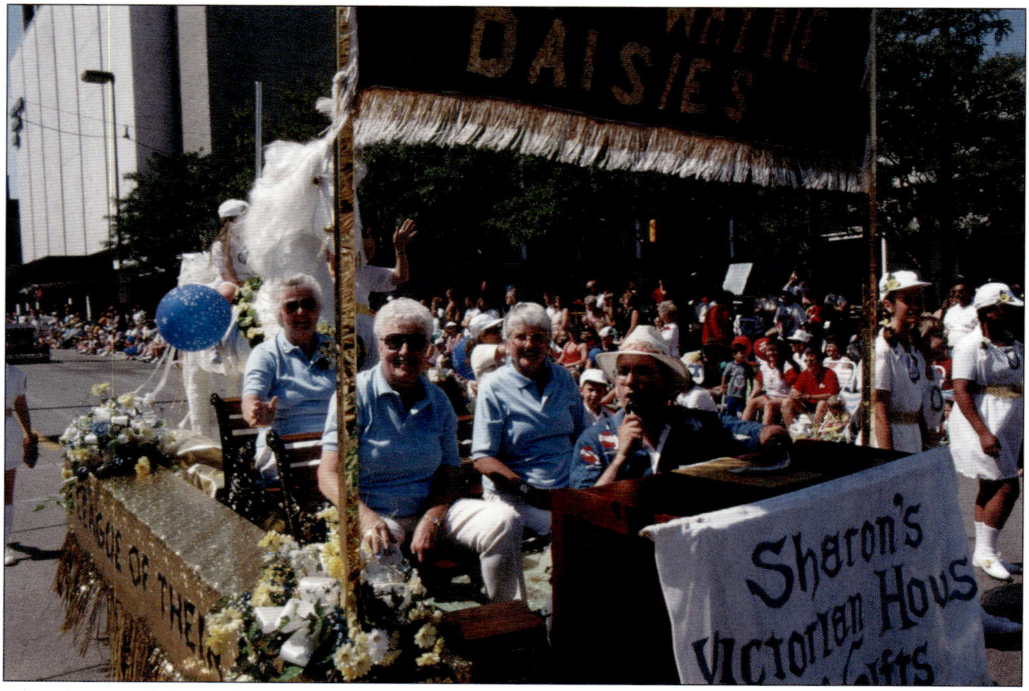

The theme of the 27th annual Three Rivers Festival parade in 1995 was "Salute to the Home Team!" Parade participants celebrated their favorite sports teams in floats, balloons, walking units, and bands. Sharon's Victorian House of Gifts saluted the Fort Wayne Daisies with its float. The Fort Wayne Daisies were an all-female baseball team that played in the All-American Girls Professional Baseball League from 1945 through 1954.

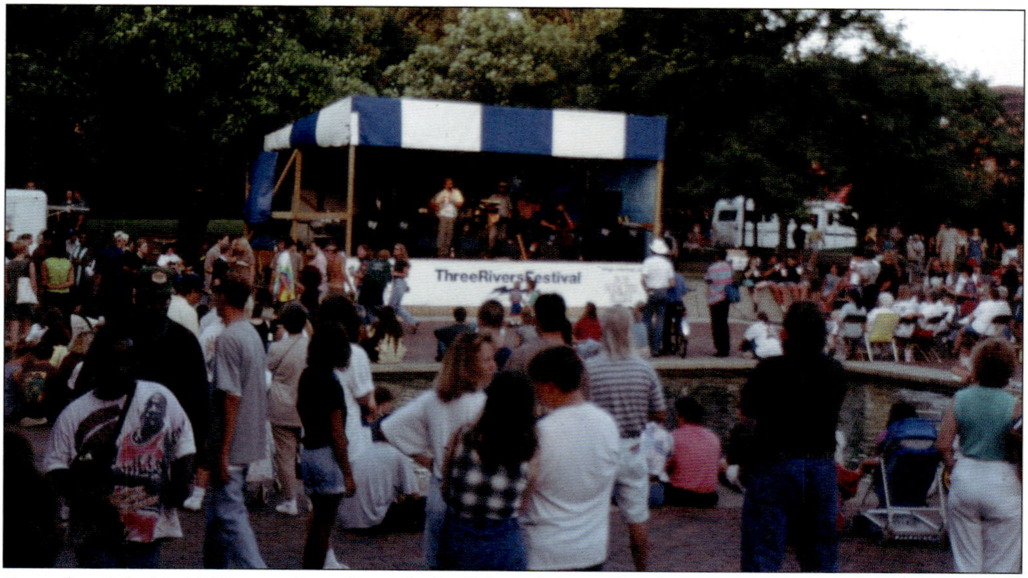

Saturday, July 13, 1996, was the official kickoff day of the 28th Three Rivers Festival. In anticipation of the festival's future move to the new Headwaters Park, the festival Emporium and Club TRF were set up on the fringes of the park. Art in the Park was once again held in Freimann Square, which is conveniently located two blocks from Headwaters Park. Pictured is the Art in the Park jazz stage.

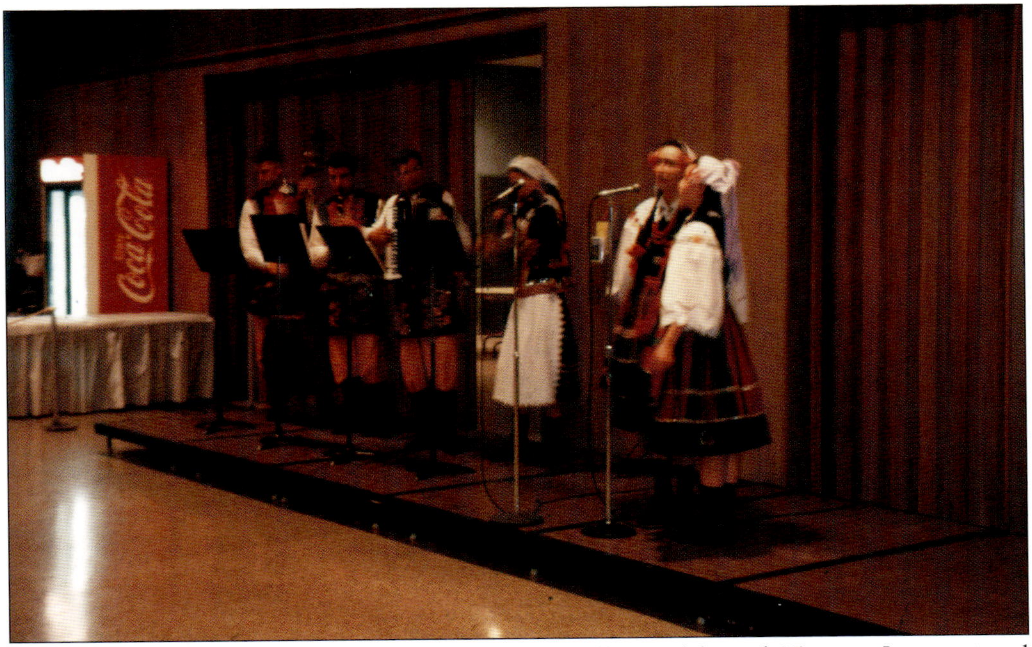

In 1996, the Three Rivers Festival's International Village celebrated 25 years. International Village was a five-day event that celebrated the many different cultural groups found in Fort Wayne. Each day featured traditional food and displays of the traditions, culture, history, and people from different areas of the world who chose to make Fort Wayne their home. Monday, July 15, 1996, was Polish and African American Day at International Village. Above, a group of Polish signers in traditional dress perform for the crowd on the International Village stage on July 15. Below, a festival guest purchases food during Filipino Day on Wednesday, July 17, at International Village. Guests could dine on delicious traditional Filipino food such as lumpia, adobo, pancit, and fried rice.

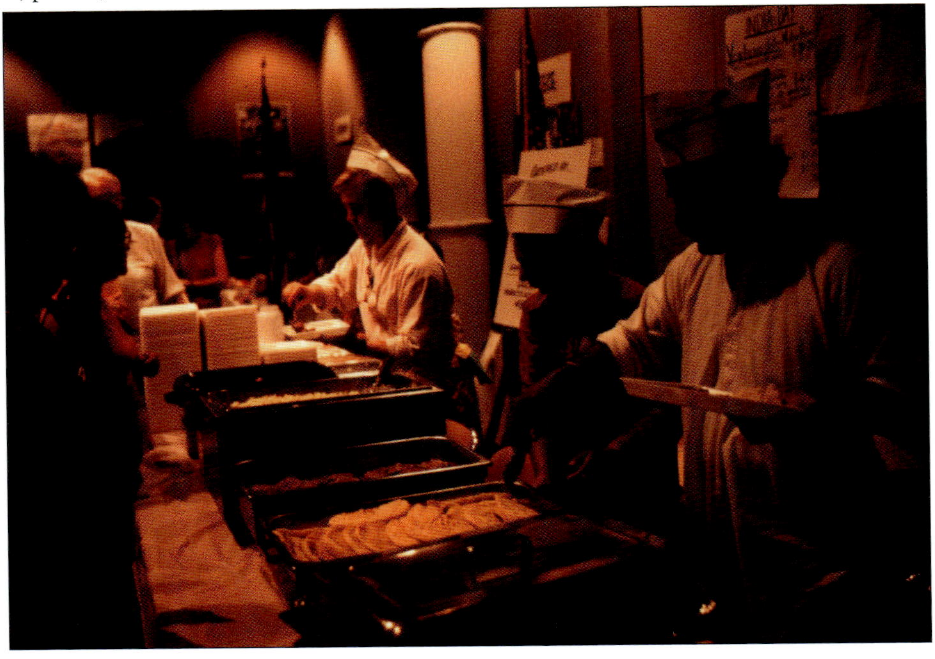

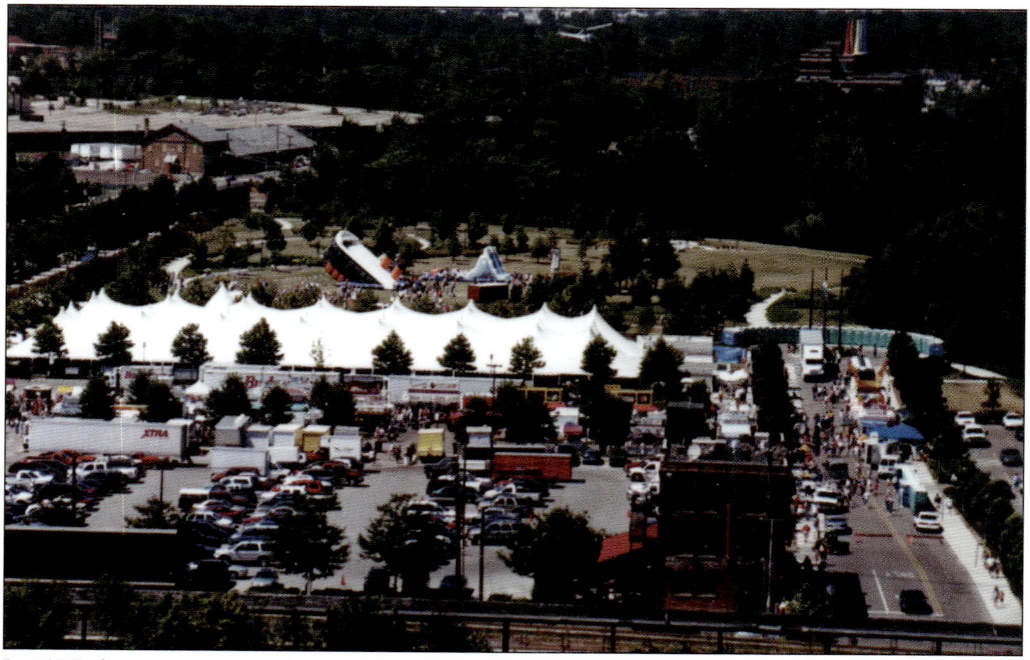

In 1997, the construction of Headwaters Park was completed, and the Three Rivers Festival moved into its new permanent home after years of being moved from place to place in downtown Fort Wayne. Headwaters Park offered the opportunity to expand many events and add new ones. Shown here is an aerial view of the 29th Three Rivers Festival in its new home in Headwaters Park.

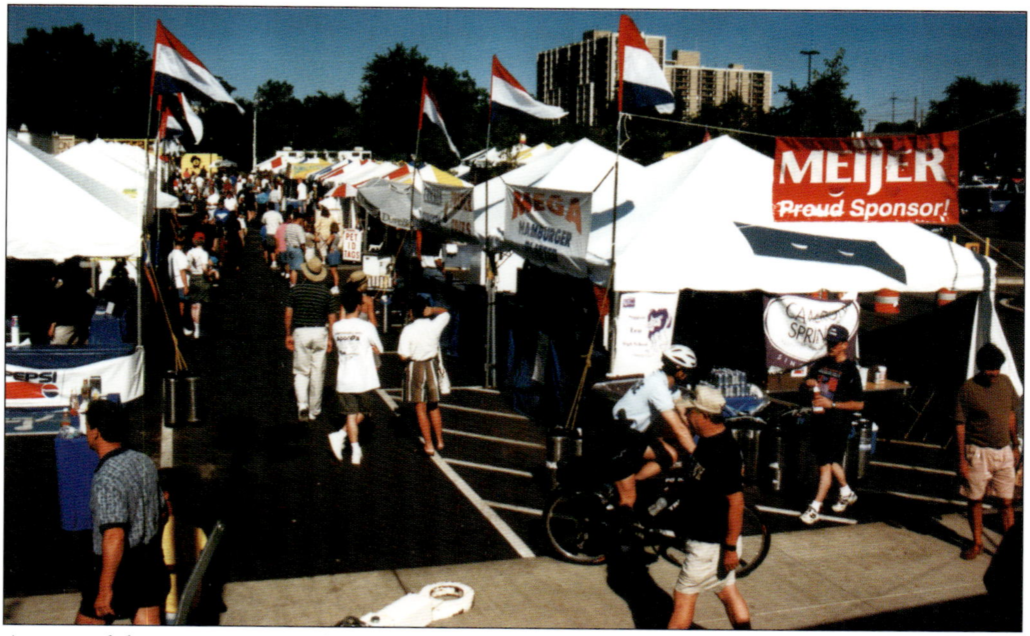

As part of the move in 1997, the festival attempted a new look with the Meijer Food Alley. The traditional colorful food trailers filled with tasty deep-fried food were replaced by a sea of white tents offering a variety of healthier food options. This change produced a multitude of letters to the editor and complaints from the community over the loss of Junk Food Alley. Pictured is the Meijer Food Alley.

The 29th Three Rivers Festival saw nine days of family, friends, and community in its new home at Headwaters Park. Sunday, July 20, 1997, brought the firework finale, and after everyone went home, the festival staff and board celebrated a great week with the annual water fight in the entertainment tent. Board past president Tony Burrus is pictured dressed, armed, and having a blast during the staff/board water fight.

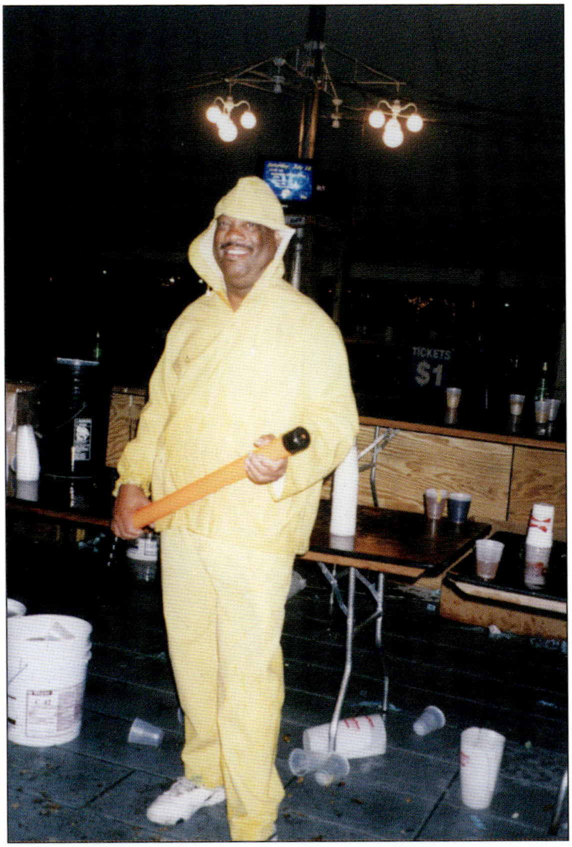

The year 1998 marked 30 years of the Three Rivers Festival. Junk Food Alley returned to the festival and moved into its new home at Headwaters Park after hundreds of complaints over its removal in 1997. Thousands of community members and visitors visited the alley for their favorite junk food. Pictured are hungry people in search of the perfect late-night treat.

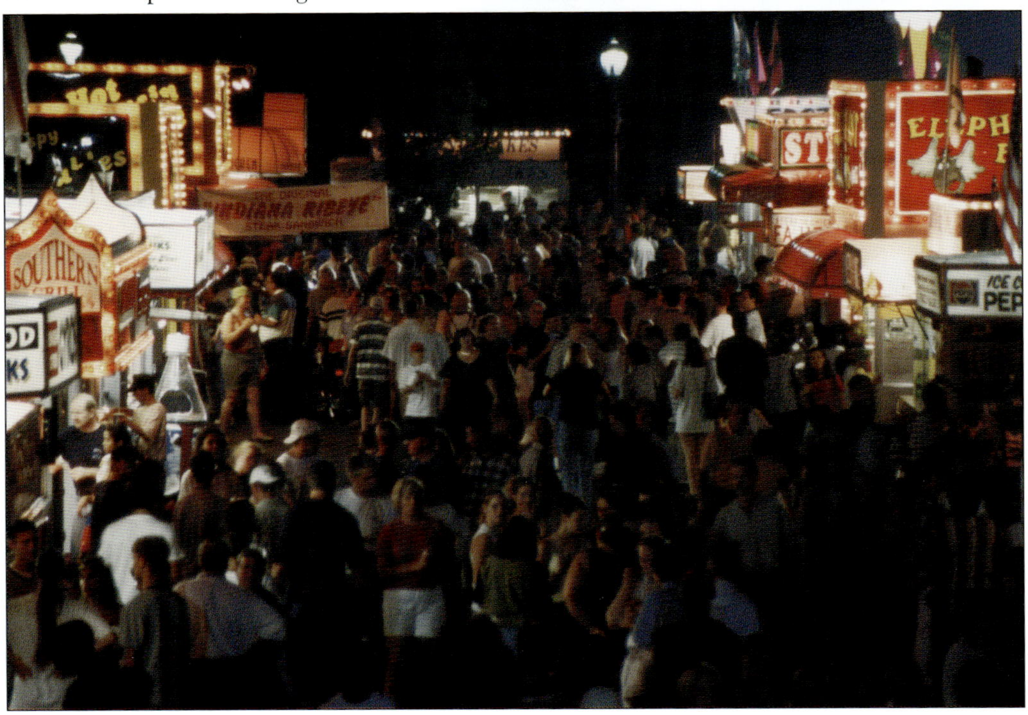

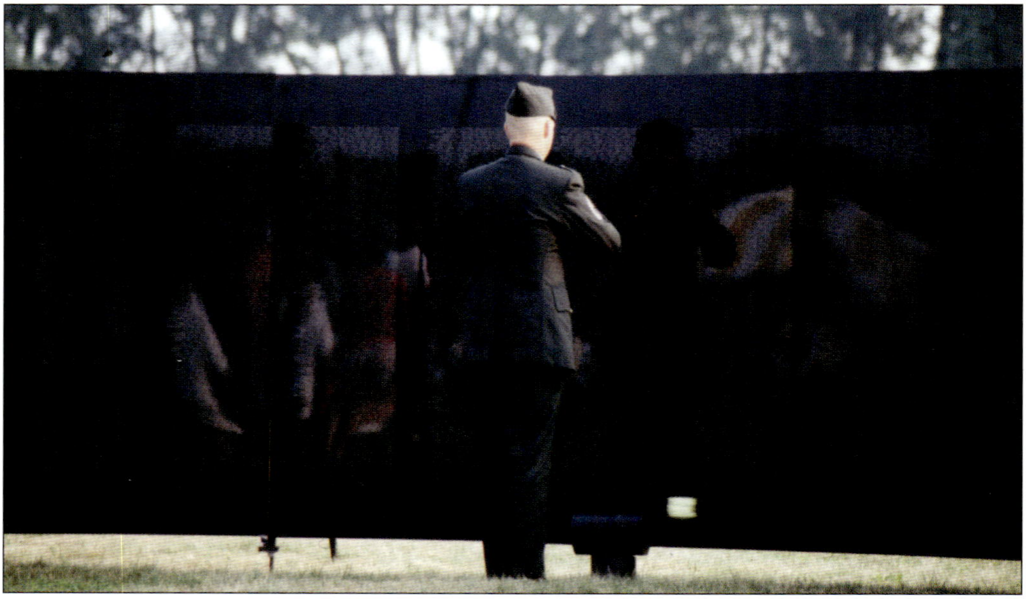

In 1998, the Three Rivers Festival parade theme was "Everyday Heroes;" this theme was carried throughout the festival in its many events. The Wall That Heals, a replica of the Vietnam Veterans Memorial in Washington, DC, was brought to the IPFW campus from July 16 to July 18. Visitors could also learn about the lives of Vietnam veterans in the Wall That Heals Museum.

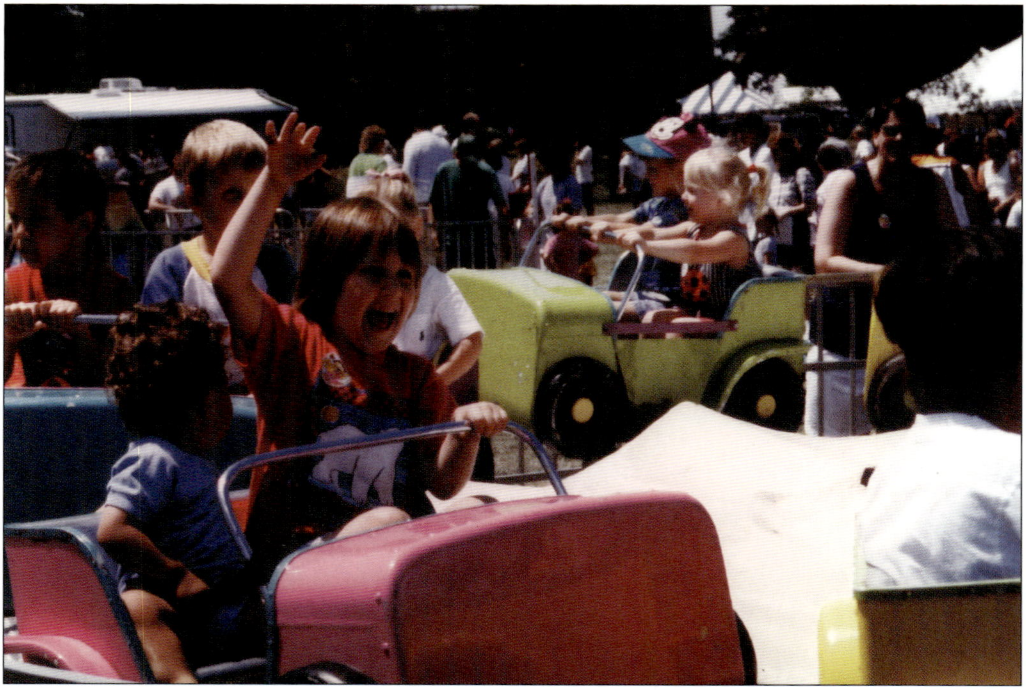

Children's Fest grew in attendance in 1998, with over 8,000 families attending the event. Children's Fest added new educational and entertaining activities such as an archaeological dig, the Milk Mustache Mobile, and carnival rides. Peg Perego and the Three Rivers Festival gave away motorized ride-on cars to children during the event. Here, children enjoy the amusement rides on Friday, July 17, 1998, at Children's Fest.

Four

1999–2008

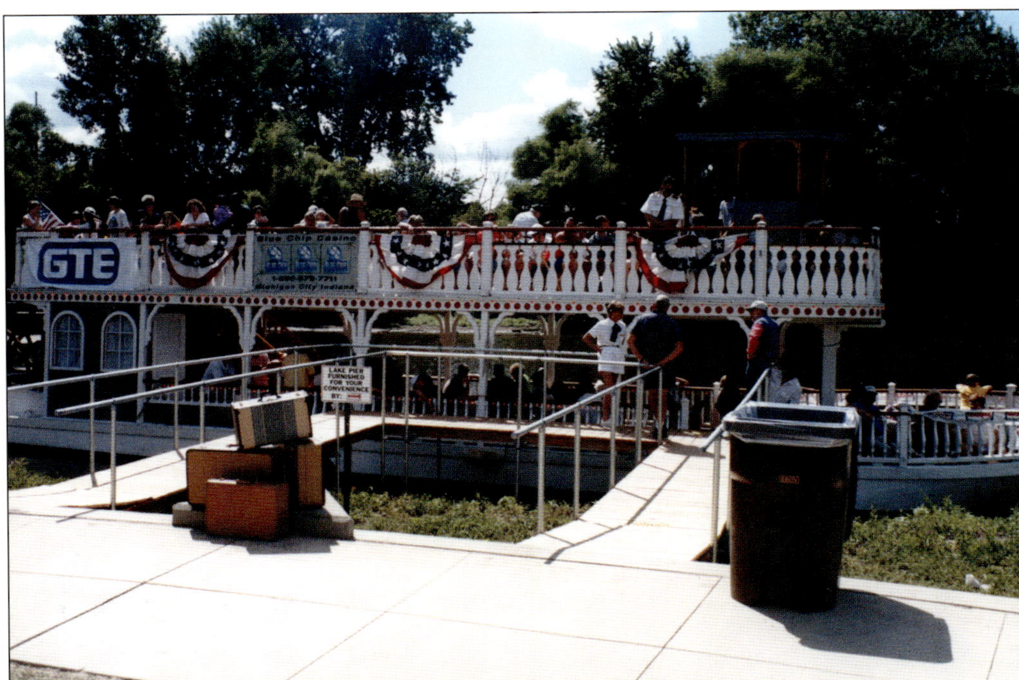

The 31st Three Rivers Festival experienced a week of sunshine and near perfect weather. Art in the Park was expanded to include Main Street and Freimann Square, the Market Place made its debut in Headwaters Park West, and the festival enjoyed crowds in excess of 500,000. Here, festival guests are arriving back to the festival after enjoying a historic tour of the St. Mary's River on the *Princess Laura*.

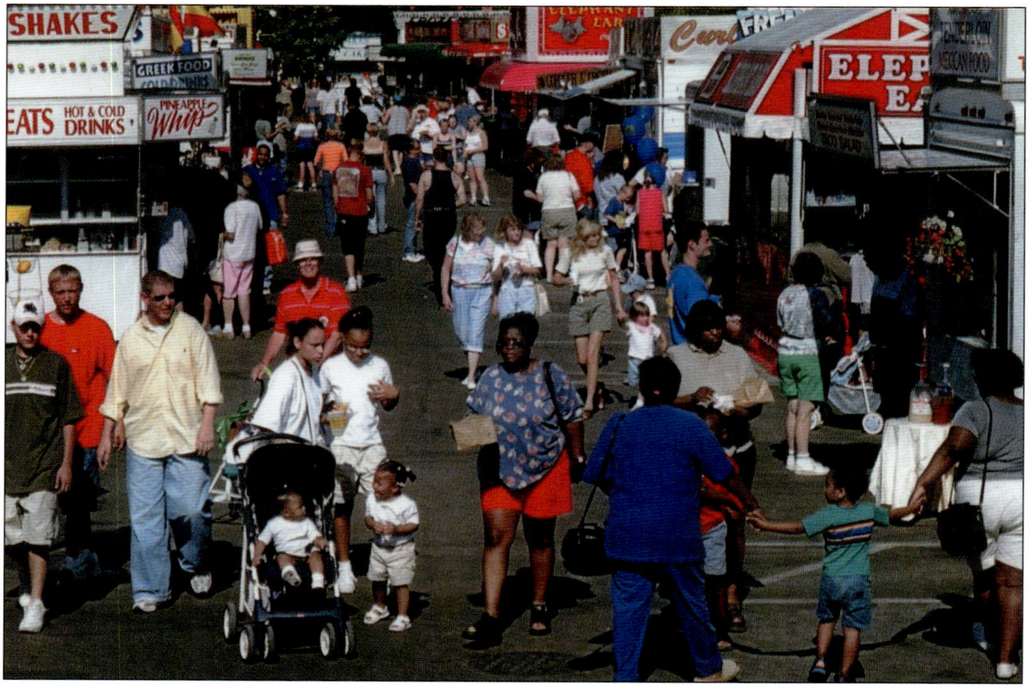

One of the most popular attractions at the Three Rivers Festival has always been the food. Elephant ears, funnel cakes, barbecue ribs, grilled chicken, fried cheese, caramel apples, and lemon shake-ups were just a few of the items available in Junk Food Alley. In 1999, Junk Food Alley reported record sales. Pictured are guests hunting for the perfect treat on July 12, 1999. (Courtesy of Samuel Hoffman, the *Journal Gazette*, Fort Wayne, Indiana, 1999.)

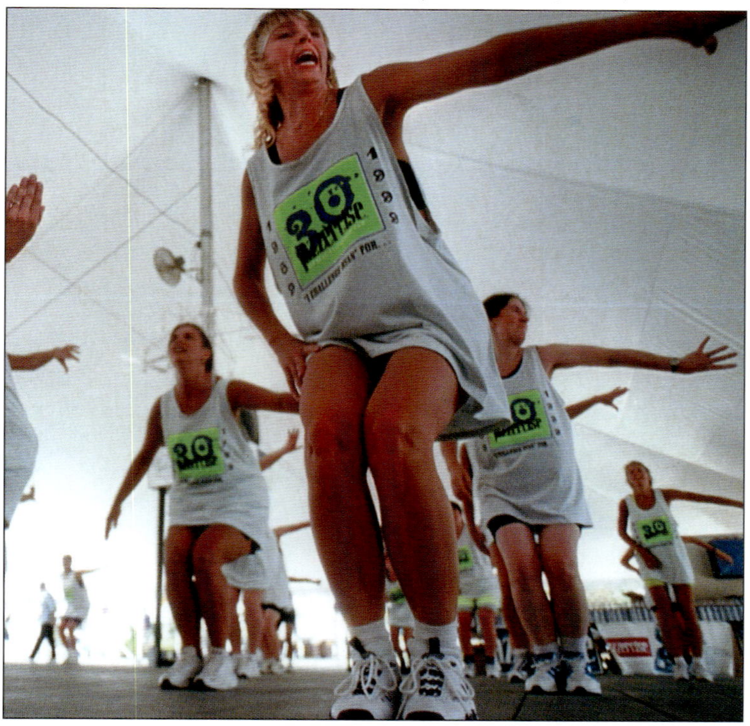

Since the start of the festival in 1969, local organizations have planned and hosted a variety of the events held each year. These affiliated events allow the festival to provide the community with numerous ways for people to come together and create great memories. Betsy Meinzen (pictured) and Paula Peeper hosted a Jazzercise session on the activity stage during the lunch hour on July 14, 1999. (Courtesy of Cathie Rowand, the *Journal Gazette*, Fort Wayne, Indiana, 1999.)

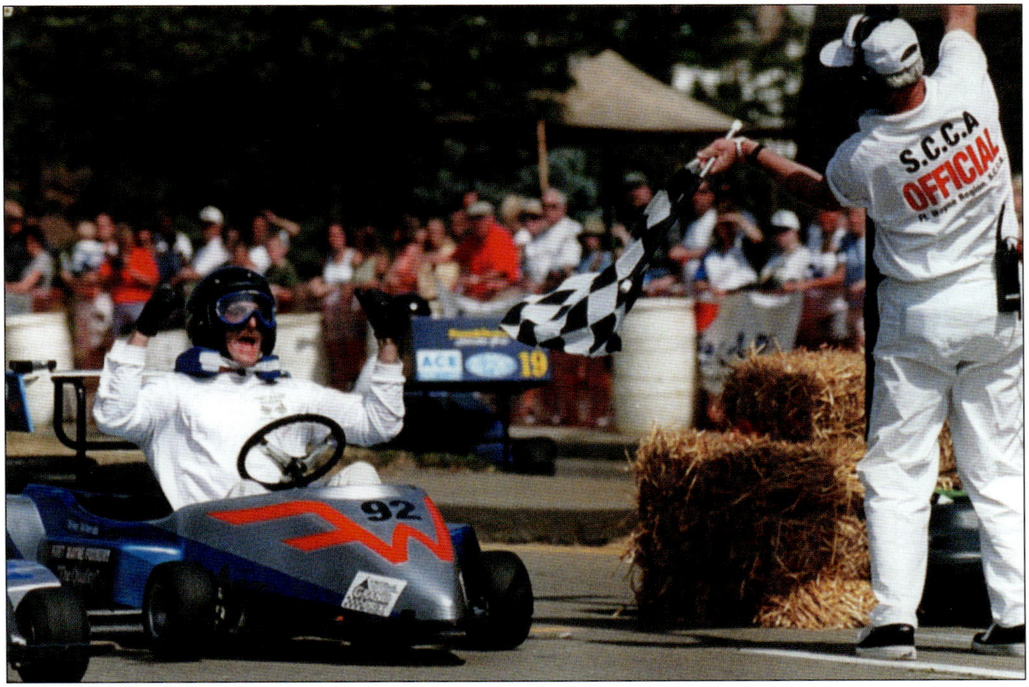

The final day of the 31st Three Rivers festival was filled with fun family-friendly events. Guests could enjoy a junior tennis tournament, reenactments at the fort, a radio-controlled air show, or the Tower Bank Junior Achievement Grand Prix. Local companies sponsored Indy-style go-carts that raced through the city to raise funds for Junior Achievement. Pictured is Ed Gervais waving the checkered flag during the grand prix on Sunday, July 18, 1999. (Courtesy of Eric Thomas, the *Journal Gazette*, Fort Wayne, Indiana, 1999.)

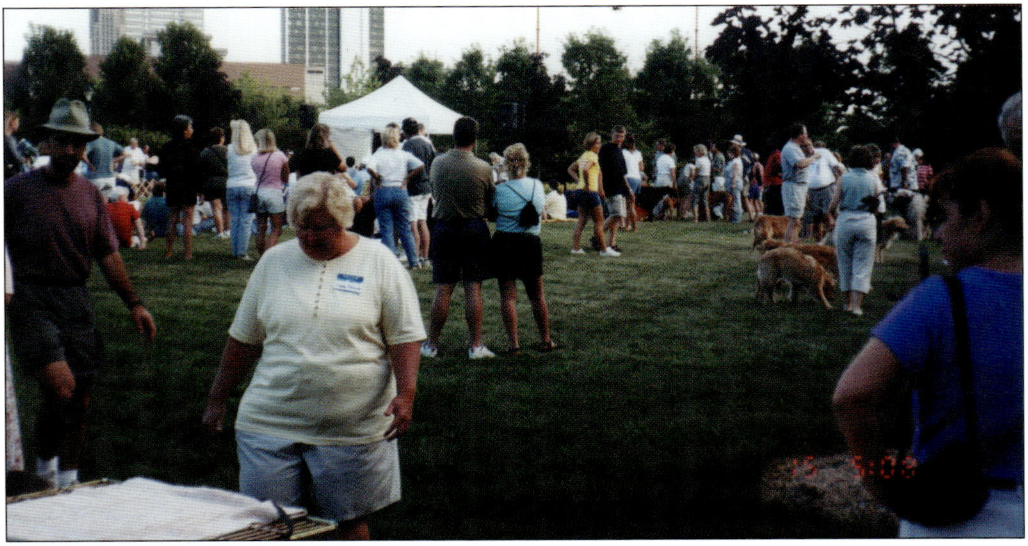

The turn of the 21st century brought the 32nd Three Rivers Festival. This year the festival brought back old favorites and introduced new events. The festival board focused on emphasizing youth and family activities by hosting a talent show, two concerts for teenagers, a BMX stunt show, and a performance by the Peru Circus. The Northeaster Indiana Kennel Club hosted an educational purebred dog show on July 10, 2000.

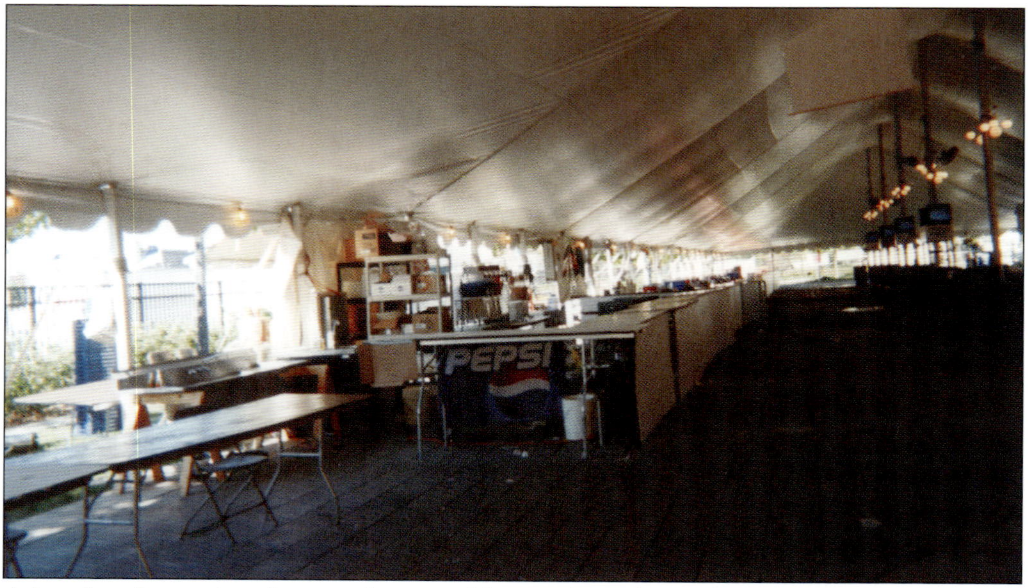

A lot of work goes into hosting the second-largest festival in Indiana. Each year, the festival board, staff, and committees spend 11 months planning and organizing the festival and nine days setting it all up. Volunteers, staff, and board members spend long days getting everything in place and ready for opening day. Pictured is the completed bar inside the festival plaza before opening on Friday, July 7, 2000.

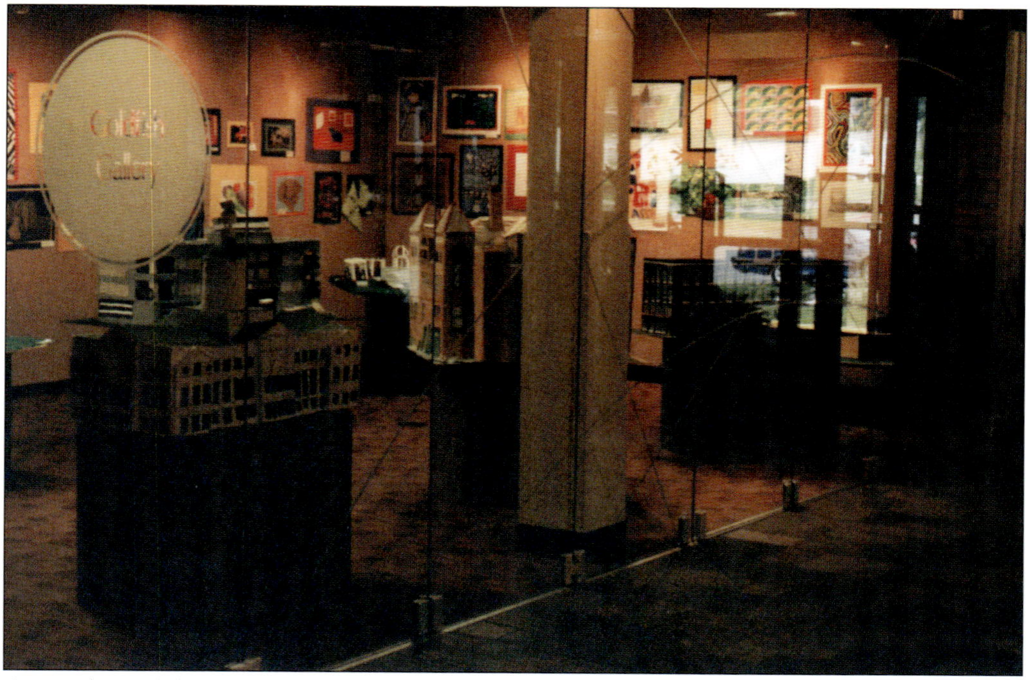

Art in the Park has been a traditional festival event since 1974. Artists from across the country participate in the two-day juried fine art event in Freimann Square. In 2001, guests could stroll through the park looking at art, enjoying music, or participating in the Chalk Walk. Pictured are replications of city buildings by students, which were on display at the Standard Federal Plaza during Art in the Park.

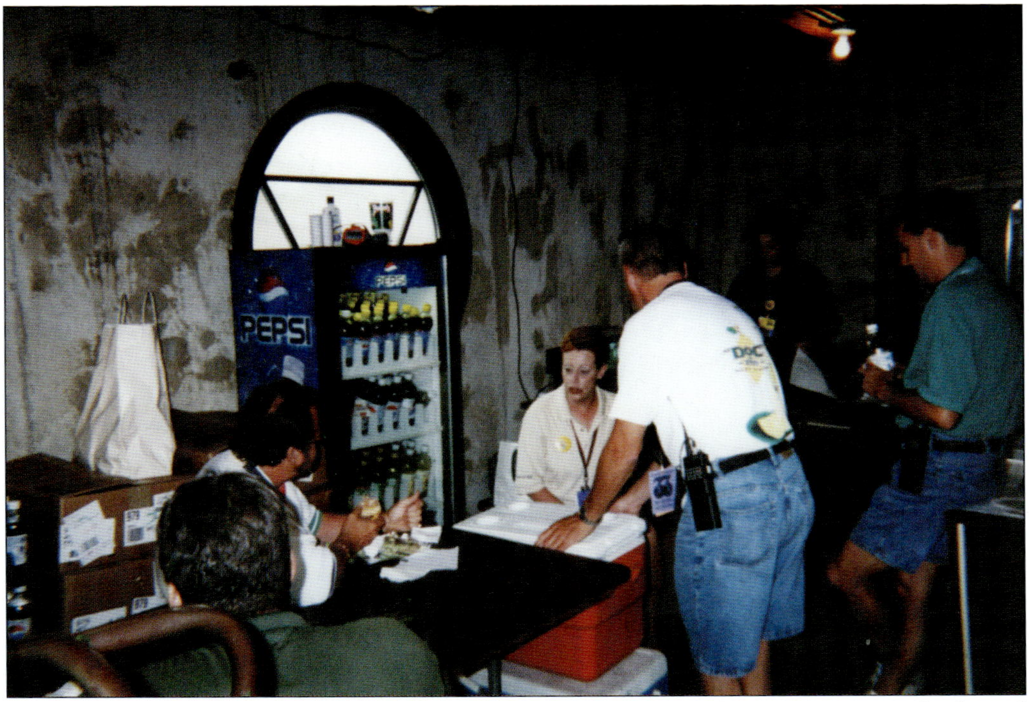

Thousands of people came out to Headwaters Park in 2001 to enjoy the many activities the festival had to offer on July 14–22. While the city was celebrating the summer and having fun, behind the scenes, festival staff was at work making sure everything was running smoothly. Staff, board, and committee members and volunteers worked hundreds of hours over the course of nine days, usually working from 16 to 18 hours a day. Tasks such as cleaning up Junk Food Alley, restocking the bar, putting up signs, refueling light towers, assisting vendors, keeping an eye on the weather, delivering ice, and making trips to the bank were just a few of the hundreds of jobs done each day. Above, festival staff is in the bunkhouse at Headwaters Park. Below, Mike Holley and Kathleen Alter make a logistics run in Headwaters Park West.

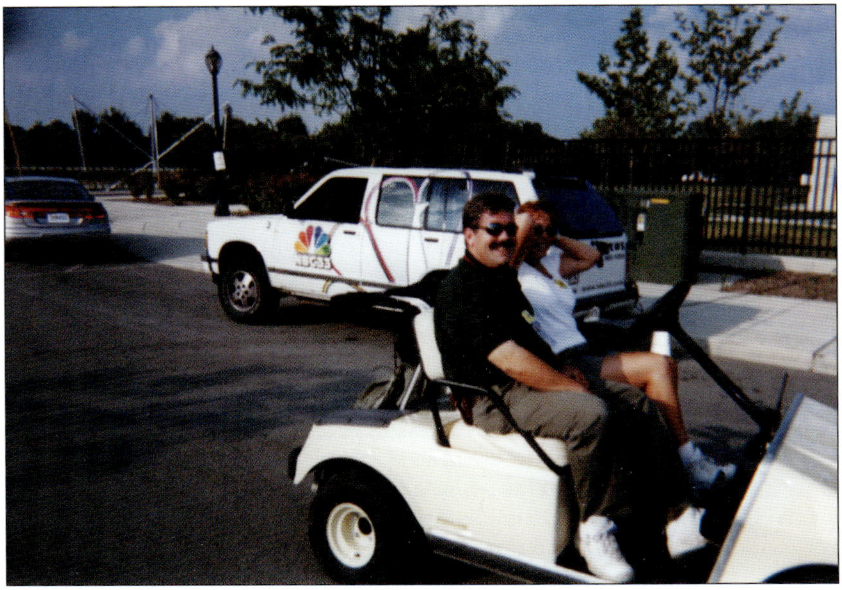

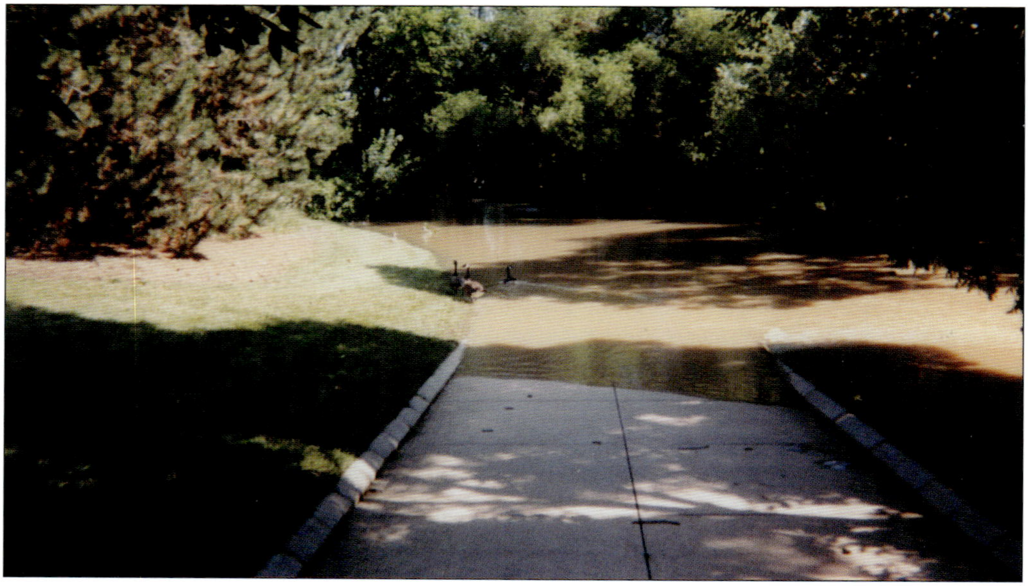

On June 26, 2002, Fort Wayne experienced flooding as the city's rivers crested their banks after receiving eight inches of rain in a single day. The festival grounds in Headwaters Park were soaked, and many of the park paths were still flooded and unusable. While the flooding caused some delays in setup, the festival marched on and opened as scheduled on July 13, 2002. Here, geese are swimming on lover's lane.

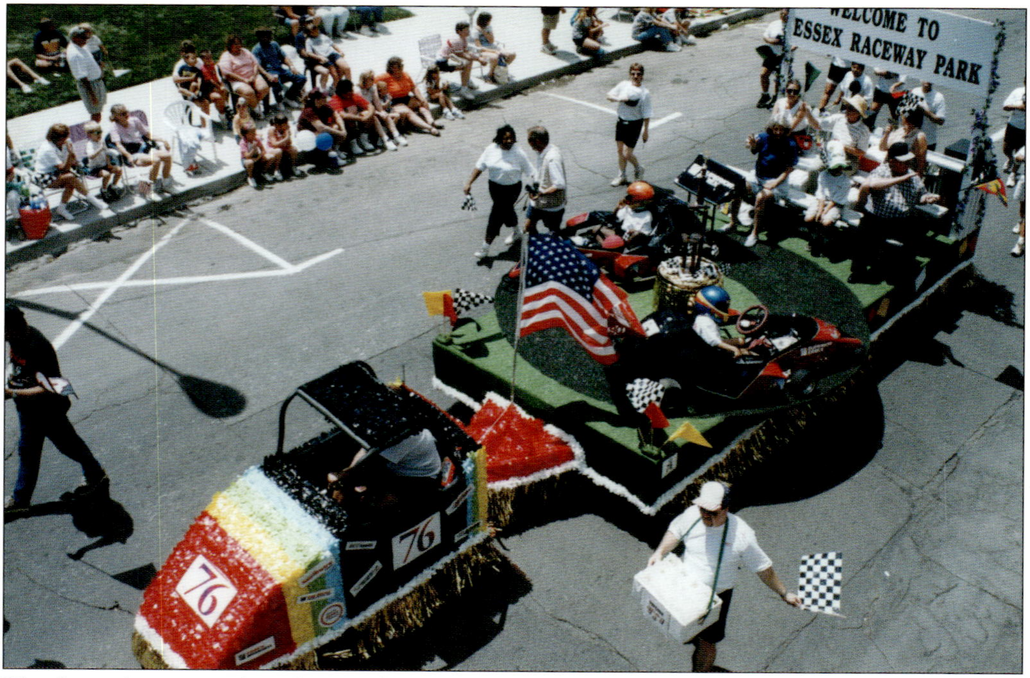

The festival was proud to show its love of this country during the 34th year of the event. The parade theme for 2002 was "Proud to be an American," which was reminiscent of the patriotic wave that gripped the nation after the terrorist attacks the prior September. Floats, balloons, marching bands, and walking units were decorated in the stars and stripes. The Essex Raceway float proudly flew the American flag.

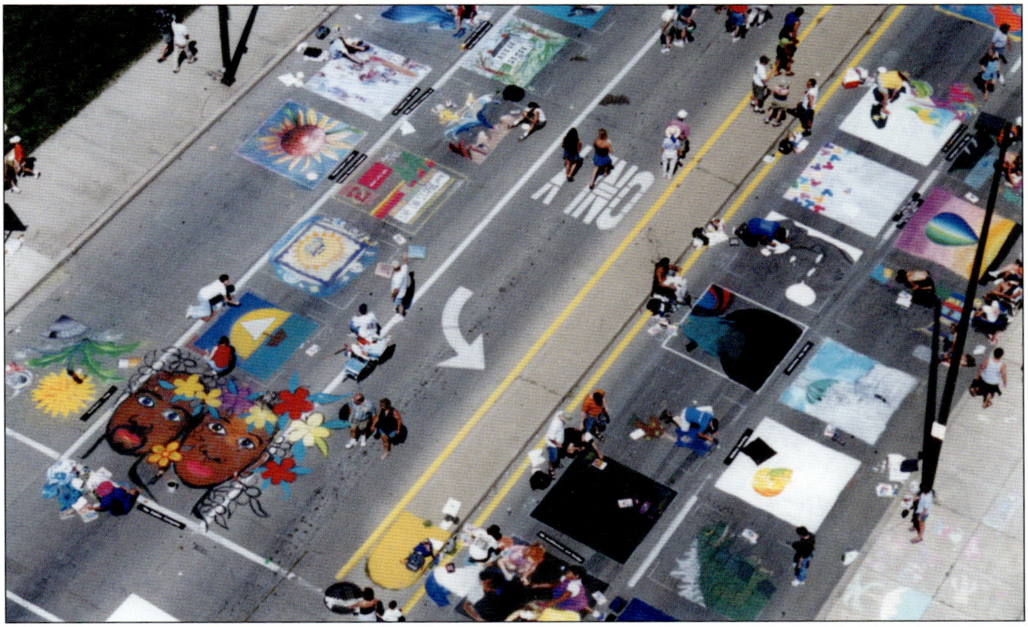

During the 34th Three Rivers Festival, the Fort Wayne Museum of Art held the Chalk Walk event for the second time, in conjunction with Art in the Park. Main Street was closed and marked off in 10-foot squares for artists to draw in. Hundreds of artists participated in the event, creating unique, beautiful, and colorful art to share with the community. Pictured is Chalk Walk on Sunday, July 15, 2002.

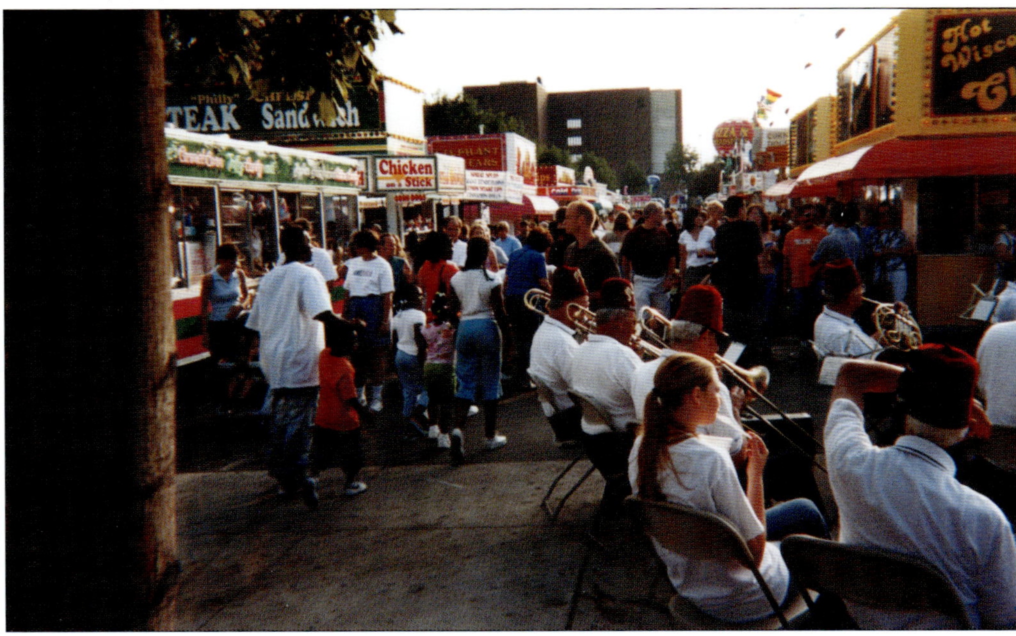

The Three Rivers Festival celebrated its 35th year in 2003. There were several new celebratory events such as a cake decorating contest, Make Me an Idol contest, Fun over Fifty for seniors, children concerts, and Christmas in July. The annual police versus fireman softball game was held in honor of servicemen killed in the line of duty. Pictured here, the Shriner Band plays for festival guests in Junk Food Alley.

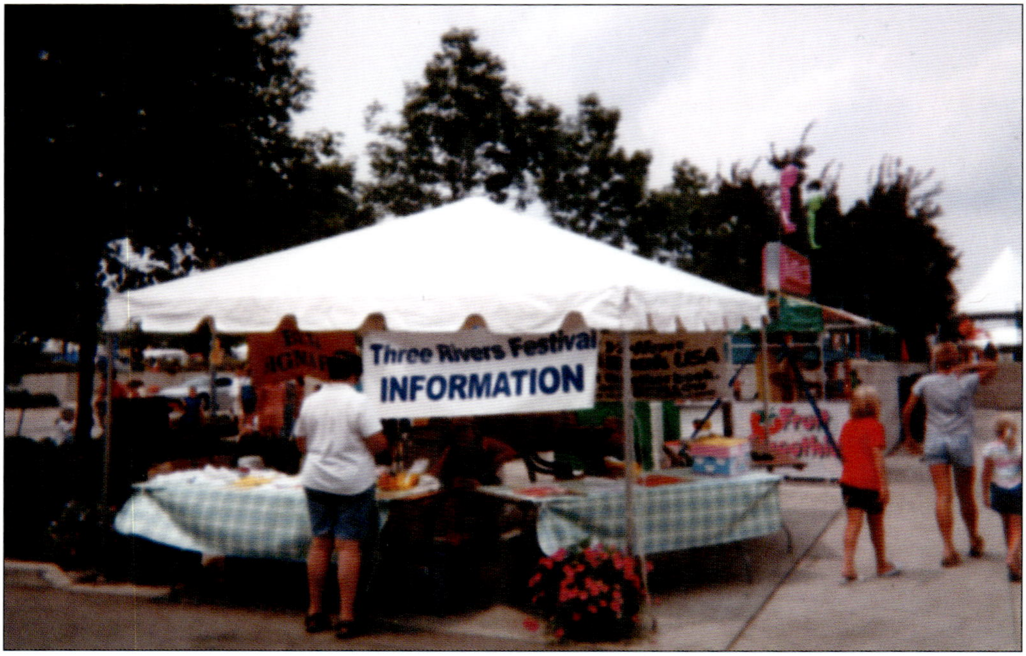

The Three Rivers Festival has always depended on donations, registration fees, and profits from sales to finance the festival each year. In 1969, the festival committee asked for $500 donations from local businesses, along with $10,000 from the city to host the festival. In 1974, the festival committee started selling yearly buttons with the festival theme, which is still done today. The festival also raised funds by selling T-shirts, hats, and beverages. The beer tent was a great source of revenue for the festival, as were the refreshment stands that volunteers manned. The ladies of the local chapter of Beta Sigma Phi sorority helped the festival for many years by staffing the information and souvenir booth. Pictured above is the 35th festival information booth in Junk Food Alley. Below, Tim Schieferstein retrieves Pepsi to restock the bar in 2003.

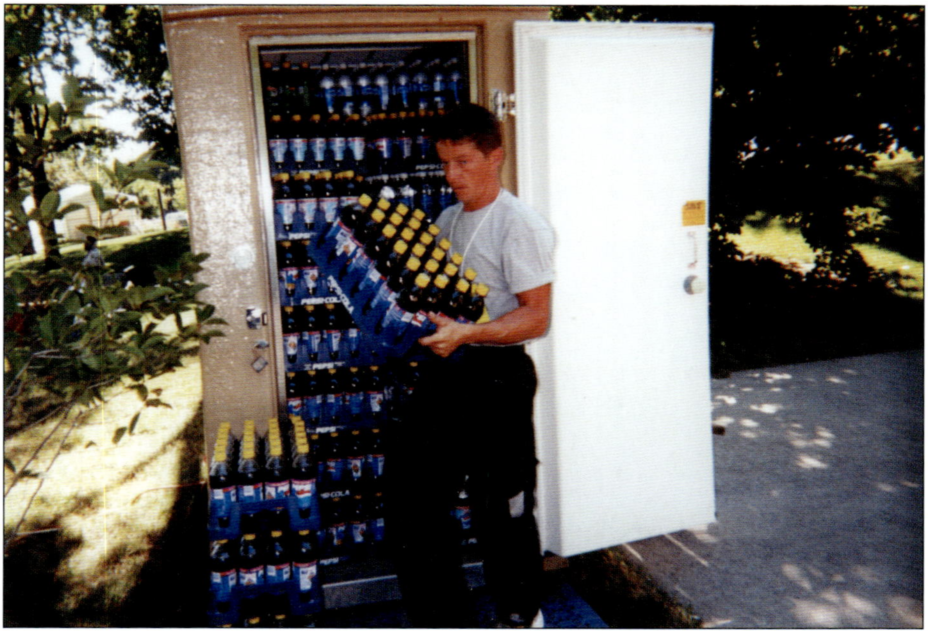

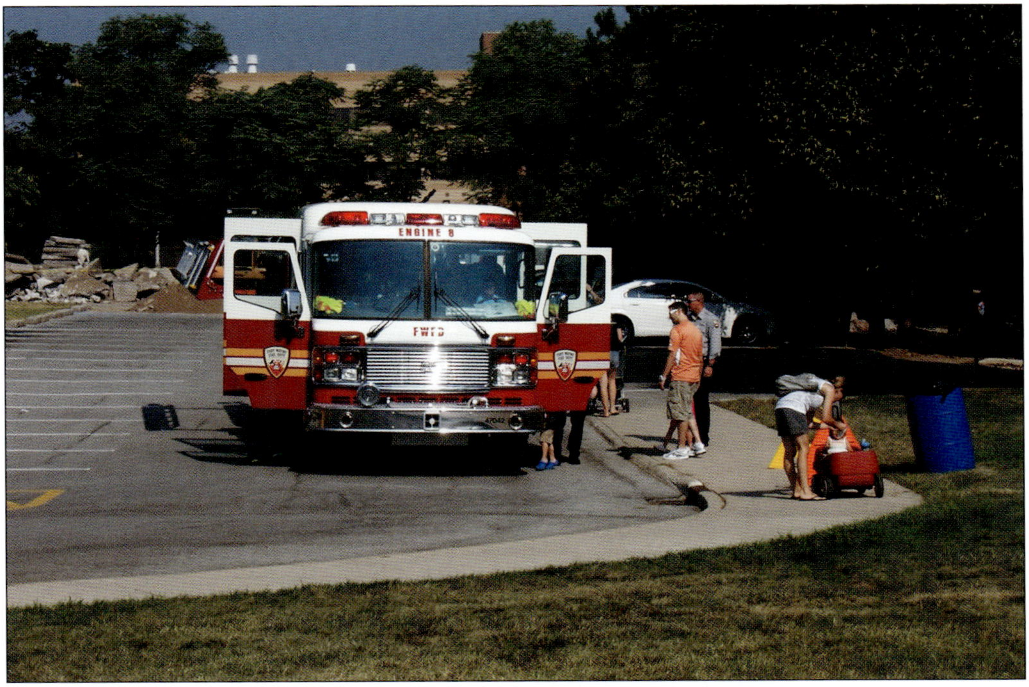

The 36th Three Rivers Festival was held July 10–18, 2004, with the theme "Community Spirit—Letting it Soar." This year the festival featured motocross races, a parade sign contest using the festival theme, and the opening night band—Blue Oyster Cult. The festival also incorporated Fort Wayne's citywide fitness initiative and hosted walks, runs, bike rides, and a body building contest. The annual Children's Fest was held July 16–17 on the campus of IPFW and featured free educational activities, performances, caricatures, face painting, rides, a diaper dash, and food. Pictured above, the Fort Wayne Fire Department brought out a fire truck for kids to climb in and learn about fire safety. At right, Fort Wayne's favorite Komets hockey mascot, Icy, came out to hang out with the kids on Saturday, July 17, 2004.

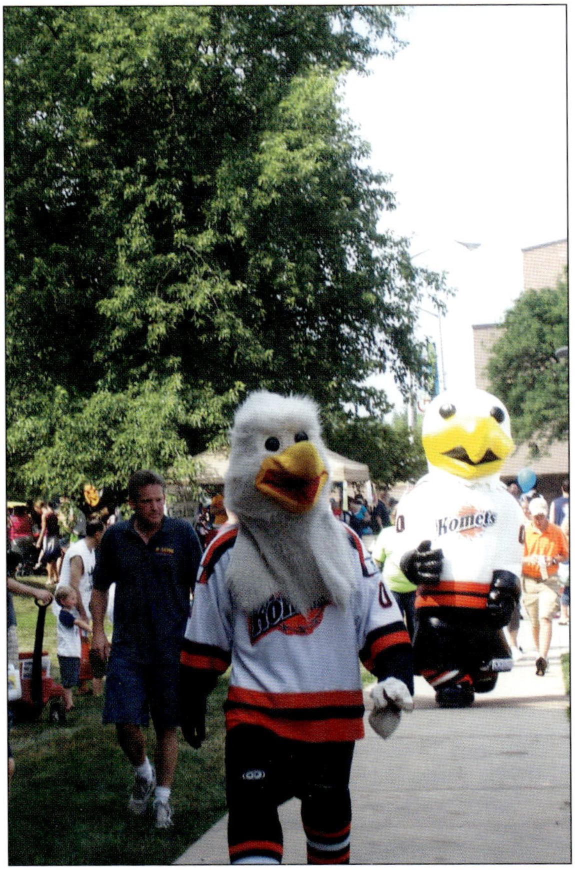

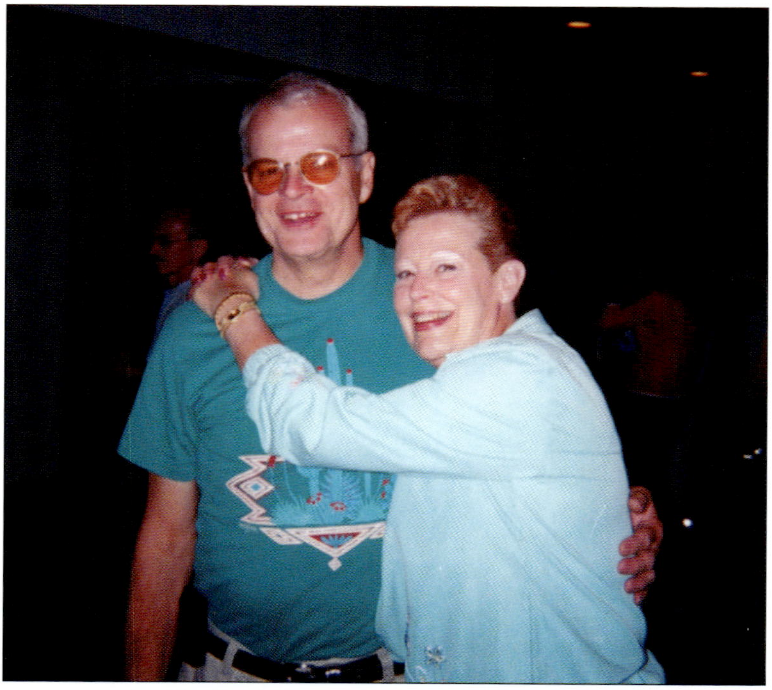

The most important piece of the festival has always been the volunteers. Thousands of volunteers have donated their time to the festival for over four decades, but only one has done so continuously since 1970. Dave Auman has volunteered for 48 festivals and has worked every job from logistics to EMT to serving on various festival committees. Pictured is Auman with Ava Kiefer during the 36th festival in 2004.

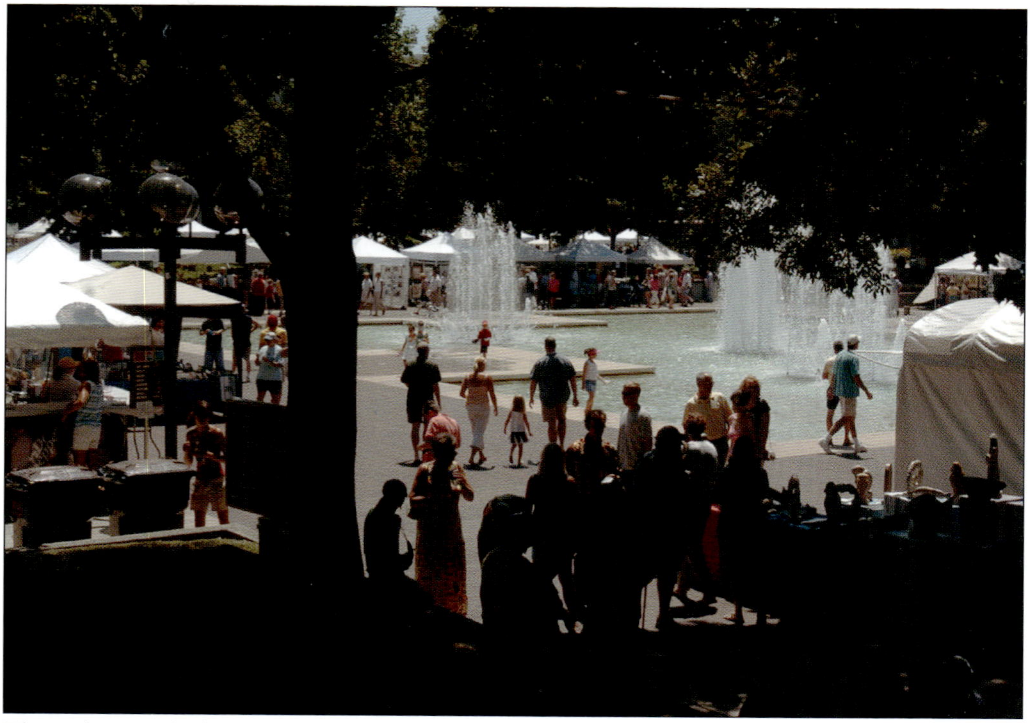

The 37th annual Three Rivers Festival opened on Saturday, July 9, 2005, with beautiful sunny skies and near perfect 74-degree weather. Festival guests enjoyed the arts and crafts on display and for sale in Art in the Park and Crafter's Market the first weekend of the festival, along with watching artists create pictures at the Chalk Walk. Here, patrons enjoy the art in Freimann Square on Sunday, July 10, 2005. (Courtesy of Samuel Hoffman, the *Journal Gazette*, Fort Wayne, Indiana, 2005.)

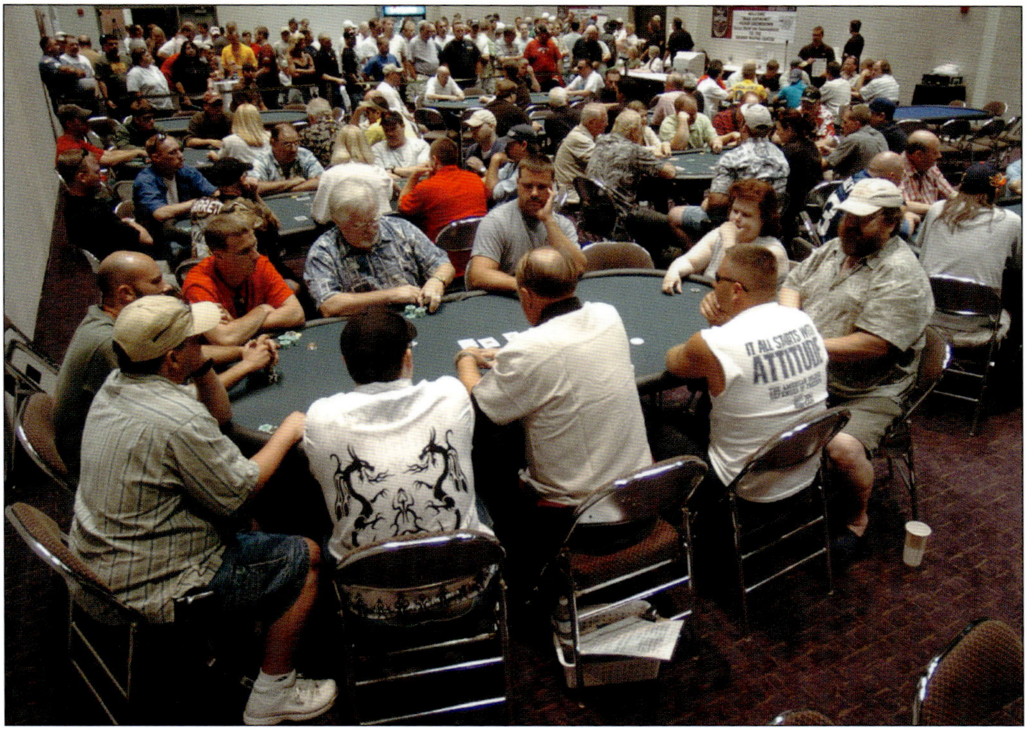

One of the highlights of the festival's opening day in 2005 was Mad Anthony's Poker Showdown. The event was held in the Anthony Wayne ballroom at the Grand Wayne Center and featured multiple poker tables, where participants played for a seat at the main table. The main tournament took place at 2:00 in the afternoon with a prize pot of $25,000. Pictured are poker players competing to win the tournament. (Courtesy of Samuel Hoffman, the *Journal Gazette*, Fort Wayne, Indiana, 2005.)

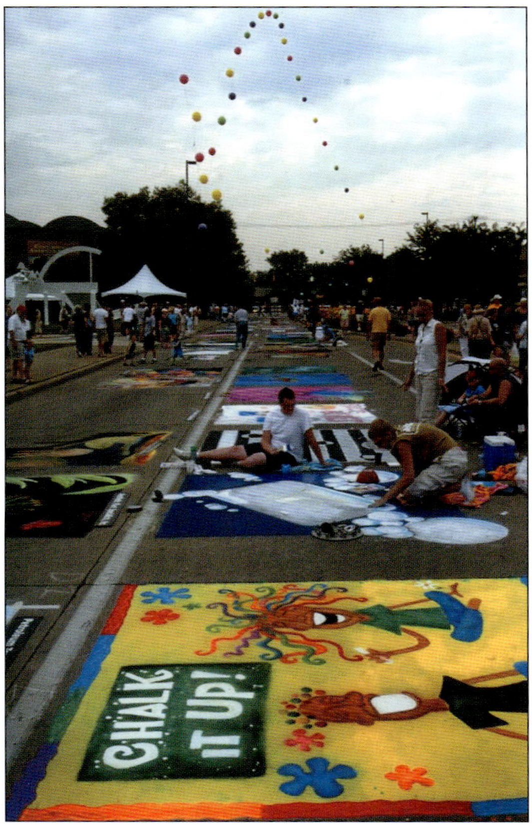

In its seventh year in 2006, the Fort Wayne Museum of Art provided a canvas for hundreds of local and regional artists to create colorful art on Main Street during the Chalk Walk at Art in the Park. Festival guests enjoyed watching the street come to life with colorful chalk, paint, and pastels. Here, Chalk Walk artists complete their works of art on Sunday, July 9, 2006. (Courtesy of Samuel Hoffman, the *Journal Gazette*, Fort Wayne, Indiana, 2006.)

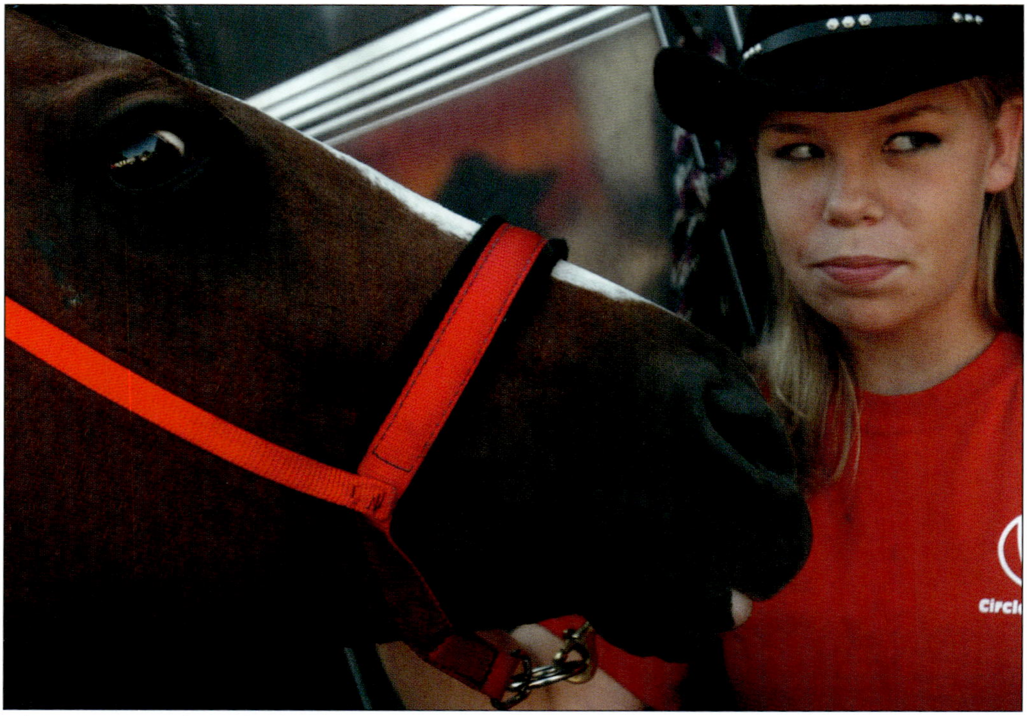

July 8–16, 2006, brought the 37th Three Rivers Festival. Opening the festival for the 37th time was the annual parade with a theme of "Celebrate Learning." The grand marshals were the superintendents from Fort Wayne Public Schools, and the parade featured over 10 marching bands from area schools. Over 90 artists performed on various stages, including the main stage in the Meijer Event Pavilion. New events included a coffee brewery tour, NASCAR race cars, Build a Bear, Best Buy Fun Zone, and a Lego exhibit. Rain tried to dampen attendees' spirits for over three days, but finally let up in time for the big fireworks finale on the last day. Pictured above, a horse named Cheyenne and Missy Nolan, from Circle W Riders, wait for the parade to start. Below, the Wayne High School Marching Band performs during the parade. (Both, courtesy of Samuel Hoffman, the *Journal Gazette*, Fort Wayne, Indiana, 2006.)

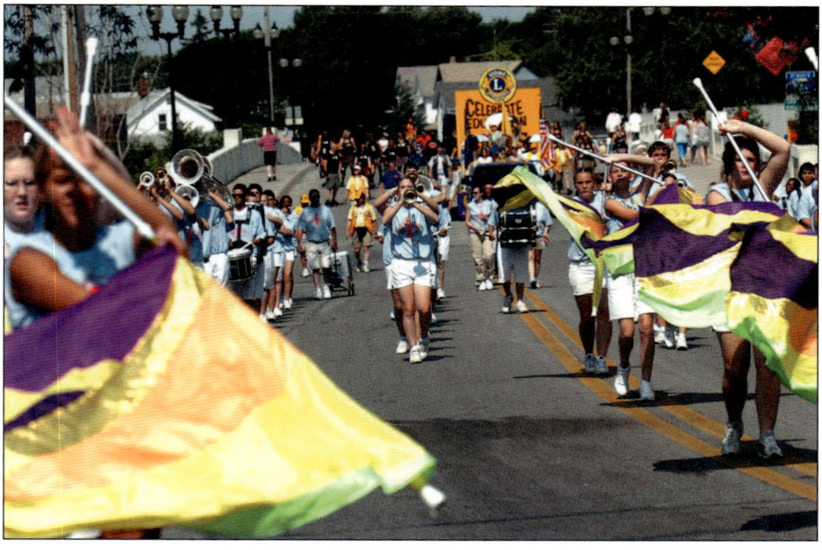

The year 2007 was the first time the Three Rivers Festival had a title sponsor. Fort Wayne Newspapers took on the role with a generous donation to the festival. Once again, the festival expanded Art in the Park. Guests could enjoy the Higher Grounds Café and visit the Hoagy Carmichael exhibit. Guests also enjoyed the Fort Wayne Museum of Art's annual Chalk Walk, along with entertainment on the Arts United Stage in front of the Arts United Center on Main Street. Around 100 artists set up shop in Freimann Square to display and sell their handcrafted fine art. At right, an artist works on a painting during Art in the Park on Saturday, July 15, 2007. Below, festival patrons stroll along the artist booths on Main Street on Sunday, July 16, 2007.

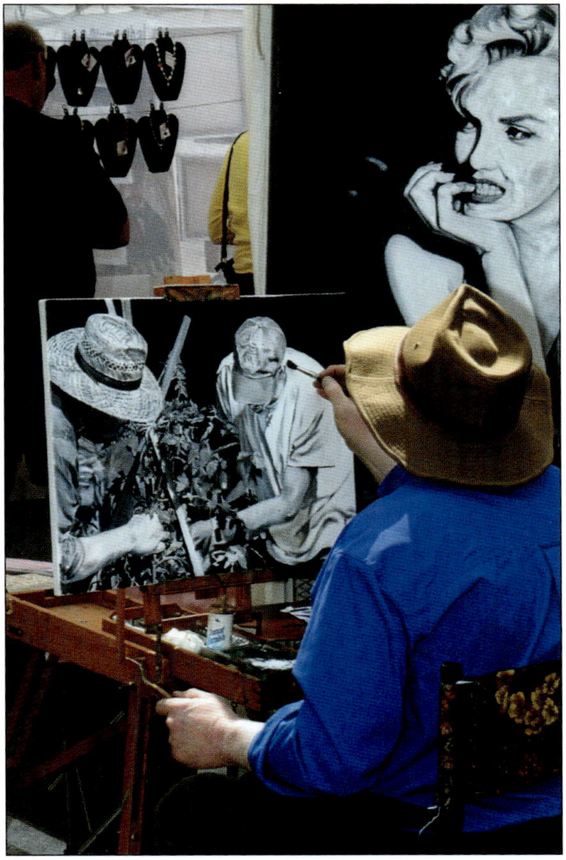

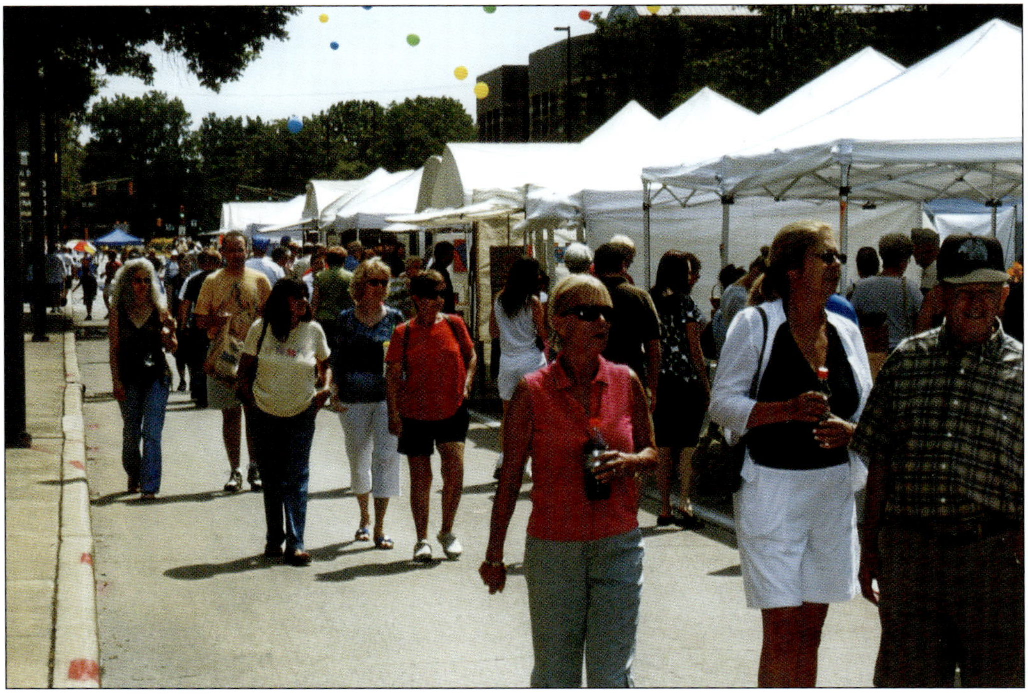

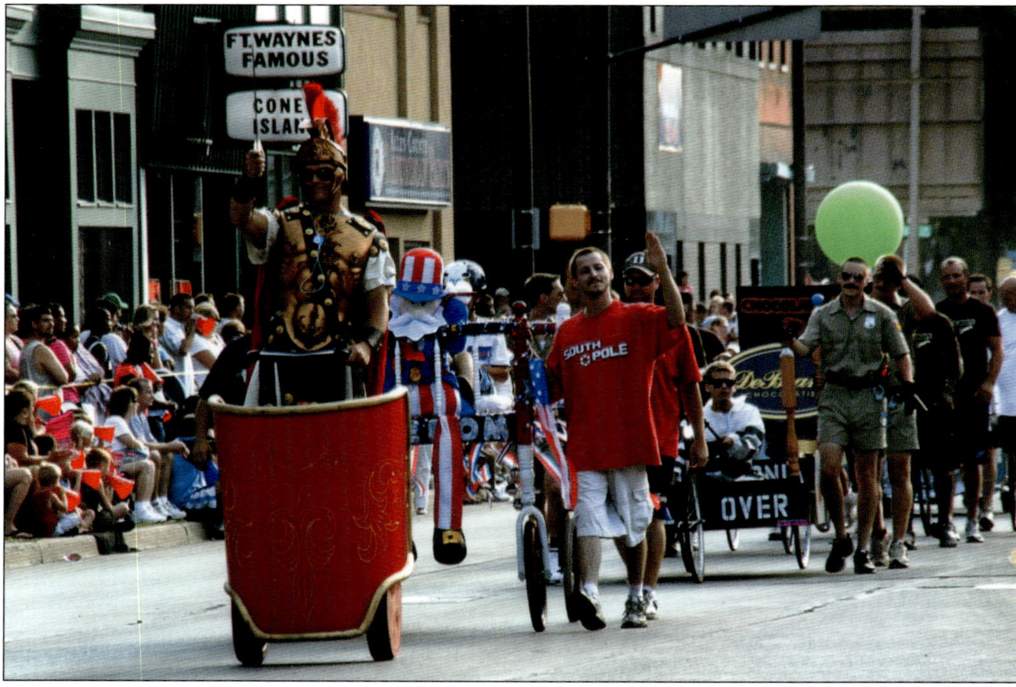

Fort Wayne Newspapers' title sponsorship was not the only festival "first" in 2007. The Meijer Event Pavilion opened for the first time on Friday, July 13, with evening karaoke. For the first time, the bar served not only draft or fountain drinks but also beverages in cans. The midway featured amusement rides, helicopter rides, the Nintendo Wii touring unit, and the Batmobile. The annual parade, Waiter & Waitress Contest, Children's Fest, bed race, and Junk Food Alley took place as usual to the delight of the community. Above, a Roman gladiator rides in his chariot during the parade lap of the annual bed race on Wednesday, July 18, 2007. Below, a team of doctors race their bed to the finish line on Main Street.

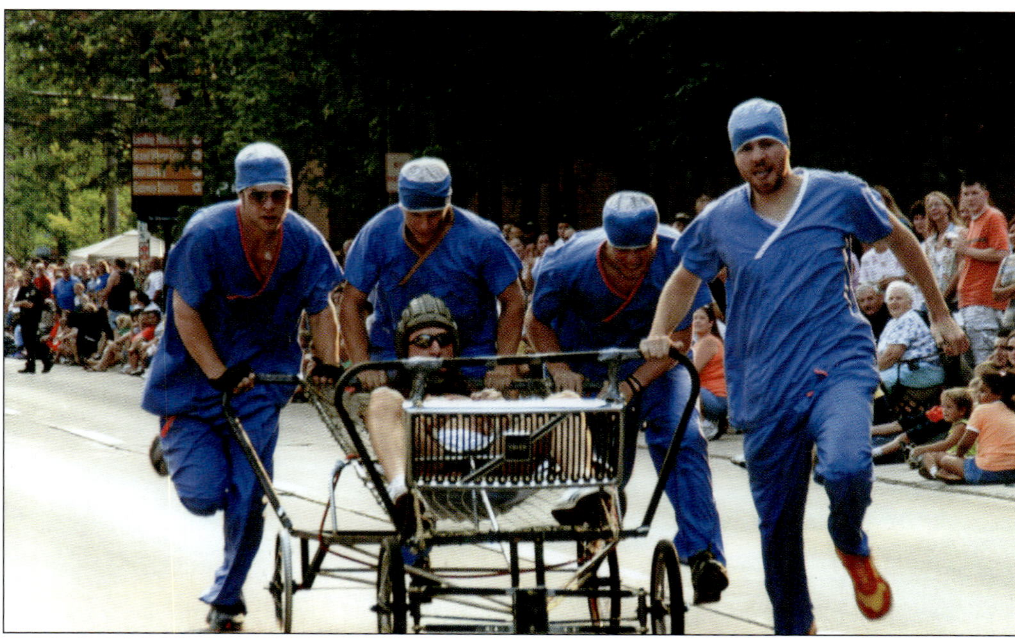

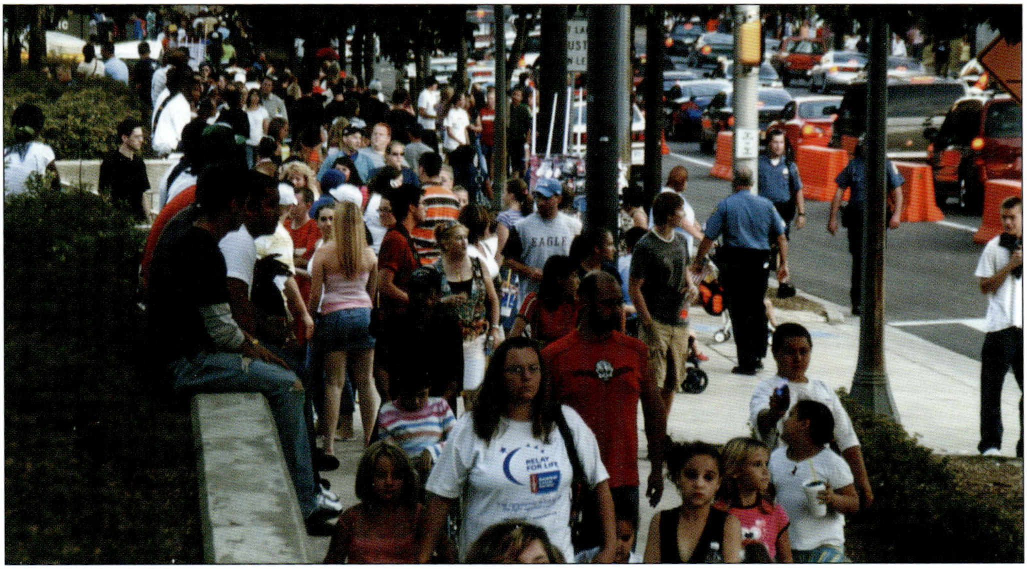

The Meijer Event Pavilion provided nightly concerts and events for the community during the 39th festival in 2007. Featured bands were Sevendust, Dark Star Orchestra, and the Georgia Satellites. Other events included a gospel fest, the Summit City Poetry Slam and Art Showcase, and Fiesta Night on Wednesday. Here, festival guests fill the sidewalk in front of the Meijer Event Pavilion on Saturday, July 15, 2007.

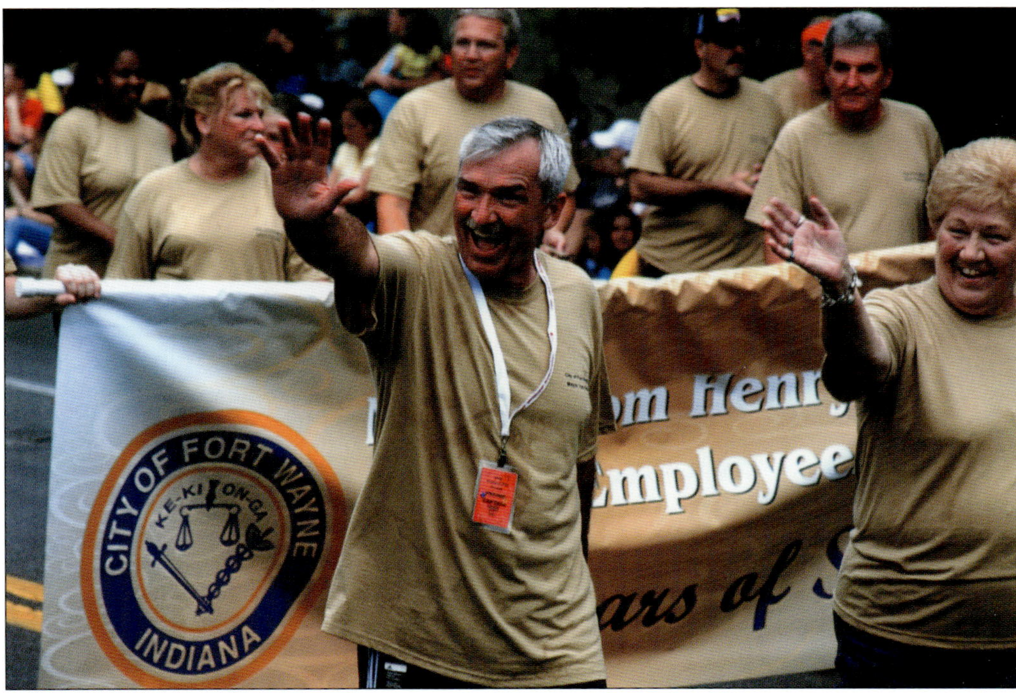

The Three Rivers Festival marked its 40th year in 2008. The festival celebrated its anniversary by adding new events, including a karaoke competition with $7,500 in prizes, a hot dog eating contest, and Fest Unlimited. This was the first year the parade allowed participants to hand out candy to kids along the parade route. Pictured is Mayor Tom Henry waving to the crowds during the 40th parade.

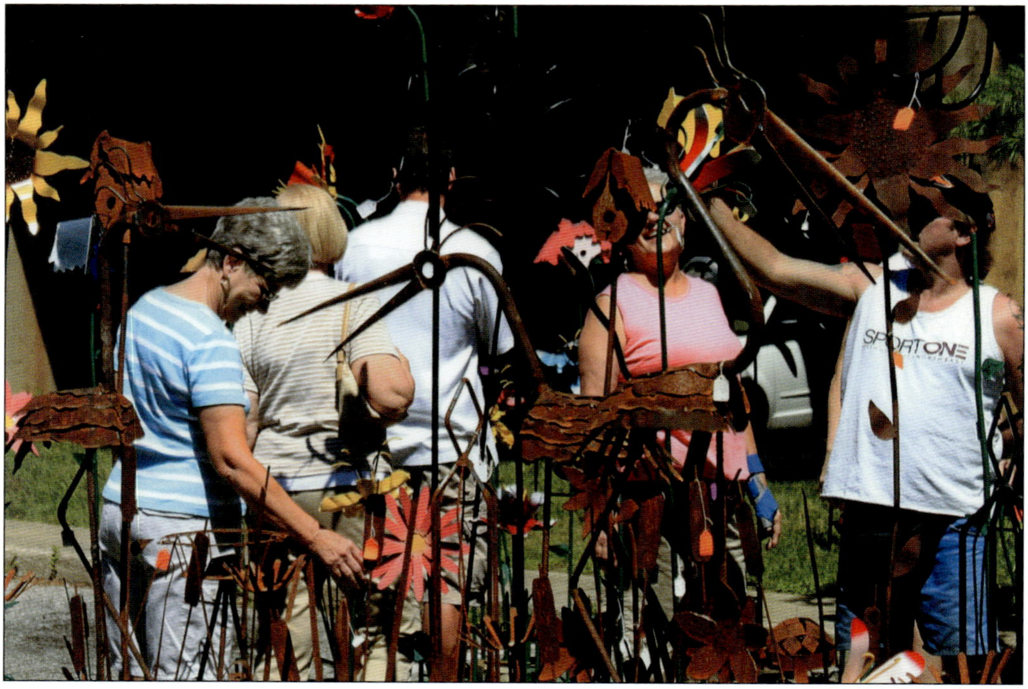

The Crafter's Market featured the handmade crafts of local artisans. Festival guests shopped for handmade soaps, lotions, jewelry, garden sculptures, hair bands, and much more. The Crafter's Market was held in the Freimann Square parking lot, in conjunction with Art in the Park on Saturday and Sunday, July 12–13, 2008. These shoppers are picking out handmade metal garden sculptures to take home during the 40th festival.

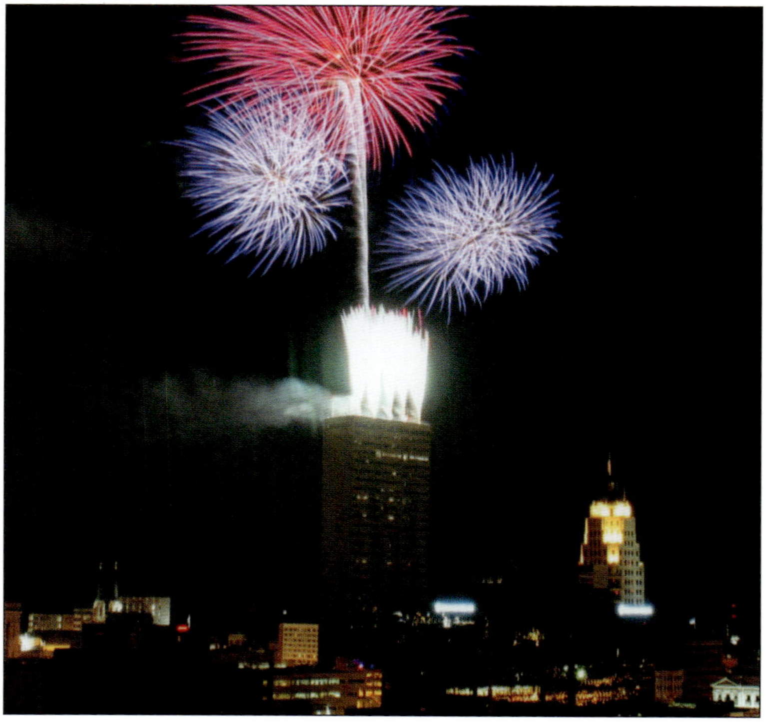

The 40th Three Rivers Festival ended on Sunday, July 20, 2008. The festival had a week of beautiful, sunny skies and temperatures ranging from 74 to 85 degrees. Hundreds of thousands of people came out to the festival to enjoy its many events, thrilling rides, entertaining concerts, and tasty food. The festival wrapped up with the annual fireworks finale from atop the Summit Square building.

Five

2009–2017

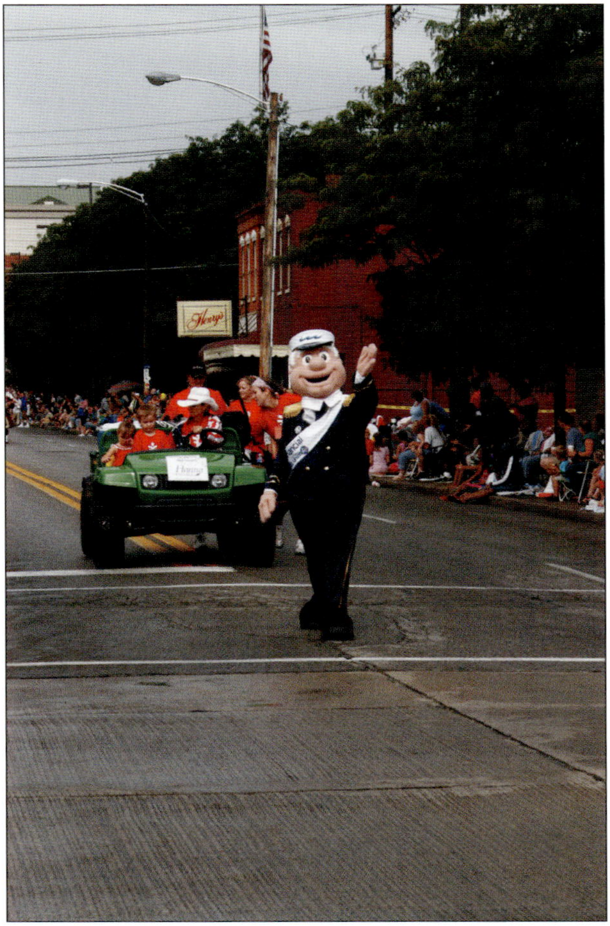

"Imagine This!" was the theme for the 41st festival. Fort Wayne's Lloy Ball, a 2008 Olympic men's volleyball gold medalist, served as the parade's grand marshal on July 11, 2009. His success at the Olympics coincided with the festival theme, making a dream and vision into reality. The festival's mascot, Admiral Andy, is walking down Main Street in the 41st Three Rivers Festival Parade.

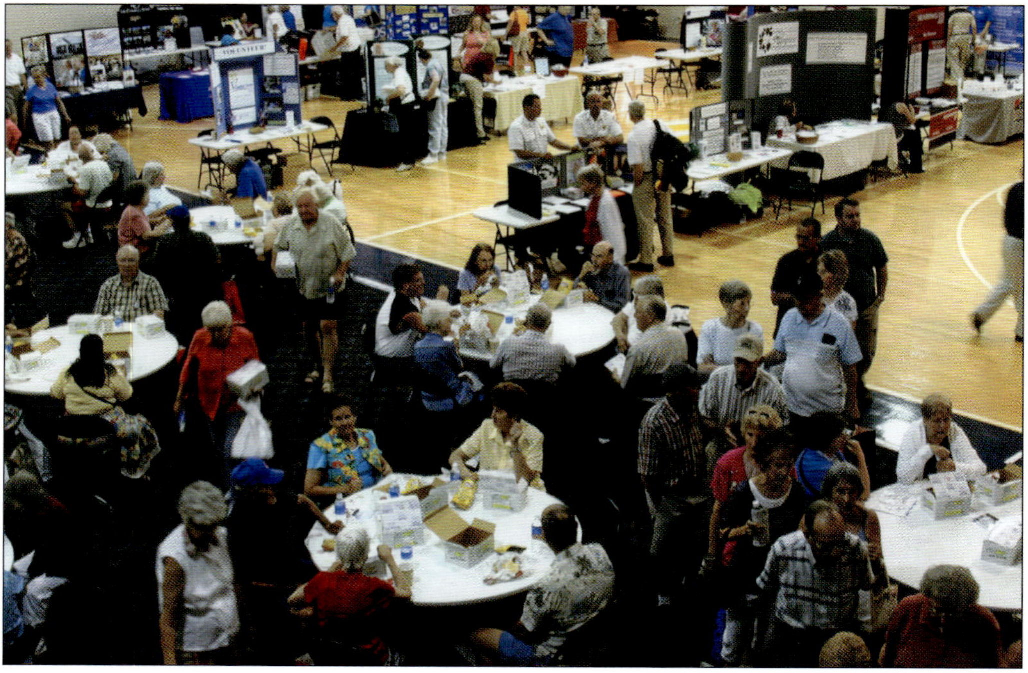

As in the past, the festival staff and board worked hard to bring in events at a low cost or for free in 2009. Over 80 percent of festival events were free and available to all. Super Seniors Day, the bed race, Art in the Park, Waiter & Waitress Contest, and Children's Fest were all free events. Many of the festival's affiliated events, such as Chalk Walk, Family Fun Day at the Courthouse, Antiques in the Park, and the Barr Street Market were also free in 2009. Above, seniors enjoy a day of euchre, bingo, live music, and lunch during Super Seniors Day at the Imagine School on Wells Street. Below, the Superior Van and Mobility team line up at the starting line during the bed race on Wednesday, July 15, 2009.

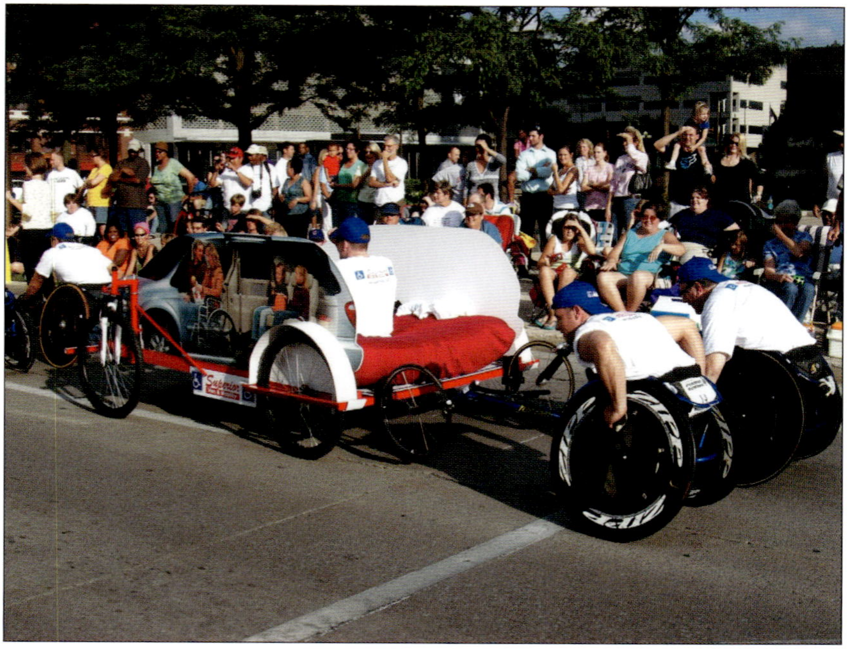

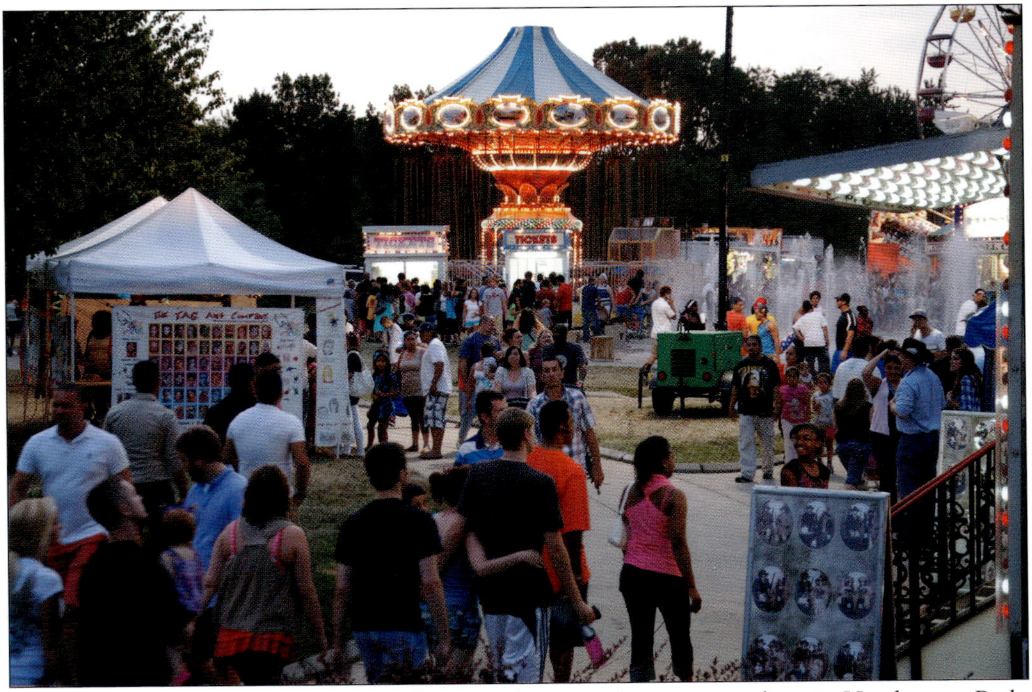

Fest Unlimited was brought back for the second year to the great meadows in Headwaters Park. Festival guests of all ages enjoyed the thrilling amusement rides and carnival games. Guests also had the opportunity to get their face painted or take an old-fashioned photograph in the park. Pictured here, Fest Unlimited was packed with people enjoying an evening at the festival on Saturday, July 11, 2009.

Bikers from all over Fort Wayne and the surrounding area descended on Headwaters Park West for Bike Night on Monday, July 12, 2010, during the 42nd Three Rivers Festival. Riders and enthusiasts enjoyed the Thunder and Lightning in the Fort ride-in event, parade, and bike show. Here, festivalgoers check out the motorcycles lining South Calhoun Street during the bike show in 2010.

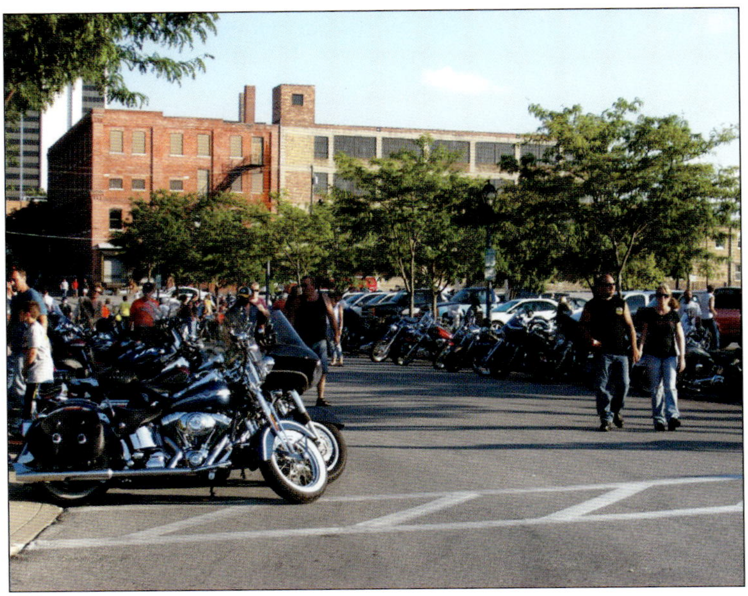

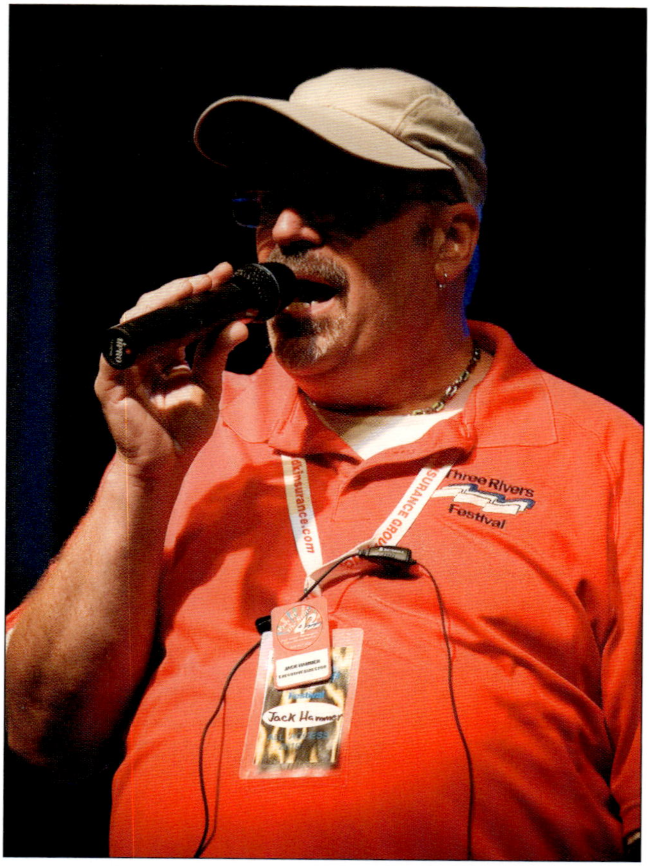

The year 2010 was a hard one for the festival. It found itself without a director and facing financial hardship just months before the 42nd festival was to open in July. Dave Bleke, board president, asked local radio personality Jack Hammer to join the festival as interim executive director. Hammer happily took the position and started out raising funds and putting the festival in order. With the help of the board of directors, committee members, and volunteers, the festival went off without a hitch on Friday, July 9, 2010. At left, Hammer introduces the concert headliner, Pink Droyd, in the festival plaza on Friday, July 9, 2010. Below, Dave Bleke is dunked in the beer trough on the last night of the festival, Saturday, July 10, 2011.

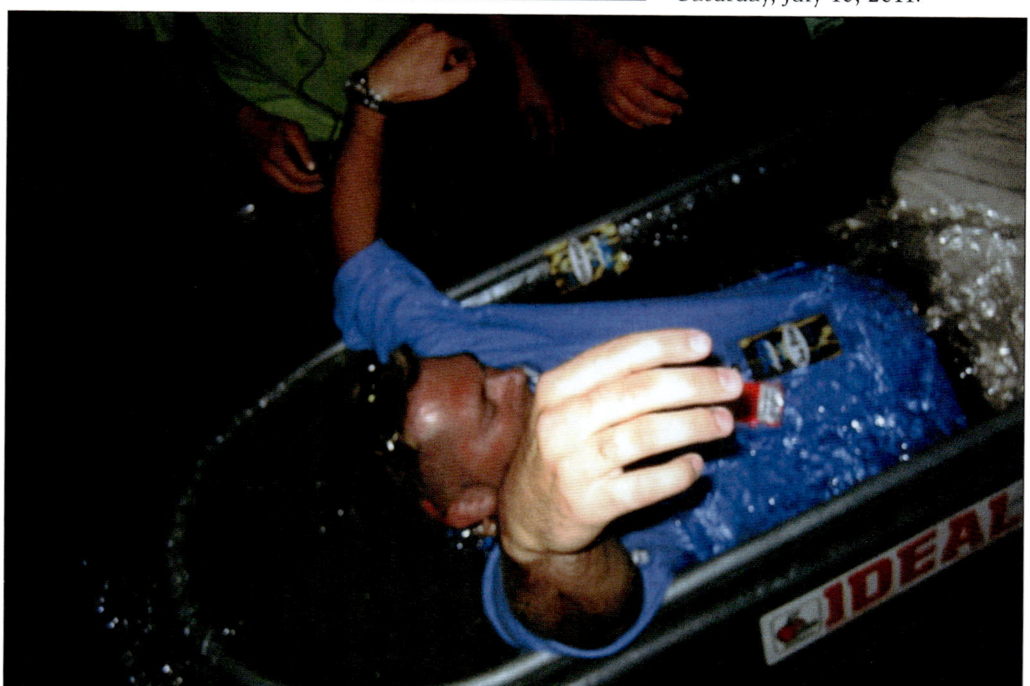

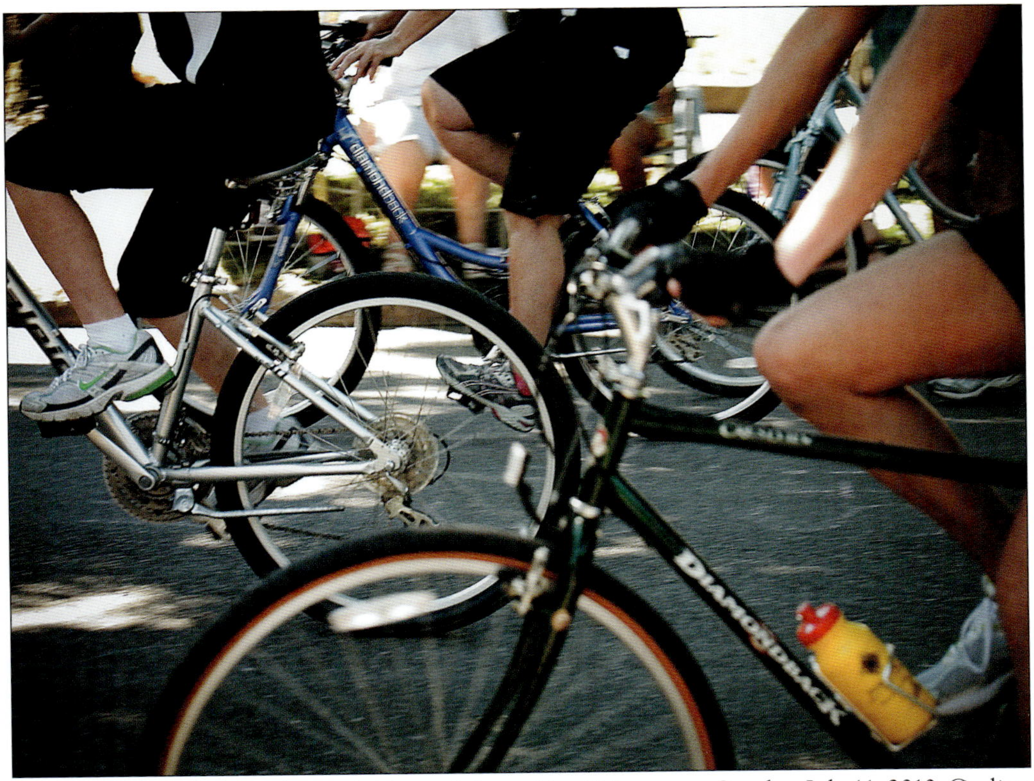

The Three Rivers Festival Bicycle Tour celebrated its 39th year on Sunday, July 11, 2010. Cyclists began the tour at the Hickory Center School on the northwest side of Fort Wayne and rode through gently rolling to moderate hills on routes of 14, 25, 52, 63, or 100 miles through Allen, Whitley, and Noble Counties. Here, a colorful array of bikes pedal through the county during the annual bike tour.

In 2009, the Three Rivers Festival teamed up with the Miss Three Rivers Pageant. Each year in September, a new Miss Three Rivers Festival and Miss Three Rivers Festival Teen is crowned. The title holders serve as ambassadors for the festival in the community. From left to right are 2011 title holders Taylor Knox, Alexa Marascovich, Emily Eshbach, and Courtney Jurick.

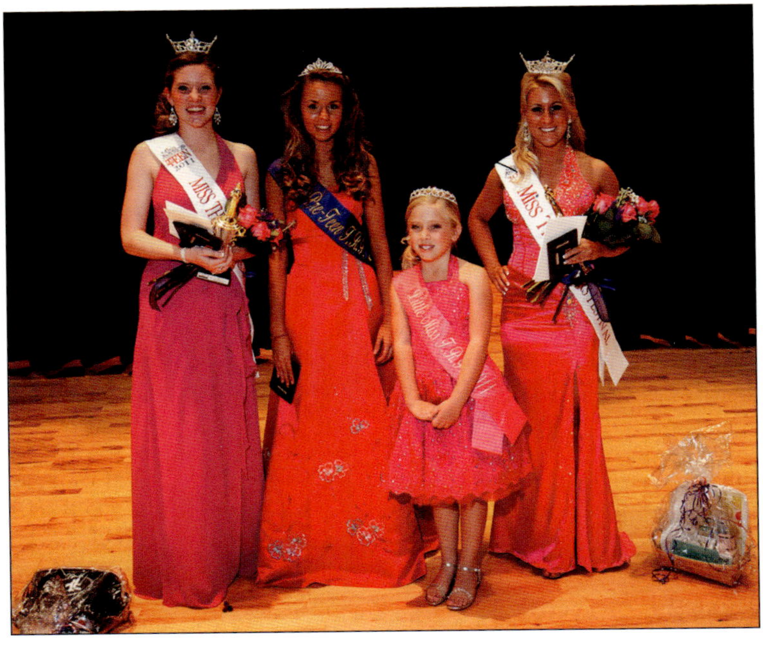

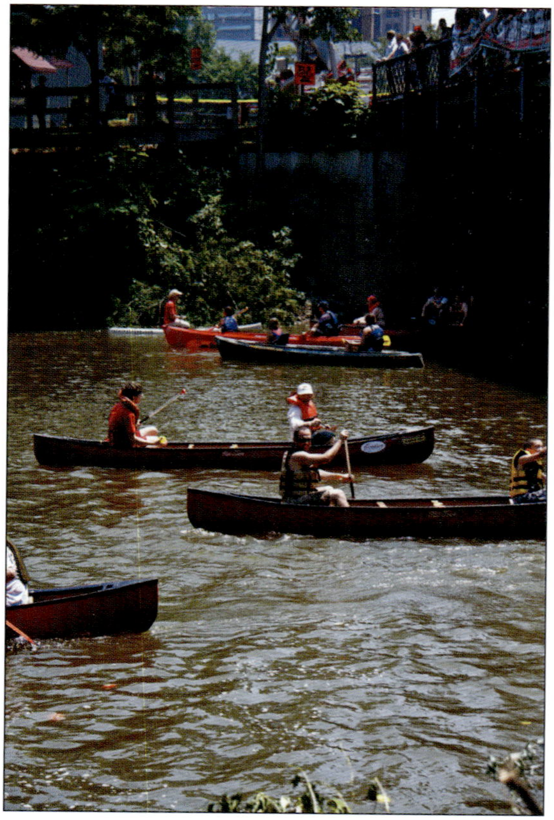

River Games debuted during the 43rd festival in 2011. Festivalgoers could participate in a canoe race, which ran from the Wells Street Bridge to the Spy Run Bridge and back. They could also test their paddling skills on the canoe obstacle course. With obstacles to weave through, flags to retrieve, and giant cascades of water to navigate, the course made for the wettest and fastest race the festival had ever seen on the river. Water Wars was a team contest on the St. Mary's River. Three-person teams went head-to-head with water balloon launchers. At left, participants in the canoe race paddle to the finish line at the Wells Street Bridge on Sunday, July 10, 2011. Below, Adam Ehle, Dave Bleke, and Craig Griffith launch balloons at their opposing team from a raft in the St. Mary's River.

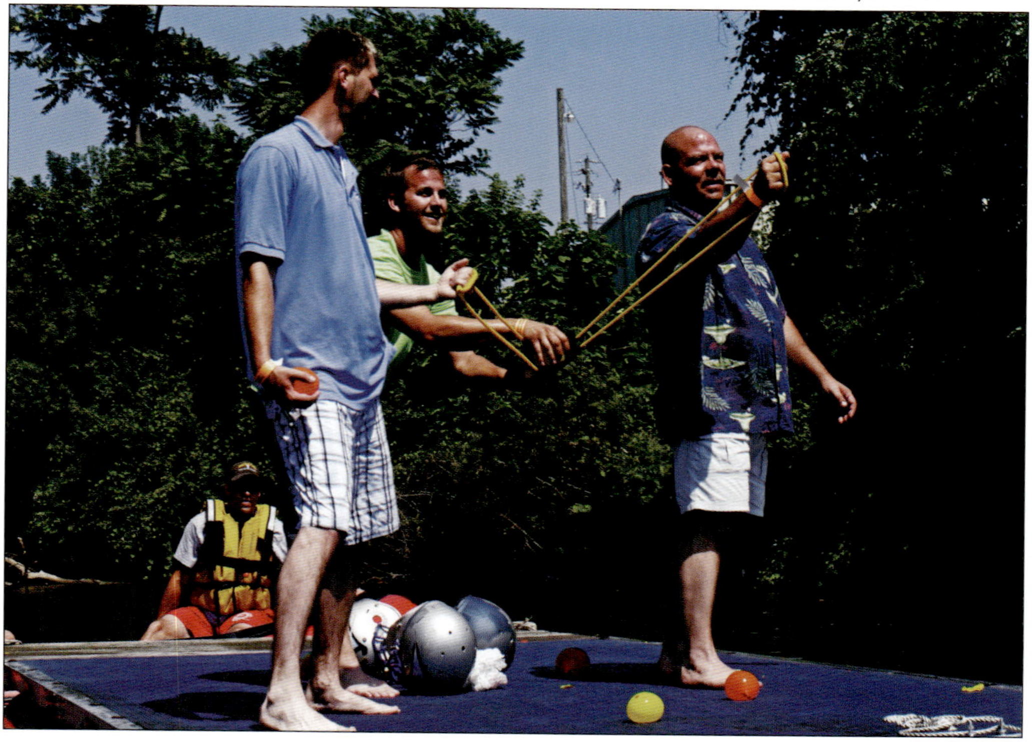

On Wednesday, July 13, 2011, Science Central (Fort Wayne's interactive museum for science, math, and technology) hosted the Catapult Chaos Competition. Contestants in the contest created and built a catapult or trebuchet to hurl objects at targets and then competed to see whose machine could throw an object the farthest. Here, two different sized trebuchets are lined up at Science Central during the competition.

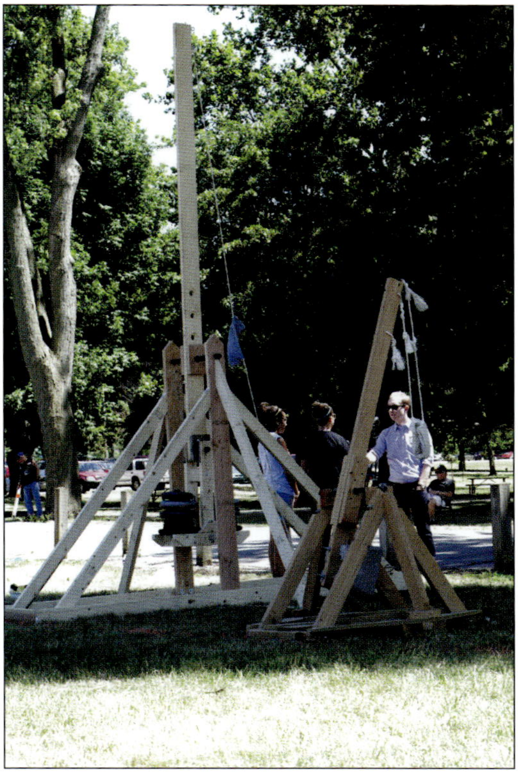

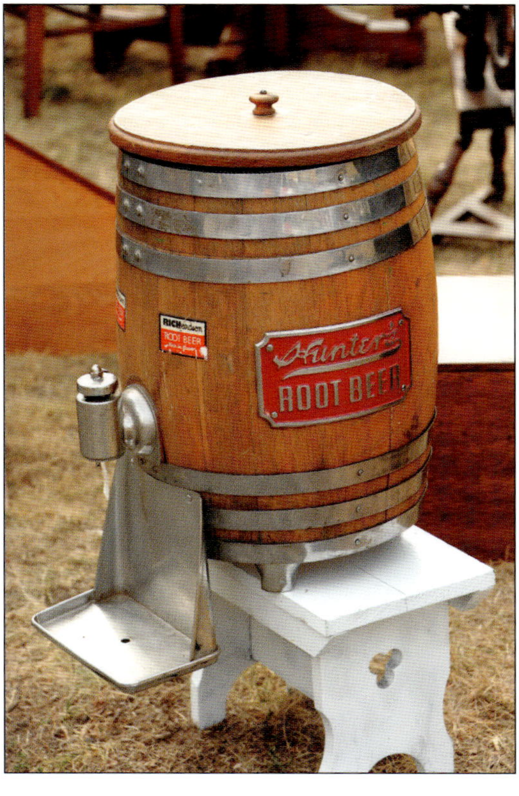

The 44th Three Rivers Festival opened on Friday, July 13, 2012. The first weekend of the festival was packed with events old and new. Antiques in the Park, a longtime festival event, was held in the historic McCulloch Park on Saturday and Sunday, July 14–15, 2012. The antique show offered furniture, primitives, glassware, garden decor, and classic antiques for sale. An antique Hunter's root beer barrel dispenser is pictured here for sale.

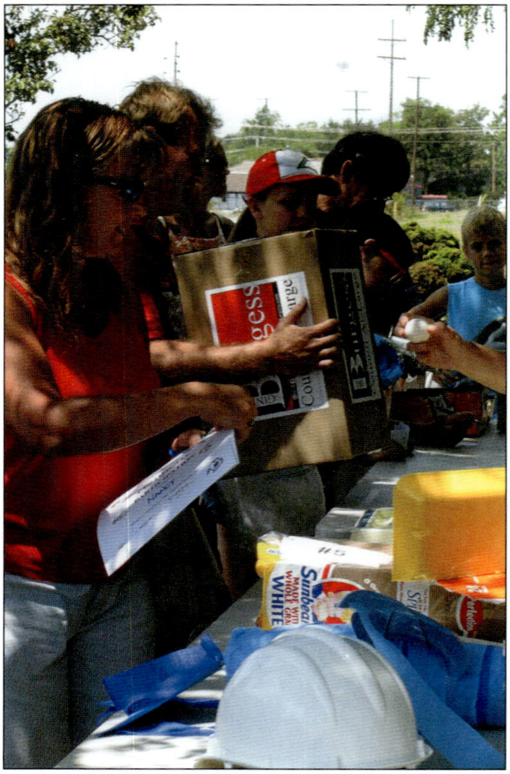

The Three Rivers Festival has always offered family-friendly events and entertainment since it began in 1969. The 44th festival continued this tradition with a long list of events that everyone could enjoy. Science Central hosted the Egg Drop Eggstravaganza on Sunday, July 15, 2012. Children and adults had the opportunity to display their creative talents by designing a container or craft that would keep an egg from breaking when dropped off the roof of the three-story building. At left, contestants line up to register for the egg drop and receive their egg. After receiving their eggs, the contestants packed them in their containers for the drop. Below, the first egg is dropped from the roof of the Science Central building.

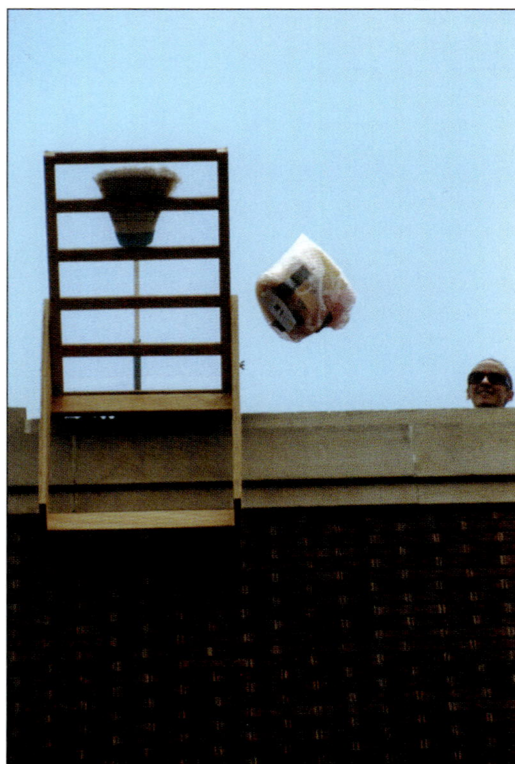

Each year, thousands of people come to the festival to enjoy junk food, music, thrilling rides, and beautiful art. However, some come out for the pets! Each year, the festival has a dog and/or cat show for the animal lovers of the world. On Saturday, July 14, 2012, the American Cat Fancier Association held a show of over 100 cats of 30 different breeds. Pictured here is a white oriental cat.

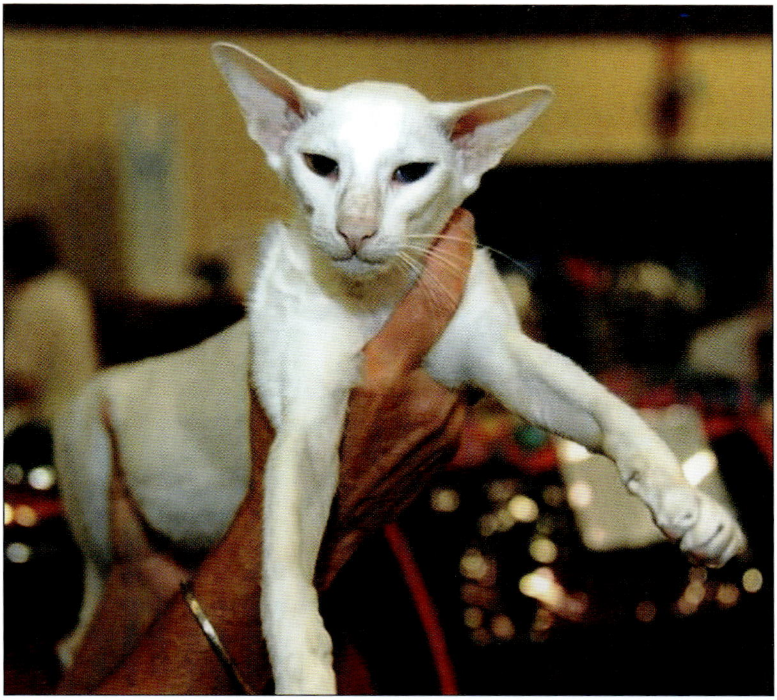

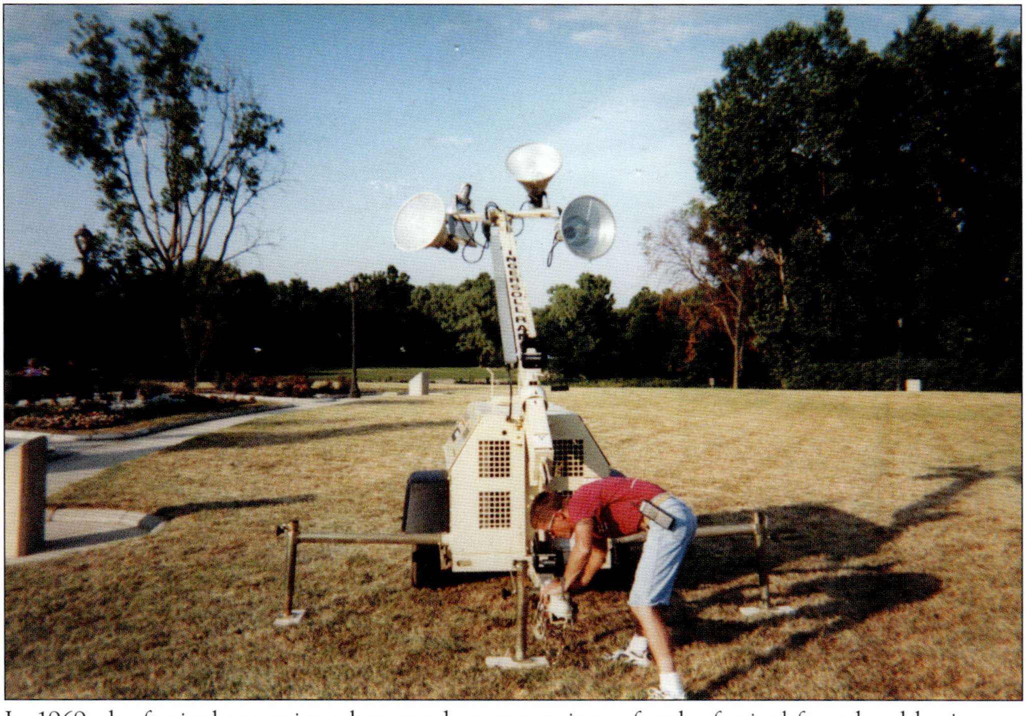

In 1969, the festival committee borrowed necessary items for the festival from local businesses and the city. As the festival has grown, the number of required items has increased. The festival now owns enough equipment to fill two semitrailers and two storage rooms, but still has to rent items such as forklifts, tents, chairs, and toilets. Here, Tim Schieferstein sets up a light tower in Headwaters Park in 2013.

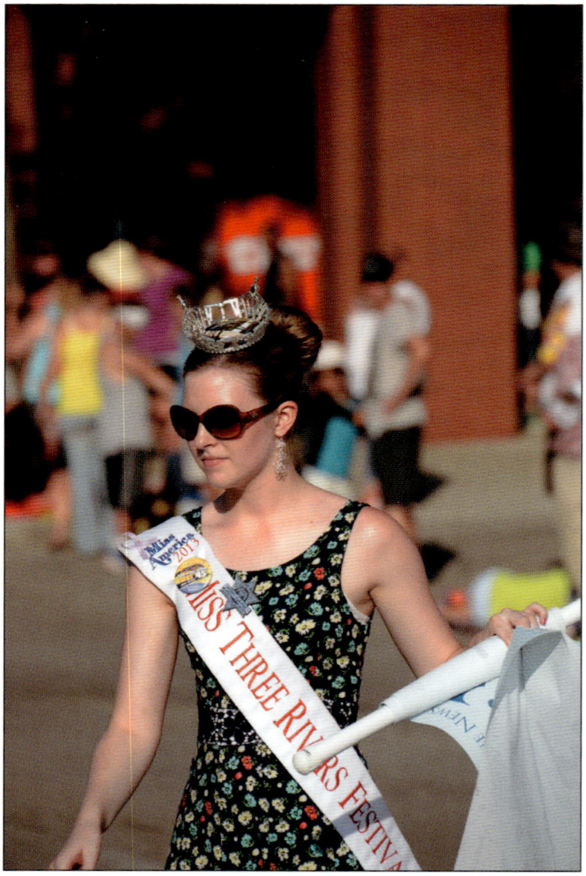

Each year, the current Miss Three Rivers Festival and Miss Three Rivers Festival Teen volunteer their time at the festival. The girls participate in the parade on Saturday morning, help in sponsor hospitality at night, serve as a customer during the Waiter & Waitress Contest, hold the finish line during the bed race, and visit children at Children's Fest. Pictured is Miss Three Rivers Festival 2013, Taylor Knox, at the bed race.

The 45th festival welcomed the return of the raft race after a 15-year hiatus. The raft race was ended after 1998 due to river conditions at the time. After years of cleanup by the City of Fort Wayne, the rivers were ready to welcome rafts again. Teams competed for speed or creativity for $14,000 in cash prizes. The GI Joe's Army Surplus team is pictured in its Viking ship.

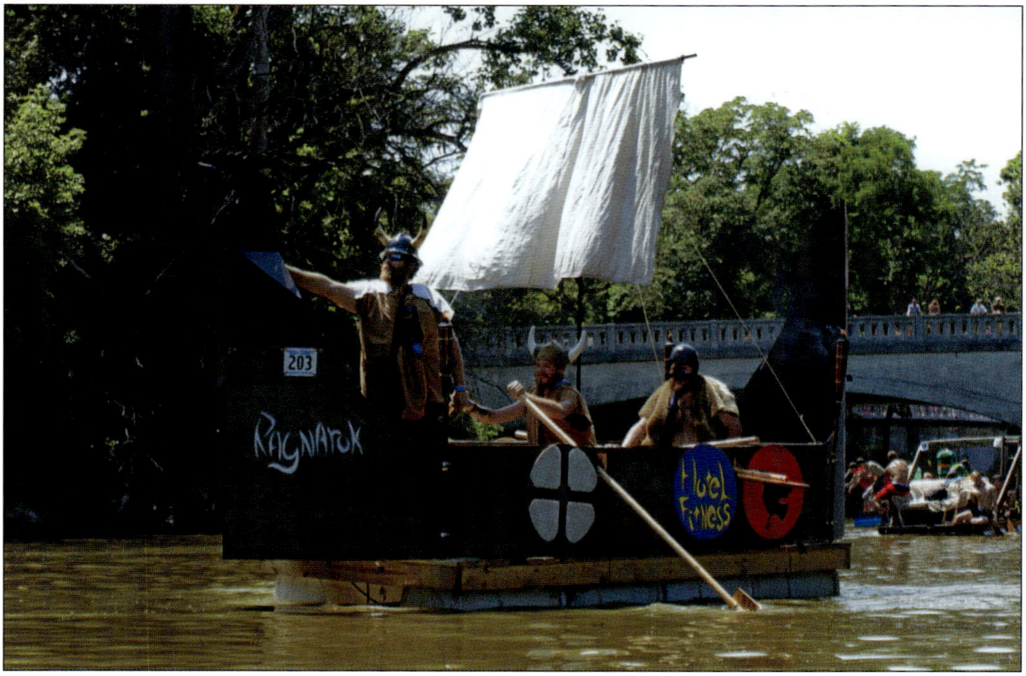

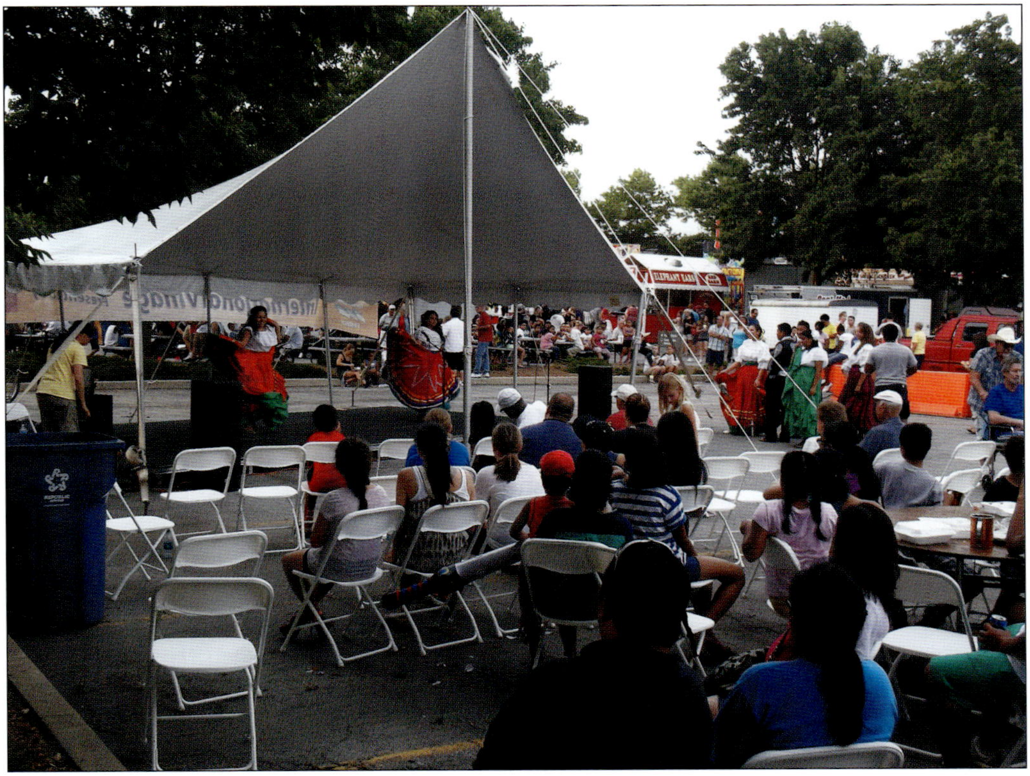

The last weekend of the 45th festival welcomed the opening of International Village. The event was moved to a new home next to Junk Food Alley in 2013. Festival guests could learn about the traditions and heritage of different cultural groups that live in Fort Wayne. Guests enjoyed ethnic foods, along with traditional songs and dances on the village stage. Here, Mexican women perform traditional dances on Friday, July 19, 2013.

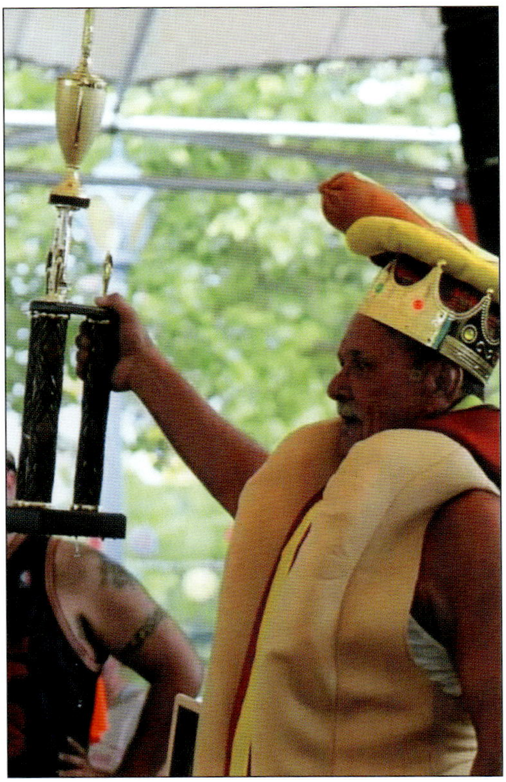

In 2014, the Three Rivers Festival helped the Coney Island Weiner Stand celebrate its 100th anniversary by hosting a coney-dog eating contest. Preliminary rounds for the contest were held at Deer Park Irish Pub on June 7, 2014, with the top 10 contestants moving on to the competition finale at the Festival Plaza on Saturday, July 12. The coney champion, who ate 19 coney dogs, is pictured here.

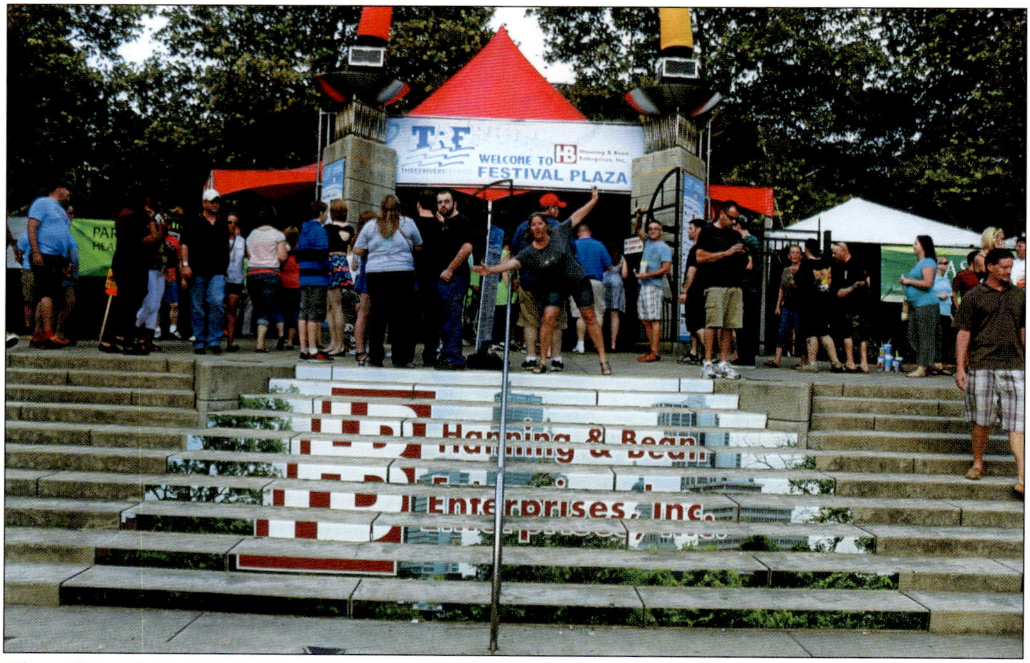

The 46th Three Rivers Festival offered exciting new events for 2014. The Indianapolis Colts brought their popular Fan Fest to the festival on Friday, July 11. Festival guests could meet the Colts players and cheerleaders, get autographs, and test their football skills. The Festival Plaza offered many exciting concerts, including Cheap Trick on Friday and the Under the Sun tour featuring Smash Mouth, Sugar Ray, Blues Traveler, and Uncle Cracker on Saturday, July 12. Family Fun Day was held for the first time on Wednesday, July 16, which featured three children's bands in Festival Plaza: the Tim Harrington Band, Jug Huffers, and the Atomic Sharks. Above, a large line formed in front of Festival Plaza and down the sidewalk for the Under the Sun concert. Below, Sugar Ray performs his hit song "Every Morning" for the crowd.

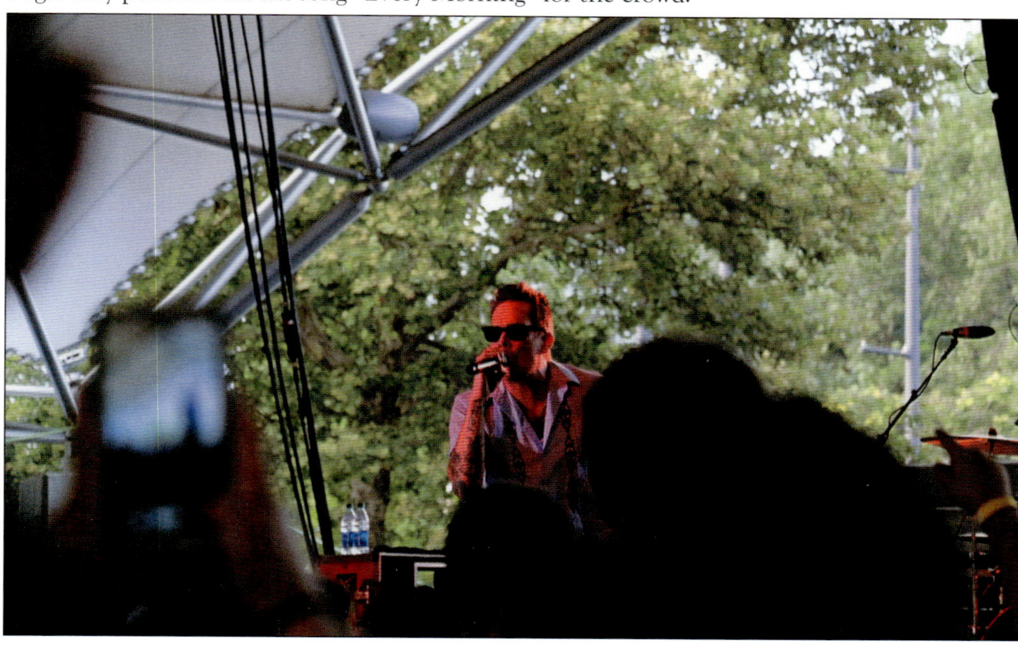

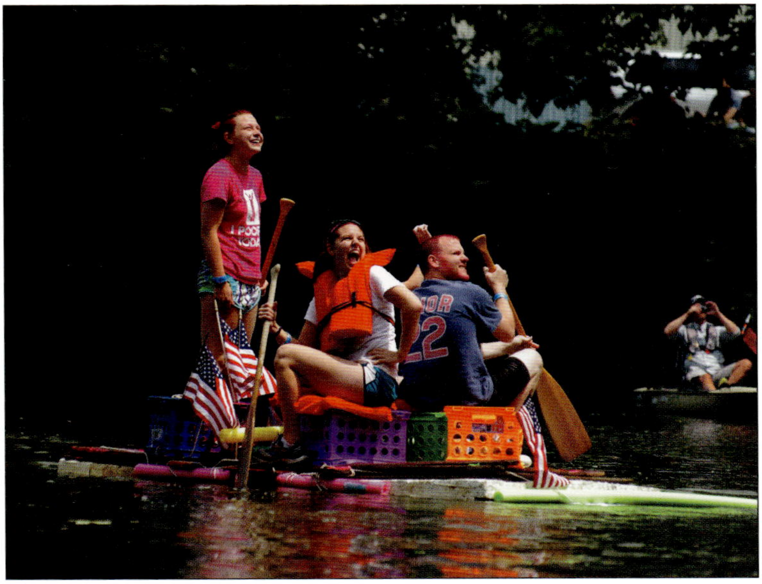

At 1:00 in the afternoon on Saturday, July 19, 2014, the banks of the St. Mary's River were lined with spectators anxious for the start of the raft race. Fifty-five rafts of all shapes, sizes, and designs lined up at the Main Street Bridge for a fun and challenging day on the river. This team, with its improvised raft, is having fun during the raft race.

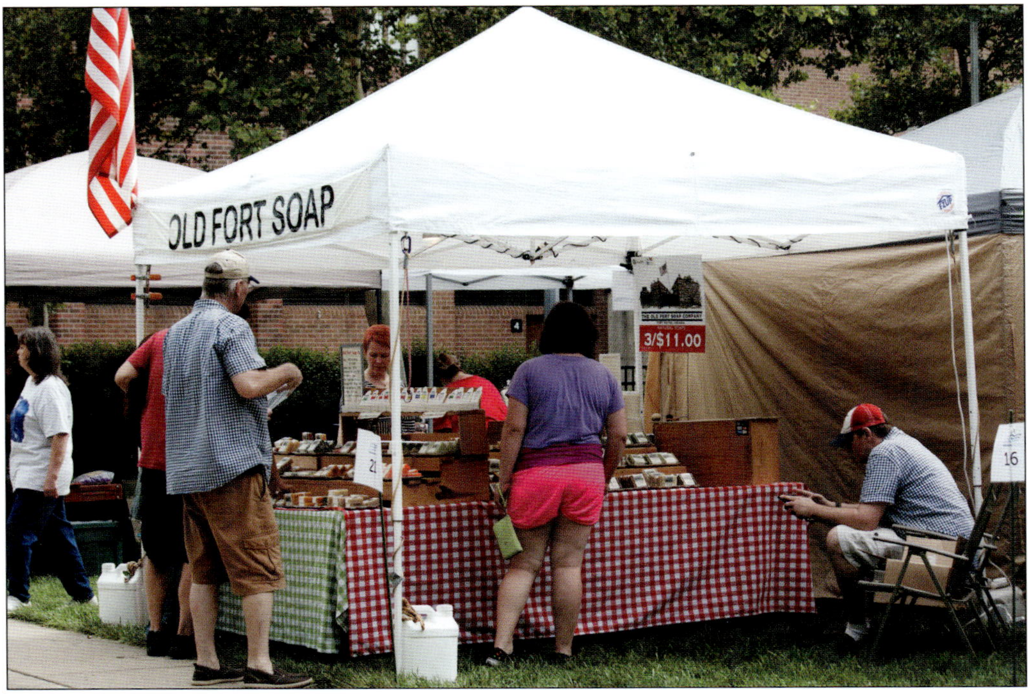

The Three Rivers Festival celebrated its 47th year in 2015. The festival met many challenges that year with constant rain all week long. The rain resulted in both the raft race and river excursions being cancelled, and the midway had to be evacuated once due to storms. However, with all the rain, people still came out to enjoy festival events. Here, guests shop for handmade soaps in the Crafter's Market. (Courtesy of Erin Graf Photography.)

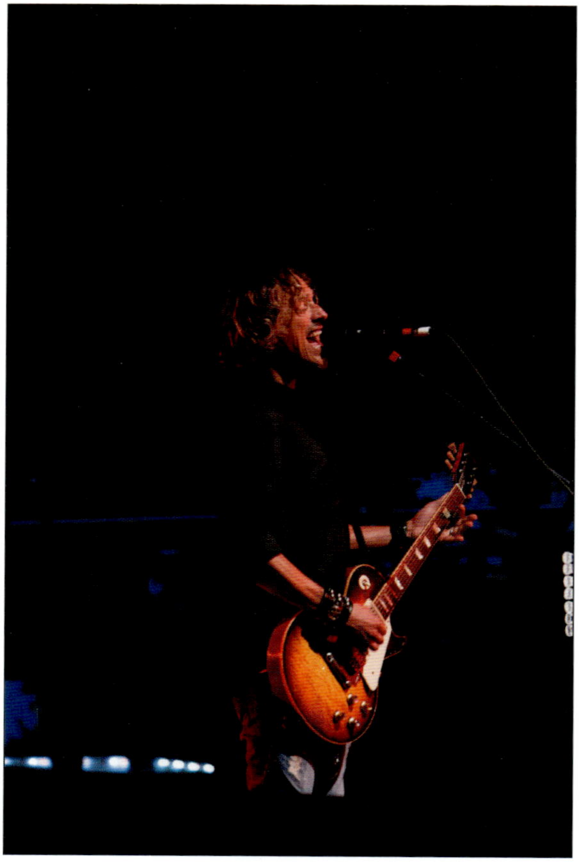

Even though rain poured on the festival day and night, Festival Plaza was packed with people who braved the weather to see the Summerland Tour and rock the night away to Everclear, the Toadies, Fuel, and American Hi-Fi on Saturday, July 11, 2015. For those who enjoy international music, a rare sunny day brought the Wisla Folk Dance Group from Plock, Poland, Fort Wayne's sister city, to International Village for a performance on Friday, July 17, 2015. After the group's performance, the festival's executive director, Jack Hammer, provided the group with wristbands for the midway and made sure they enjoyed the delicious food in Junk Food Alley. At left, guitarist Brett Scallions of Fuel performs on the festival stage on Saturday, July 11, 2015. Below, the Wisla Folk Dance Group from Plock, Poland, sings for the crowd on Friday, July 17.

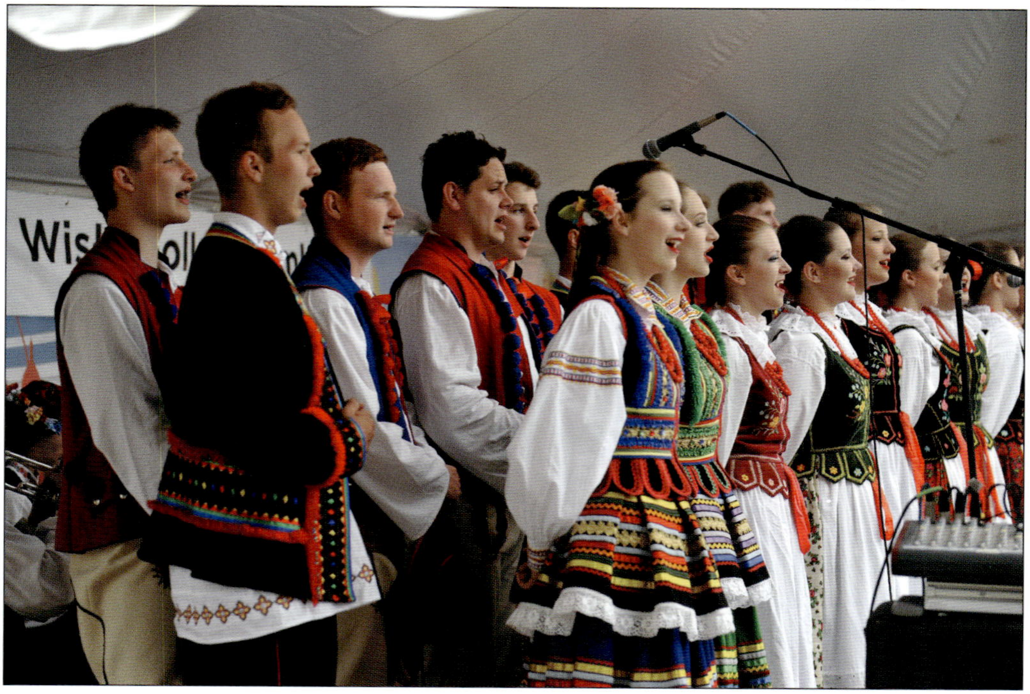

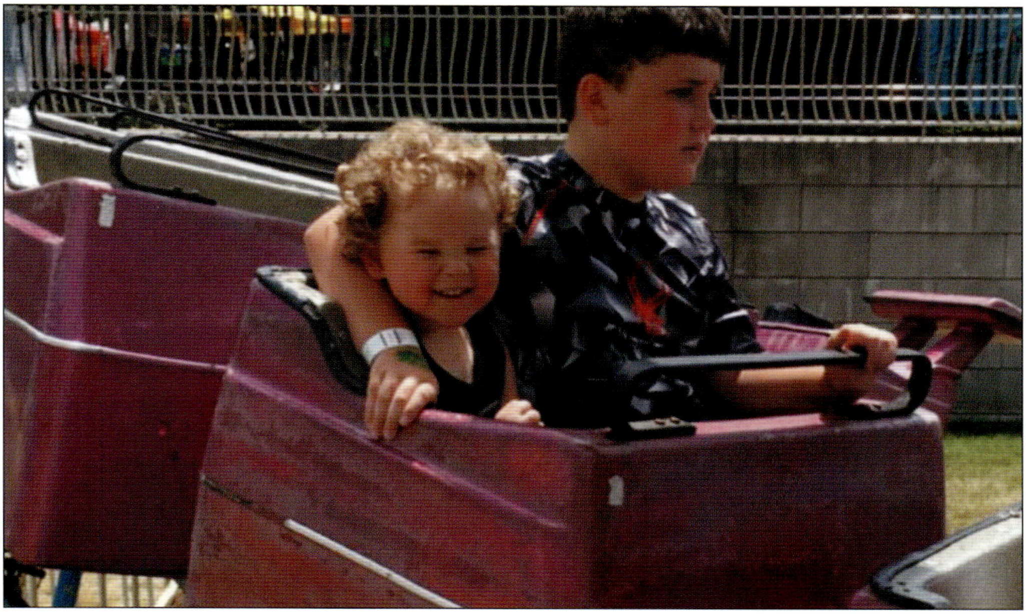

The second annual Family Fun Day was held on Wednesday, July 15, at the Festival Plaza. Over 1,000 children enjoyed games, face painting, animal encounters, prizes, and an appearance from Spiderman and Elsa. The Atomic Sharks entertained the children with their fun island music. The fun continued all day in the midway with discounted ride wristbands. Families could also learn about animals and farming and pet a cow, mini-horse, or goat in the festival's Petting Farm in Headwaters Park West. A ride around downtown in a helicopter was offered for those who enjoyed a more thrilling festival experience. Above, Zerek Graf enjoys his first roller coaster ride with his older brother Kaiden Graf-Martz during Family Fun Day. Below, Penny the goat poses for the camera during Family Fun Day on Wednesday, July 15, 2015. (Both, courtesy of Erin Graf Photography.)

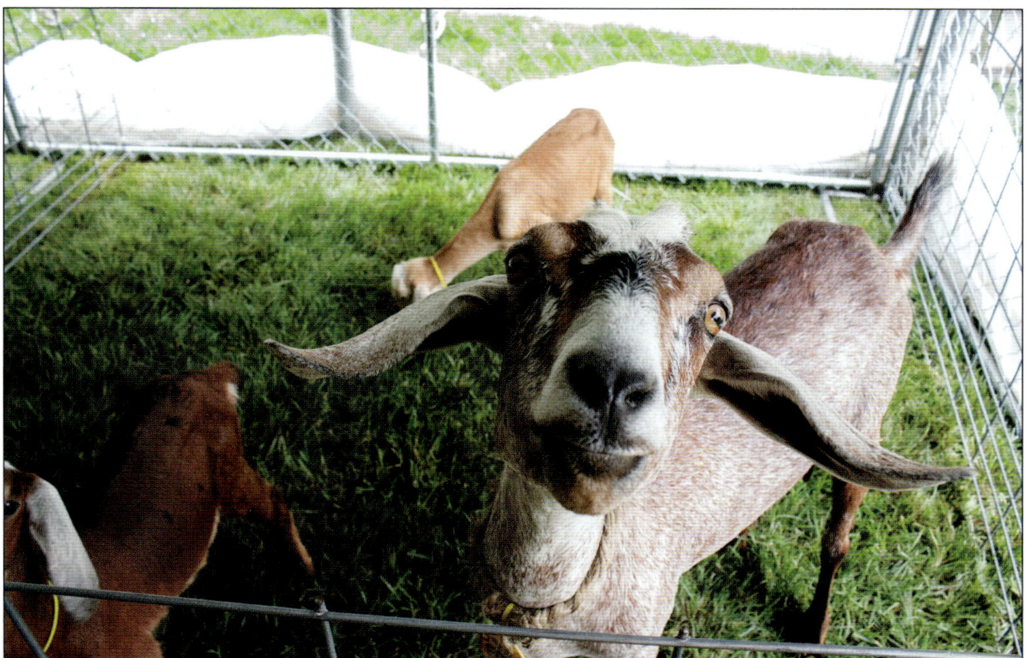

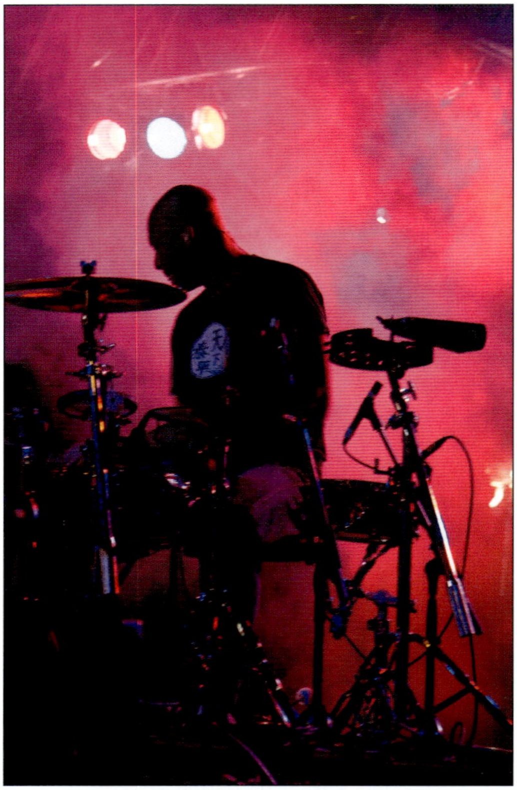

The State of Indiana turned 200 years old in 2016. To celebrate the state's bicentennial, the Three Rivers Festival board and staff dedicated the 48th festival to the celebration. The festival was accepted by the state as an official bicentennial legacy project. The theme of the annual parade was "Indiana's Bicentennial: Celebrate History—Ignite the Future." The week provided nothing but clear and sunny skies, which was much welcomed by festival staff after the rain in 2015. The 48th festival brought the Ford Super Duty Tour, Spam American Tour, and the Sprint Mobile Store to the festival midway. At left, Better Than Ezra performs during the Summer Daze concert on Saturday, July 9. Below, Pink Droyd closes out the festival on Saturday, July 16, 2016. (Both, courtesy of Erin Graf Photography.)

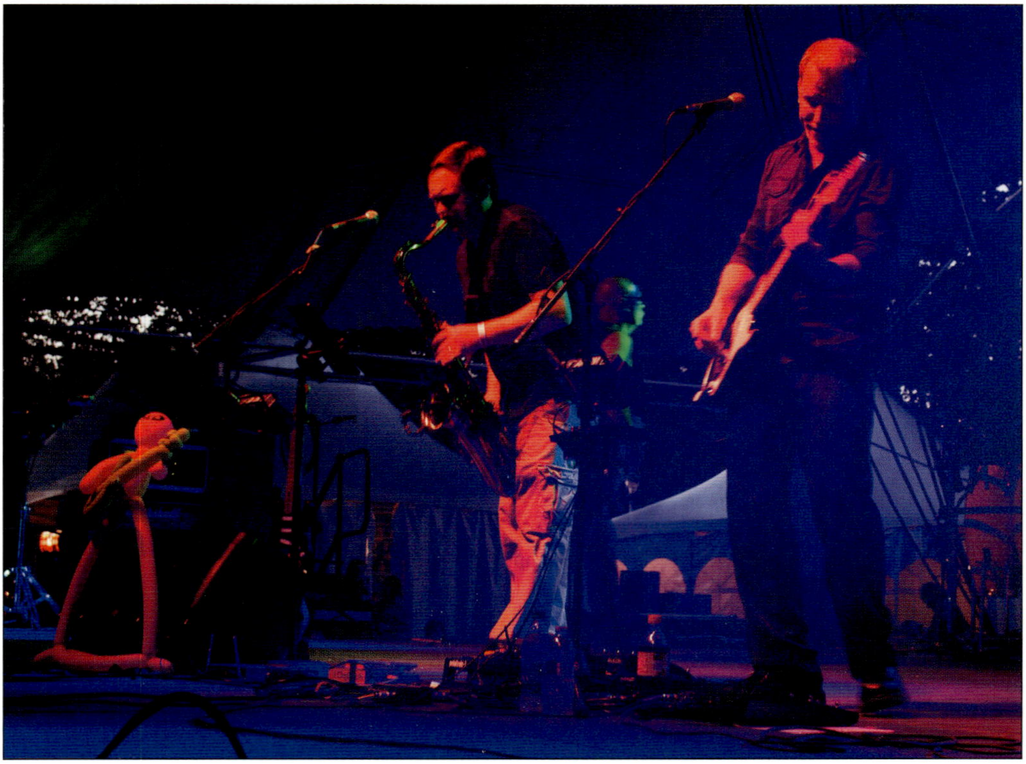

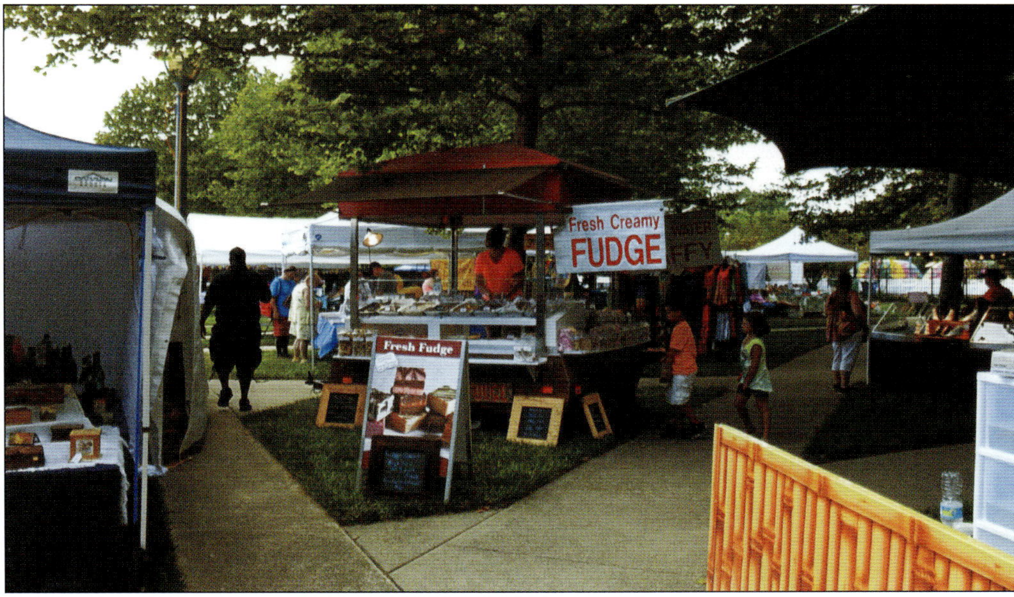

The Crafter's Market and the Marketplace were combined into the Emporium in 2016. The Emporium offered festival guests the opportunity to buy unique handmade items by local crafters, along with manufactured items and services. The Emporium also offered food that could not be found in Junk Food Alley, including a coffee shop. Here, children stop by Old World Fudge for some sweet treats on Saturday, July 9, 2016. (Courtesy of Erin Graf Photography.)

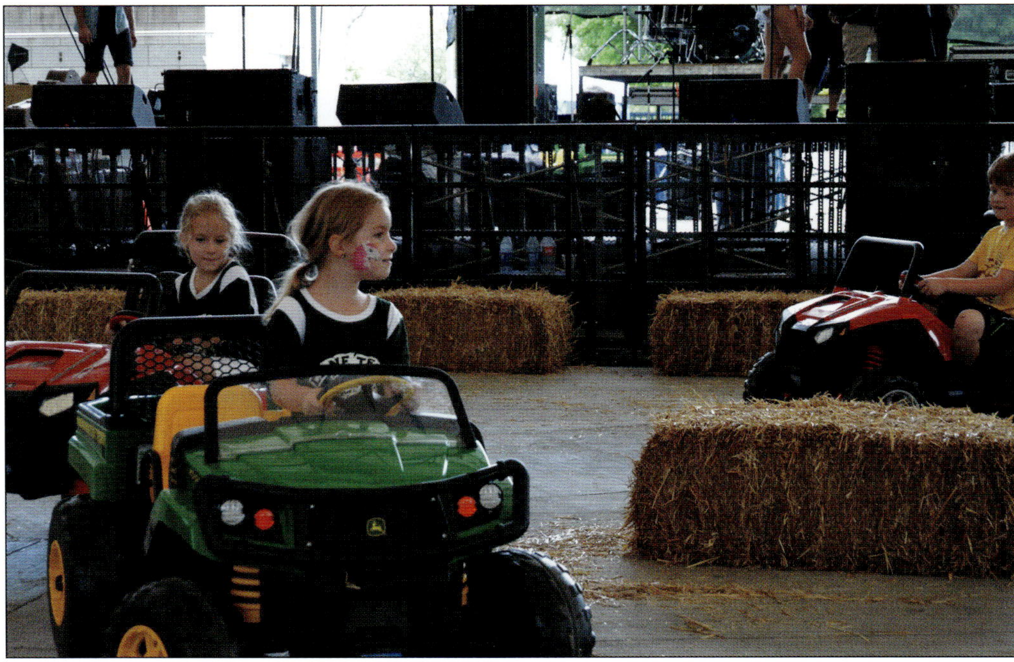

Family Fun Day was back in 2016. This event had grown from a few bands in the plaza in 2014 to having over 20 games and activities in 2016. Edy's Ice Cream provided a fun game and free ice cream, Peg Perego brought out its Little Gator track, and Indiana Wild brought interesting animals to share with the children. From left to right are Harleigh, Addy, and Sean Lane riding Little Gators.

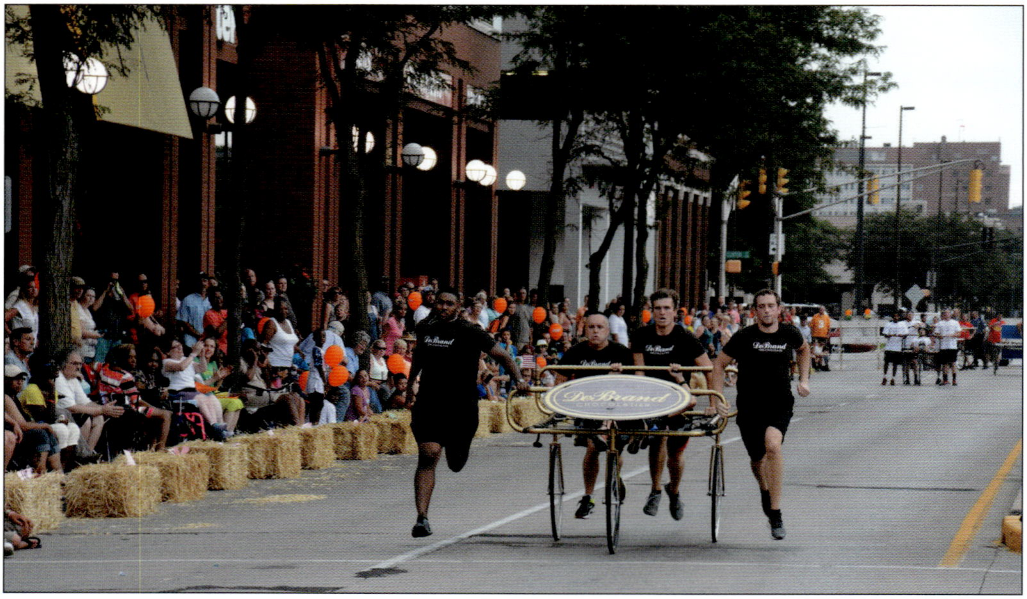

The annual Three Rivers Festival bed race is an honored tradition for many of its participants, especially for DeBrand Chocolatiers. DeBrand was the winner of the bed race in 2012, 2013, and 2014. The team lost its title in 2015 but came back with a vengeance to win the race in 2016. Here, the DeBrand team is running a heat in the 2016 bed race on July 13.

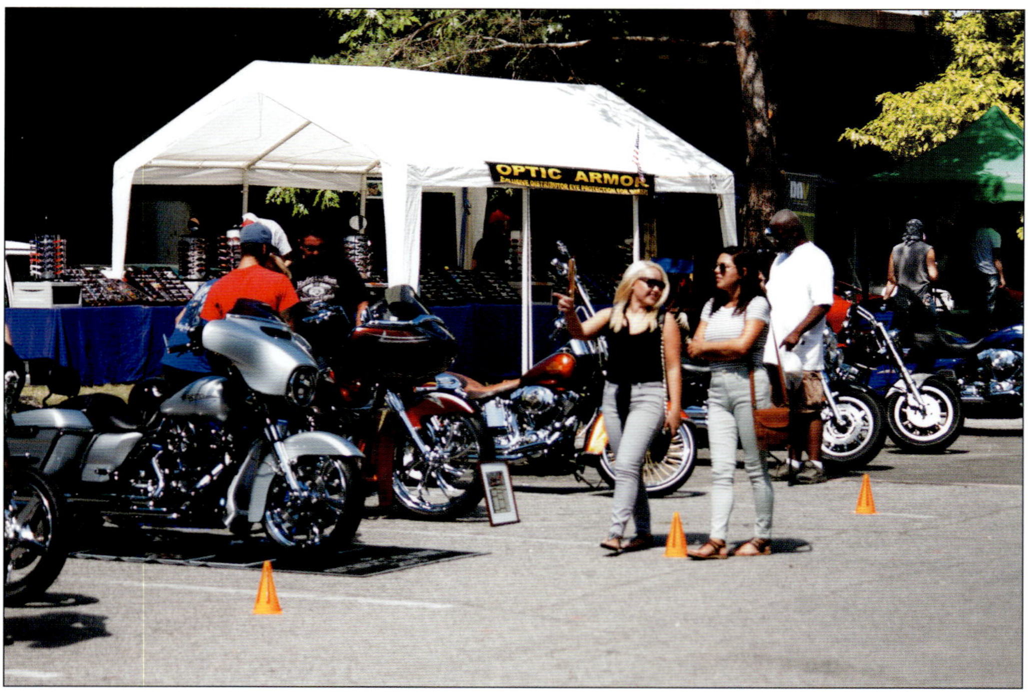

The last day of the 48th Three Rivers Festival featured the annual Bike Night and fireworks finale. Bike Night was hosted by 469 Cycle and featured a bike show with cash prizes and motorcycle vendors in the Freimann Square parking lot. Festival guests enjoyed checking out the many custom bikes at the show. Here, guests stroll through the bikes in Freimann Square on Saturday, July 16, 2016.

The Three Rivers Festival marked 49 years in 2017. "Superheroes" was the theme of the 49th annual parade, and it featured floats, walking units, and balloons all decked out in superheroes of every kind. The festival welcomed its own superhero, title sponsor Ruoff Home Mortgage, to the festival in 2017. Here, American Landmaster honors the United States with the help of Captain America. (Courtesy of Erin Graf Photography.)

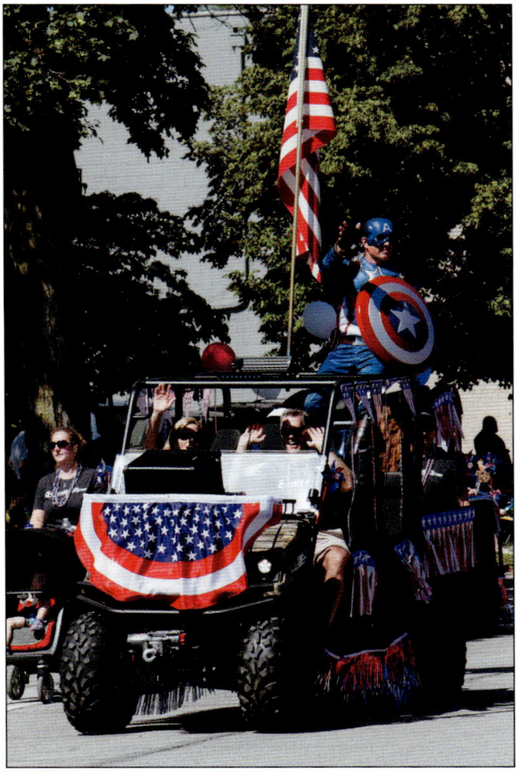

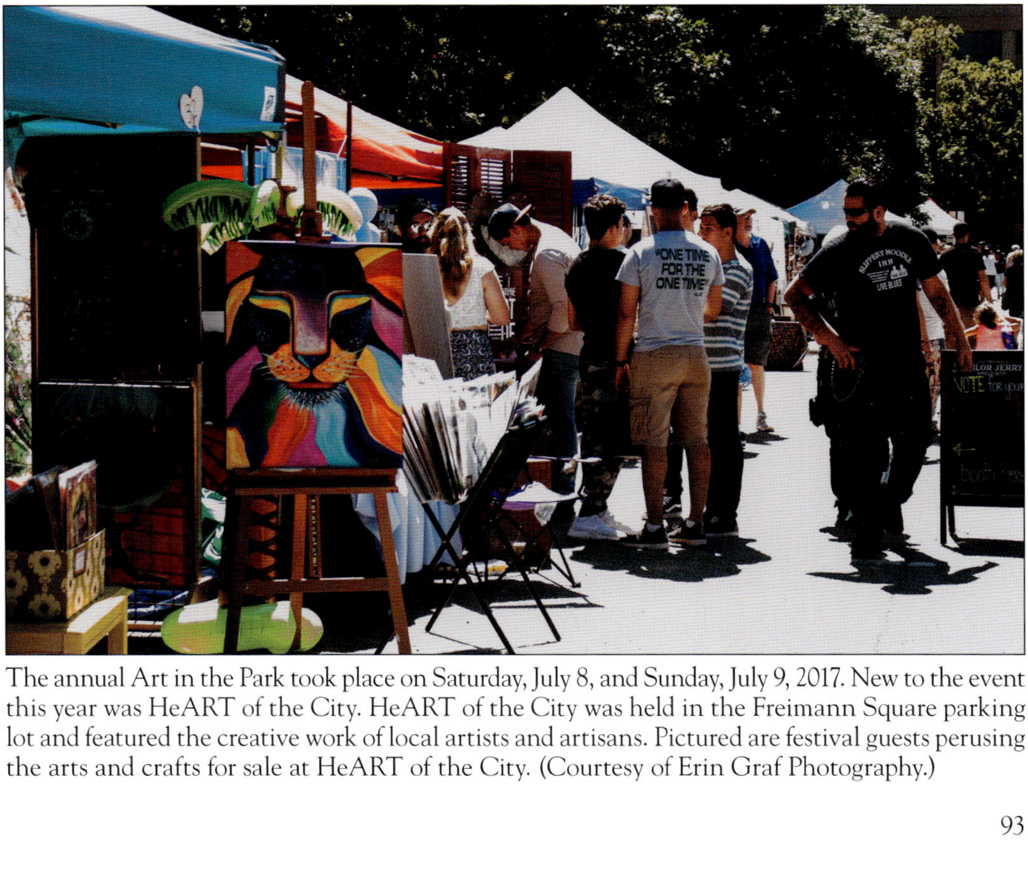

The annual Art in the Park took place on Saturday, July 8, and Sunday, July 9, 2017. New to the event this year was HeART of the City. HeART of the City was held in the Freimann Square parking lot and featured the creative work of local artists and artisans. Pictured are festival guests perusing the arts and crafts for sale at HeART of the City. (Courtesy of Erin Graf Photography.)

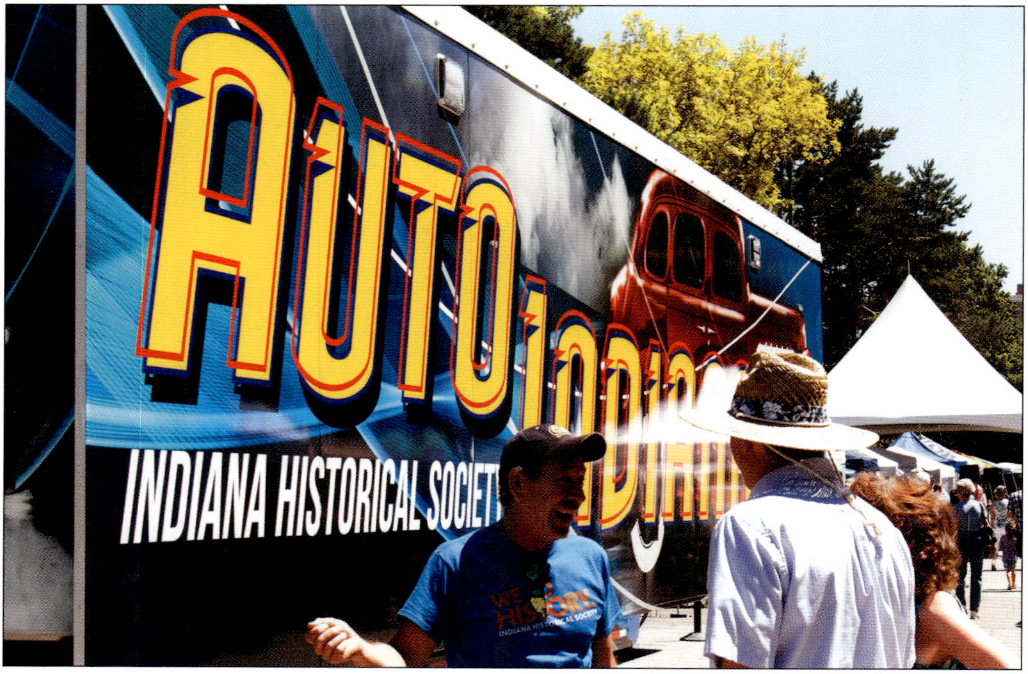

In 2017, the Indiana Historical Society designed and built a traveling exhibit on the history of the automotive industry in Indiana. The festival was excited to host the History on Wheels: Auto Indiana exhibit during the first weekend of the 49th Three Rivers Festival. The exhibit consisted of a 53-foot, double-expanding semitrailer, which housed state-of-the-art interactive educational displays. The exhibit covered the history of more than 100 Indiana automakers and manufacturers, along with delving into the lives of Hoosier innovators and inventors. The exhibit was free and open to all festival guests. Above, Mark McNees, from the Indiana Historical Society, welcomes a guest to the exhibit. Below, a model Indy 500 car awaits a visitor while guests investigate the artifacts in the glove box display on Saturday, July 8, 2017. (Both, courtesy of Erin Graf Photography.)

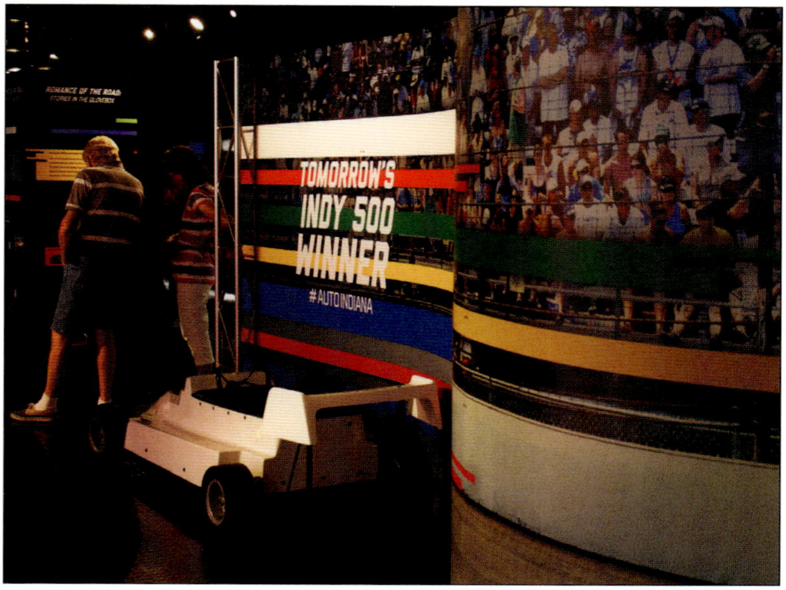

Monday, July 10, 2017, dawned as a bright, sunny, and hot day. The festival was in full swing, and hundreds of people were enjoying their day. The annual Waiter & Waitress Contest was held in Festival Plaza that evening and went off without a hitch. Over 30 teams from local restaurants competed for the coveted trophy. Here, the Trolley Steaks and Seafood team await their turn in the competition. (Courtesy of Erin Graf Photography.)

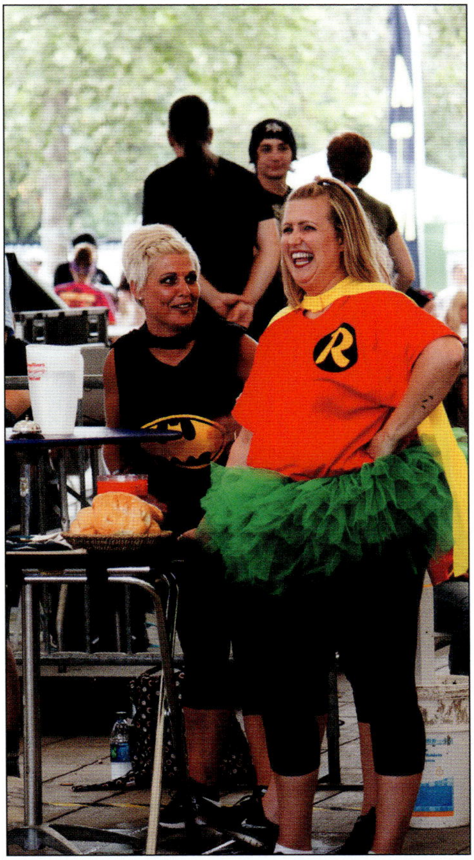

The 49th Three Rivers Festival closed for the year on Saturday, July 15, 2017. People from all over the city came out to the festival to enjoy their last corn dog, lemon shake-up, amusement ride, and concert of the year. Here Come the Mummies rocked out the festival stage with its very entertaining funk-rock show. The midway was packed and lit up on the last night of the festival. (Courtesy of Chad Smith.)

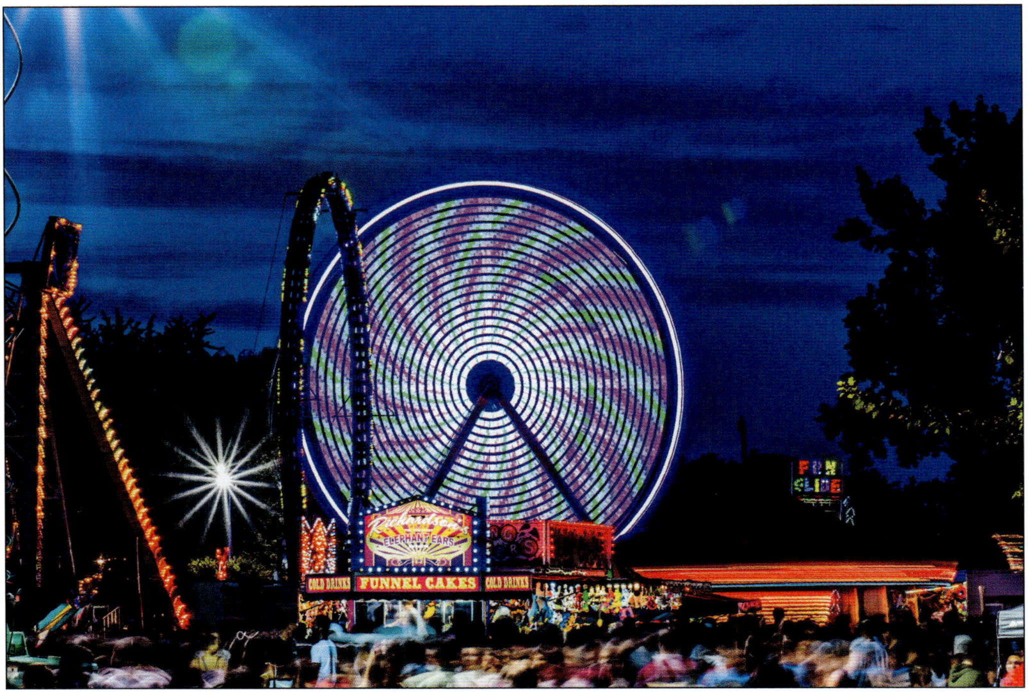

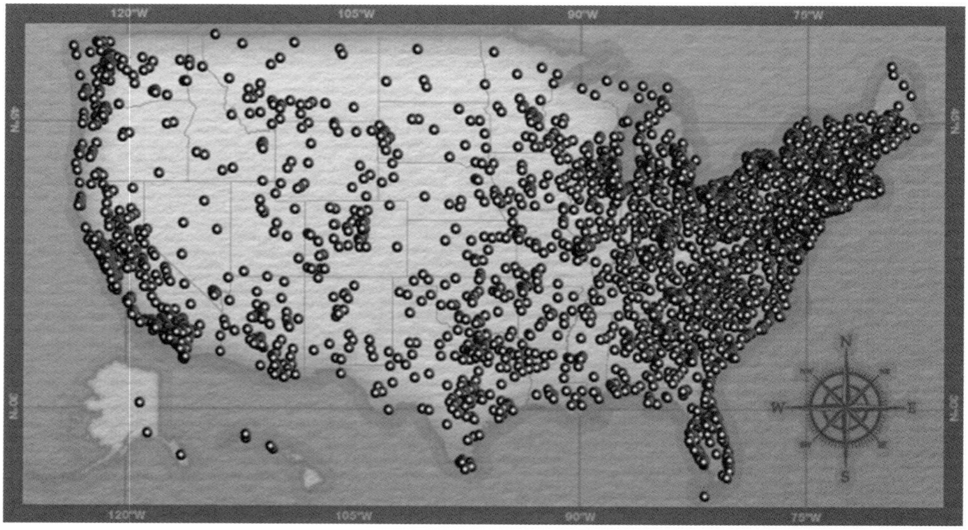
120°W
105°W
90°W
75°W